LETTING ISLAM BE ISLAM

LETTING ISLAM BE ISLAM

SEPARATING TRUTH FROM MYTH

Stephen M. Kirby Ph.D.

ISBN 1478118296

ISBN-13 978-1478118299

CreateSpace

Moderate Islam

These descriptions are very ugly, it is offensive and an insult to our religion. There is no moderate or immoderate Islam. Islam is Islam and that's it.

Turkish Prime Minister Recep Tayyip Erdogan commenting in August 2007 on the term "moderate Islam."

I was the first to expose the notion of "moderate Islam," which is used as a means to canonize a "non-Islamic Islam." I don't know why they call it "moderation." This "moderation" means violation [of the laws] of Islam.

Then-Egyptian Presidential Candidate and Former CAIR Official Bassem Khafagy, March 14, 2012
(The Middle East Media Research Institute (MEMRI), Clip No. 3372).

Modern Islam

Islamic modernism is a reform movement started by politically-minded urbanites with scant knowledge of traditional Islam. These people had witnessed and studied Western technology and socio-political ideas, and realized that the Islamic world was being left behind technologically by the West and had become too weak to stand up to it. They blamed this weakness on what they saw as 'traditional Islam,' which they thought held them back and was not 'progressive' enough. They thus called for a complete overhaul of Islam, including—or rather in particular—Islamic law (sharia) and doctrine (aqida). Islamic modernism remains popularly an object of derision and ridicule, and is scorned by traditional Muslims and fundamentalists alike.

The 500 Most Influential Muslims 2011, The Royal Islamic Strategic Studies Center (Amman, Jordan), p. 19.

Table of Contents

Introduction i

1. The Importance of the *Tafsirs* 1
The *Tafsirs* 1
"An American take on the Quran" 6
No Compulsion in Islam 8
Eid Greeting from ISNA 11
Hurt no one so that no one may hurt you 16
Do not throw yourselves into destruction 18

2. The *Hadiths* and *Sira* 23
The *Hadiths* 23
The *Sira* 26

3. Doctrine of Abrogation 27
Introduction 27
Banning Alcoholic Drinks - all Medinan Verses 29
Other Examples 31

4. The Significance of Muhammad 34
The Life of Muhammad 34
The Wives of Muhammad 42
The "Slave Concubines" of Muhammad 49
How the Muslims viewed Muhammad 51
Lying about Muhammad 52
Those Who Criticize or Revile Muhammad 54
Stoning Adulterers 58
Muhammad and Slaves 69
Cutting Off a Thief's Hand 75
Muhammad and Violence in General 78
Muhammad Forgetting Verses from the Koran and Prayers 82
Digging Up the Graves of Non-Muslims to Build His Mosque... 84
How Muhammad Used the Mosque 85

Muhammad's Statements about Homosexuality 86
Muslims Can't Inherit from Non-Muslims and Vice-versa..........87
A Reminder 87

5. The Religion of Peace 89
Introduction 89
Chapter 9, Verse 5 - The "Verse of the Sword" 89
Chapter 9, Verse 12 92
Chapter 9, Verse 23 94
Chapter 9, Verse 29 95
Chapter 9, Verse 30 97
Chapter 9, Verse 32 98
Chapter 9, Verse 33 99
Chapter 9, Verse 63 100
Chapter 9, Verse 73 101
Chapter 9, Verse 111 103
Chapter 9, Verse 123 104
Summary 105

6. The Religion of Peace, Redux 107
Introduction 107
Chapter 5, Verse 3 108
Chapter 5, Verse 17 109
Chapter 5, Verse 32 110
Chapter 5, Verse 33 114
Chapter 5, Verse 51 115
Chapter 5, Verse 55 117
Chapter 5, Verse 57 117
Chapter 5, Verse 65 118
Chapter 5, Verse 66 120
Chapter 5, Verse 69 121
Chapter 5, Verse 82 122
Summary 124

7. No Compulsion in Islam? 127
No Compulsion and the Islamic Scholars 127

Non-Muslims and Compulsion 133
Muslims and Apostasy 139
Conclusion 151

8. Three Religions with the Same God? 153
Introduction 153
Al-Fatihah 154
What Does the Koran Say about Jews and Christians? 159
What Did Muhammad Say about Jews and Christians? 182
Shirk, the Unforgiveable Sin of Christians 188
Conclusion 193

9. Christ Was Not Crucified 194
An Imposter on the Cross 194
Jesus and His Disciples were Muslims 197
Jesus will Return to Earth 200
Conclusion 203

10. Sharia Law and Women 205
Introduction 205
General Impact 206
Praying in Mosques and Participating in Prayers 213
Marriage - Introduction 218
Marriage - Coercion and Consent 219
Marriage - Prepubescent Marriage 221
Marriage - Temporary Marriage 224
Marriage - Role of the Guardian 227
Marriage - "Protecting" the Wife 228
Marriage - Beating Wives 230
Marriage - The Price of Maintenance 234
Inheritance 239
Divorce 240
Annulment 243
Death 244
Conclusion 245

11. Whom Your Right Hands Possess 248
Women Captives and the Koran 248
Women Captives and Sharia Law 252
Women Captives and Muhammad 253
Conclusion 259

12. The Pact of 'Umar 260
Introduction 260
The Pact of 'Umar 261

13. Why 5 Daily Prayers? 263
Making Things Easier 263
Making Things Easier in Battle 265

14. Nature of Paradise 267
Physical Description 267
Beautiful Virgin Wives 270
Beautiful Immortal Boys Serving Wine 276
Demographics in Paradise 279

15. Suicide or Paradise? 281
Introduction 281
Suicide 281
Martyrdom in Allah's Cause 284
Conclusion 293

16. Changing Islam? 294
Introduction 294
The First Obstacle - the Koran 294
The Second Obstacle - Muhammad 300
The Third Obstacle - It's Been Decided 301
Conclusion 307

17. A Forum on Being an American Muslim 308

18. Muslim-Americans 311
How Many Muslim-Americans? 311
"Suicide Bombing" 313
View of Al-Qaeda 316
American Mosques and their Religious Leaders (*Imams*) 318
Praying with Women 322
Conclusion 323

19. Handling the Koran at Gitmo 325

Chronology 334

Bibliography 380

Introduction

The Arabic word 'Islam' simply means 'submission', and derives from a word meaning 'peace'. In a religious context it means complete submission to the will of God.[1]

Especially since the *jihadist* attacks against the United States on September 11, 2001, we have heard numerous non-Muslims, including many of our political leaders, telling us what Islam *is*. Their favorite mantras are:

1. Islam is a religion of peace.

2. The "suicide bombers" and *jihadists* are "radicals" and do not follow the true teachings of Islam. In fact, these "radicals" have "hijacked Islam."

3. The "moderate," peaceful Muslims follow the true teachings of Islam.

These mantras lead us to the conclusion that the "moderate," peaceful Muslims are the orthodox Muslims, the true followers of the Doctrines in the Koran, the teachings of Muhammad, and the consensus of the authoritative Islamic scholars. In contrast, the "radicals" ignore, or pick-and-choose among the Doctrines in the Koran, the teachings of Muhammad, and the consensus of the authoritative Islamic scholars.

---

[1] From the website of the Royal Embassy of Saudi Arabia, Washington, DC. Accessible at http://www.saudiembassy.net/about/country-information/Islam/understanding_Islam.aspx.

Unfortunately, the common denominator in all of this is that many, if not most of those non-Muslims telling us what Islam *is* appear to have relatively little knowledge about Islam. For that reason, and to gain a better understanding of Islam, the focus of this book is on letting the Koran, "the Prophet" Muhammad, and the authoritative Islamic scholars tell us what Islam *is*. Fortunately, the works of many of these Islamic scholars have been translated into English by Muslims and published by Muslim publishing houses. This book relies mainly on such translations.

In these scholarly works you will often see translations of the verses in the Koran and the *hadiths* with words in parentheses. These words have been inserted by the translator to assist the reader in better understanding the particular translation.

Relying on these translated works also helps us address one of the common responses when presenting information about Islam: *That's a bad translation*. I would refer anyone saying this to contact, for example, Darussalam publications in Saudi Arabia and lodge their complaint.

Another common response when talking about Islam is: *That quote was taken out of context*. For that reason I have generally erred on the side of quoting at length, instead of providing a summary. This allows, for example, a statement by Muhammad to be seen in its full context. And it can then be so presented when you are talking with others about Islam.

We can apply this approach to understanding the phrase *fighting in Allah's Cause*. You might hear the explanation that this means some kind of internal personal struggle to make oneself a better Muslim. However, here is how Muhammad explained it:

> *Narrated Abu Musa: A man came to the Prophet and asked, "O Allah's Messenger! What kind of fighting is in Allah's Cause? (I ask this), for some of us fight because of being enraged and angry and some for the sake of their pride and haughtiness." The Prophet raised his head (as the questioner was standing) and said, "He who fights that*

Allah's Word (i.e. Allah's Religion of Islamic Monotheism) should be superior, fights in Allah's Cause."[2]

So we can see from the context that *fighting in Allah's Cause* has nothing to do with an internal personal struggle to make oneself a better Muslim. This will be further illustrated in Chapter 15, *Suicide or Paradise?*.

The last three chapters of this book look at Islam and the United States. In Chapters 17 and 18 we will examine some attitudes and disturbing trends among Muslim-Americans. In Chapter 19 we will look at the 2003 Department of Defense (DOD) order on how the Korans of the detainees at Guantanamo Bay were to be handled. By Chapter 19 you will have a better understanding of the book that DOD ordered to be treated with "respect and reverence."

To clarify, verses in the Koran are mentioned two ways in this book: Chapter 9, Verse 5, or 9:5.

All dates used in this book are Anno Domini.

So now sit back and let the Koran, Muhammad, and the authoritative Islamic scholars tell you what Islam *is*. And after finishing this book you will be in a position to start giving serious thought about the idea of a paradigm shift in applying the adjectives *orthodox* and *radical* in describing Muslims. The *orthodox* follow the Doctrines in the Koran, the teachings of Muhammad, and the consensus of the authoritative Islamic scholars; the *radicals* pick-and-choose among these. The *orthodox* quote un-abrogated verses from the Koran, authentic *hadiths*, and the consensus of the authoritative Islamic scholars to support their actions; the *radicals* have no such doctrinal support. So who are the truly *orthodox* Muslims? And who are the truly *radical* Muslims?

---

2 Muhammad bin Ismail bin Al-Mughirah Al-Bukhari, *Sahih Al-Bukhari*, trans. Muhammad Muhsin Khan, Vol. 1 (Riyadh, Kingdom of Saudi Arabia: Darussalam, 1997), Book 3, No. 123, p. 128.

People can be offended by a lie or by the truth. If it is a lie, then one should respond by identifying the lie and explaining with the truth. But if it is the truth that offends, then it is time for knowledge and reality to become more a part of one's thought process, uncomfortable as this can initially make one.

Stephen M. Kirby
September 5, 2012

1

The Importance of the *Tafsirs*

> *Ibn 'Abbas said that the Prophet said, 'Whoever explains the Qur'an with his opinion or with what he has no knowledge of, then let him assume his seat in the Fire.'*[1]

The *Tafsirs*[2]

Muslims believe the Koran is the infallible, pure word of Allah, eternal and perfect and delivered through the angel Gabriel to the final prophet Muhammad. But if you have ever sat down and read the Koran on your own, you were likely either uncertain about the meaning of the verses, or simply confused by what you were reading. This shows the importance of the *tafsirs* (commentaries on the Koran). The *tafsirs* explain the meanings and the contexts of verses in the Koran. In fact, the authoritative *tafsirs* are the primary sources for understanding the Koran, and, in effect, Islam.

So to understand the Koran we must turn to those authoritative *tafsirs*, for, as the quote above shows, it is prohibited for one to engage in *tafsir* using one's own opinion. In fact, it is prohibited to engage in *tafsir* using your own opinion even if you're correct; this is because you failed to research

---

[1] Abu Al-Fida' 'Imad Ad-Din Isma'il bin 'Umar bin Kathir Al-Qurashi Al-Busrawi, *Tafsir Ibn Kathir* (Abridged), trans. Jalal Abualrub, et al., Vol. 1 (Riyadh, Kingdom of Saudi Arabia: Darussalam, 2000), pp. 32-33. Versions of this were also reported in Abu 'Eisa Mohammad Ibn 'Eisa at-Tirmidhi, *Jami' At-Tirmidhi*, trans. Abu Khaliyl, Vol. 5 (Riyadh, Kingdom of Saudi Arabia: Darussalam, 2007), Nos. 2950-2952, pp. 274-276.

[2] Pronounced "tahfseers."

what the authoritative scholars had to say.[3] And Muhammad said that it was disbelief (*Kufr*) to argue about the Koran based only on personal opinions.[4]

Fortunately, a number of *tafsirs* by authoritative Islamic scholars have been translated into English. In this book I have relied on the following six *tafsirs*:

Tafsir Al-Qurtubi, Vol. 1

Abu 'Abdullah Muhammad ibn Ahmad al-Ansari al-Qurtubi lived from 1214-1273. His *tafsir* is "one of the great classical commentaries" which contains an "enormous wealth of traditional understanding" of the verses of the Koran.[5] This volume covers Chapters 1 and 2 of the Koran and is the only part of his *tafsir* that has been translated into English.

Tafsir Ibn Kathir

Abu Al-Fida' 'Imad Ad-Din Isma'il bin 'Umar bin Kathir Al-Qurashi Al-Busrawi lived from 1323-1396. This ten volume collection

> *is the most popular interpretation of the Qur'an in the Arabic language, and the majority of the Muslims*

---

[3] Abu 'Abdullah Muhammad ibn Ahmad al-Ansari al-Qurtubi, *Tafsir Al-Qurtubi: Classical Commentary of the Holy Qur'an*, Vol. 1, trans. Aisha Bewley (London: Dar Al Taqwa Ltd., 2003), p. 35. This is also mentioned in Abu Dawud Sulaiman bin Al-Ash'ath bin Ishaq, *Sunan Abu Dawud*, trans. Yaser Qadhi, Vol. 4 (Riyadh, Kingdom of Saudi Arabia: Darussalam, 2008), No. 3652, p. 212.

[4] *Sunan Abu Dawud*, Vol. 5, No. 4603, p. 159.

[5] *Tafsir Al-Qurtubi*, p. xv.

consider it to be the best source based on Qur'an and Sunnah.[6]

Tafsir Al-Jalalayn

This *tafsir* is the work of two people (the two Jalals):

Jalalu'd-Din Muhammad ibn Ahmad al-Mahalli - 1389-1459
Jalalu'd-Din as-Suyuti - 1445-1505

This one volume *tafsir* of 1,378 pages

> *has, since its publication more than half a millennium ago, been considered the essential first text in the study of the meaning of the Qur'an by teachers and students of the Qur'anic text throughout the entire Islamic world...It has always been held in the highest esteem by all the scholars of Islam...*[7]

Tafsir Ibn 'Abbas

Although this *tafsir* is often attributed to Ibn 'Abbas, an authoritative commentator on the Koran and Muhammad's cousin, its authorship is uncertain. However, there was a report of the text being in existence around 900.[8] Nevertheless, it is considered "a pivotal work for the study of Islamic exegesis" because, among other things:

---

[6] *Tafsir Ibn Kathir*, Vol. 1, p. 5. The *Sunnah* (pronounced "soonah") consists of the examples, ways, and teachings of Muhammad that have become rules to be followed by Muslims.

[7] Jalalu'd-Din Al-Mahalli and Jalalu'd-Din As-Suyuti, *Tafsir Al-Jalalayn*, trans. Aisha Bewley (London: Dar Al Taqwa Ltd., 2007), p. xi.

[8] *Tafsir Ibn 'Abbas*, trans. Mokrane Guezzou (Louisville, KY: Fons Vitae, 2008), p. xvi. This is the second volume in *The Great Tafsirs of the Holy Qur'an* series, sponsored by the Royal Aal al-Bayt Institute for Islamic Thought, which is

1. The core of this work consists of the traditions attributed to Ibn 'Abbas; and

2. It contains reports going back to Muhammad or Ibn 'Abbas.[9]

Tafsir Ahsanul-Bayan

In contrast to the previous four *tafsirs*, this one is a recent *tafsir* resulting from a discussion between Abdul Malik Mujahid, the Managing Director of Darussalam publishers, and his wife. The purpose was to provide a

> *commentary of the Holy Qur'an for students which should be free from the old unauthentic Israeli stories, weak and feeble sayings, philosophical and unnecessary discussions but that should reveal the exact meaning and explanation which was explained by the Prophet and his Companions.*[10]

It was originally published in the Urdu language in 1995. At this time Koran Chapters 1-41 of this *tafsir* have been translated into a four volume

---

> *an international Islamic non-governmental, independent institute headquartered in Amman, the capital of the Hashemite Kingdom of Jordan. The purpose of the Royal Aal al-Bayt Institute for Islamic Thought is to serve Islam and humanity at large. Among its objectives are: promoting awareness of Islam and Islamic thought, rectifying unsound ideas and misconceptions about Islam, highlighting the Islamic intellectual contribution and its impact on human civilization...*

From the website at http://www.aalalbayt.org/en/index.html, accessed on August 15, 2012.

[9] *Tafsir Ibn 'Abbas*, p. x.

[10] Salahuddin Yusuf, *Tafsir Ahsanul-Bayan*, trans. Mohammad Kamal Myshkat, Vol. 1 (Riyadh, Kingdom of Saudi Arabia: Darussalam, 2010), p. 9.

set. There is also a separate pocket-sized book titled *Tafsir Ahsanul-Bayan (Part 30)* which covers Koran Chapters 78-114.[11] Using this modern *tafsir* will show us that there have been no significant changes in how the Koran has been interpreted for many hundreds of years.

Al-Wahidi's Asbab al-Nuzul

Abu'l-Hasan 'Ali ibn Ahmad ibn Muhammad ibn 'Ali al-Wahidi died in 1075. This work is based on the branch of "science" of the Koran titled *Asbab al-Nuzul*, which focuses on "the occasions, reasons or causes of revelation" of a verse in the Koran.[12] However, it deals with only about 570 of the over 6,600 verses in the Koran.[13] Nevertheless, the translator of this work pointed out:

> *Not only is this book the earliest extant work in the genre, but it is also the standard upon which all subsequent works on the occasions of revelation were modelled.*[14]

And Al-Wahidi explained the significance of his book:

> *It is unlawful to advance an opinion regarding the occasions of the revelation of the Book unless it is based on narration and transmission from those who have witnessed the revelation and were aware of the occasions,*

---

[11] Salahuddin Yusuf, *Tafsir Ahsanul-Bayan(Part 30)* (Riyadh, Kingdom of Saudi Arabia: Darussalam, 2010).

[12] Abu'l-Hasan 'Ali ibn Ahmad ibn Muhammad ibn 'Ali al-Wahidi, *Al-Wahidi's Asbab al-Nuzul*, trans. Mokrane Guezzou (Louisville, KY: Fons Vitae, 2008), p. xi. This is the third volume in *The Great Tafsirs of the Holy Qur'an* series, sponsored by the Royal Aal al-Bayt Institute for Islamic Thought.

[13] Ibid., p. xiii.

[14] Ibid., p. xvi.

in that they seriously sought to know them. The Sacred Law threatens the ignorant who stumble in this science with hell fire...As for nowadays, every person invents something and contrives lies and fabrications, and by doing so he throws himself in the grip of ignorance, paying no heed to the threat issued to the ignorant regarding the occasions of different verses. This is what has driven me to dictate this book which brings together all the different occasions, so that those who seek this subject as well as those who deal with the revelation of the Qur'an can consult it, know what is true, do away with falsification and lies, and then strive to preserve it after seeking its knowledge and receiving by transmission.[15]

So now that we understand the purpose and significance of these *tafsirs*, let's put that knowledge to use by applying it to five examples:

"An American take on the Quran"[16]

On February 11, 2012 there was an article in the *Des Moines Register* about Sandow Birk, a non-Muslim artist and "surfer," who wasn't "even very religious," and who had spent most of the last six years

hand-writing an English translation of the Quran and illustrating it with scenes of modern American life.[17]

Birk explained that few Americans knew anything about the Koran, so he was

---

15 Ibid., pp. 1-2.

16 "An American take on the Quran," *Des Moines Register*, February 11, 2012, p. 1E.

17 The article did not specify whose translation of the Koran Birk was using.

attempting to create visual metaphors that go along with the text and hopefully make it more accessible to Americans, more relevant to American life.

Birk was engaging in *tafsir* even though he appeared to know little or nothing about the Koran. And some of the panels from his work had been put on display in the Faulconer Gallery at Grinnell College in Grinnell, Iowa.

The problem with this becomes very apparent by Birk's use of race cars to illustrate Chapter 100, Verses 1-4 of the Koran. Here are those verses:

By the (steeds) that run, with panting. Striking sparks of fire (by their hooves). And scouring to the raid at dawn. And raise the dust in clouds the while. [18]

Ibn Kathir pointed out that these verses referred to horses of war fighting in the cause of Allah ("*Jihad*"), the morning attacks by Muhammad on villages from which he did not hear the *Adhan* (the Muslim call to prayer), and the dust raised by those attacks.[19]

The *Tafsir Al-Jalalayn* explained that this verse was about quickly moving war horses being ridden for an attack at "first light."[20]

The *Tafsir Ahsanul-Bayan* also explained that these verses pertained to horses of war kicking up dust as they rushed to the attack.[21]

---

[18] Unless otherwise indicated, the Koran I use in this book is *The Noble Qur'an*, trans. Muhammad Muhsin Khan and Muhammad Taqi-ud-Din Al-Hilali (Riyadh, Kingdom of Saudi Arabia: Darussalam, 2007).

[19] *Tafsir Ibn Kathir*, Vol. 10, p. 566.

[20] *Tafsir Al-Jalalayn*, pp. 1348-1349.

[21] *Tafsir Ahsanul-Bayan (Part 30)*, pp. 257-259.

Al-Wahidi's Asbab al-Nuzul and the *Tafsir Ibn 'Abbas* noted that this verse was about a military expedition Muhammad had sent against the Banu Kinanah, another tribe.[22]

Race cars and an implied racing event substituting for war horses and Muslim attacks at dawn? The pitfalls of *tafsir* by personal opinion. Unfortunately, Birk's attempt at *tafsir* received recognition and also exhibit space at a college.

No Compulsion in Islam

In the first example we had a non-Muslim who appeared to have taken a creative, artistic approach to *tafsir*, instead of ensuring that his drawings reflected the consensus of authoritative Islamic scholars. In this second example we will consider an award winning biography about Muhammad. This book, *The Sealed Nectar*, was written by a Muslim, and in 1979 it was awarded first prize by the Muslim World League in the worldwide competition for a new biography of Muhammad.

And what is the Muslim World League? Here is the description from their website:

> *The Muslim World League is an international non governmental Islamic organization based in the Holy City of Makkah. It is engaged in propagating the religion of Islam, elucidating its principles and tenets, refuting suspicious and false allegations made against the religion. The League also strives to persuade people to abide by the commandments of their Lord, and to keep away from prohibited deeds.*[23]

---

22 *Al-Wahidi's Asbab al-Nuzul*, p. 257; and *Tafsir Ibn 'Abbas*, p. 888.

23 http://www.themwl.org/Profile/default.aspx?l=en. Accessed July 16, 2012.

So we would expect accurate information in *The Sealed Nectar*. However, on page 407 we find the following statement about the Treaty of Al-Hudaibiyah (March 628), a treaty between the Meccans and the Muslims, who were increasing in military strength:

> *The Muslims did not have in mind to seize people's property or kill them through bloody wars, nor did they ever think of using any compulsive approaches in their efforts to propagate Islam, on the contrary, their sole target was to provide an atmosphere of freedom in ideology or religion; "Then whosoever wills, let him believe, and whosoever wills, let him disbelieve." [18:29]*[24]

So according to this statement, the goal of the Muslims at that time was "to provide an atmosphere of freedom in ideology or religion." And a tolerant appearing verse from the Koran was provided to support this statement. But the book quoted only part of that verse. So let's take a look at the entire verse:

Chapter 18, Verse 29

> *And say: "The truth is from your Lord." Then whosoever wills, let him believe; and whosever wills, let him disbelieve. Verily, We have prepared for the Zalimun (polytheists and wrongdoers), a Fire whose walls will be surrounding them (disbelievers in the Oneness of Allah). And if they ask for help (relief, water), they will be granted water like boiling oil, that will scald their faces. Terrible is the drink, and an evil Murtafaq (dwelling, resting place)!*

---

[24] Safiur-Rahman Al-Mubarakpuri, *The Sealed Nectar* (Riyadh, Kingdom of Saudi Arabia: Darussalam, 2008), p. 407.

What does this verse mean? When we examine the *tafsirs* we find that this verse is actually a threat from Allah to non-Muslims.

Ibn Kathir explained that this verse was a threat from Allah and a warning to non-Muslims about the consequences of not believing in Islam (*The truth*):

> *Allah says to His Messenger Muhammad: "Say to the people, 'What I have brought to you from your Lord is the truth, in which there is no confusion or doubt.'"*
>
> > *Then whosoever wills, let him believe; and whosever wills, let him disbelieve.*
>
> *This is a type of threat and stern warning, after which Allah says, Verily, We have prepared meaning made ready, for the wrongdoers, meaning those who disbelieve in Allah, His Messenger and His Book...*[25]

And what Allah had made ready was fire and scalding water.

The *Tafsir Al-Jalalayn* stated that *the truth* was the Koran, and continued:

> *Then whosoever wills, let him believe; and whosever wills, let him disbelieve. This is a threat to them* [the non-Muslims].[26]

The *Tafsir Ibn 'Abbas* stated that the truth meant "there is no deity except Allah," and also stated:

> *...Then whosoever wills, let him believe; and whosever wills, let him disbelieve) this is a threat from Allah...*[27]

---

25 *Tafsir Ibn Kathir*, Vol. 6, p. 146.

26 *Tafsir Al-Jalalayn*, p. 626.

27 *Tafsir Ibn 'Abbas*, p. 367.

Al-Wahidi explained that where this verse talked about the *Zalimun*, Allah was "threatening them with hell."[28]

It is interested to note that the modern *Tafsir Ahsanul-Bayan* had no comment about this verse.

Without the *tafsirs* it would have been easy to believe that the context and the partial quote of 18:29 in *The Sealed Nectar* provided support for the claim that under Islam there has been freedom of religion. Did the author and the Muslim World League not know what the authoritative scholars said about 18:29? Were they instead engaging in *tafsir* by personal opinion, which Muhammad condemned? Or could there be another explanation?

***Eid* Greeting from ISNA**

On November 5, 2011, an *Eid Mubarak* (Blessed Festival) greeting was e-mailed out by the Islamic Society of North America (ISNA). Here is a description of ISNA from their website:

> *ISNA is an association of Muslim organizations and individuals that provides a common platform for presenting Islam, supporting Muslim communities, developing educational, social and outreach programs and fostering good relations with other religious communities, and civic and service organizations.*[29]

Once again, we would expect accurate information from this kind of group. So here is the greeting:

---

[28] *Al-Wahidi's Asbab al-Nuzul*, p. 152.

[29] http://www.isna.net/ISNAHQ/pages/Mission--Vision.aspx. Accessed July 16, 2012.

November 5, 2011

EID GREETINGS FROM ISNA

This Eid, let us reflect on and give thanks for the many blessings we were given this past year.

Let us also remember that even in times of great hardship, Allah knows best. While some blessings arrive in disguise, He will always guide us towards what is best for each of us.

eid mubarak

"...It may be that you dislike a thing which is good for you and that you like a thing which is bad for you. Allah knows but you do not know" (Quran 2:216). We at ISNA give thanks for your continued support and for your trust in ISNA to serve you. From all your friends at ISNA, we pray your family has a happy Eid and a very blessed year!

Notice the tone. The message is that on this blessed festival we need to remember that Allah knows what is best for us even in times of great hardship, and some of our blessings arrive in disguise. So trust in Allah. And the last paragraph starts out with what appears to be a supporting verse from the Koran (2:216).

As we can see, the first part of this verse was not included in the greeting. So let's look at the entire verse. The portion omitted from the ISNA greeting is underlined:

Chapter 2, Verse 216

> *Jihad (holy fighting in Allah's Cause)* [30] *is ordained for you (Muslims) though you dislike it, and it may be that you dislike a thing which is good for you and that you like a*

---

30 *Al-Jihad (holy fighting) in Allah's Cause (with full force of numbers and weaponry) is given the utmost importance in Islam and is one of its pillars (on which it stands). By Jihad Islam is established, Allah's Word is made superior, (His Word being La ilaha illallah which means none has the right to be worshipped but Allah), and His religion (Islam) is propagated. By abandoning Jihad (may Allah protect us from that) Islam is destroyed and the Muslims fall into an inferior position; their honour is lost, their lands are stolen, their rule and authority vanish. Jihad is an obligatory duty in Islam on every Muslim, and he who tries to escape from this duty, or does not in his innermost heart wish to fulfil* [sic] *this duty, dies with one of the qualities of a hypocrite.*

The Noble Qur'an, p. 50, n. 1. This footnote in *The Noble Qur'an* was used to explain the meaning of the first part of 2:190: *And fight in the way of Allah...*

The last sentence of the above paragraph was taken from a statement made by Muhammad:

> *It has been narrated on the authority of Abu Huraira that the Messenger of Allah (may peace be upon him) said: One who died but did not fight in the way of Allah nor did he express any desire (or determination) for Jihad died the death of a hypocrite.*

Abu'l Hussain 'Asakir-ud-Din Muslim bin Hajjaj al-Qushayri al-Naisaburi, *Sahih Muslim*, trans. Abdul Hamid Siddiqi, Vol. 6 (New Delhi: Adam Publishers and Distributors, 2008), No. 1910, p. 289. A version of this *hadith* is also found in *Tafsir Ibn Kathir*, Vol. 1, p. 596.

La ilaha illallah : worship only Allah

thing which is bad for you. Allah knows but you do not know.

ISNA somehow forgot that this verse is talking about *jihad* against non-Muslims. How do the *tafsirs* explain this verse?

We start with Ibn Kathir:

> *In this Ayah* [verse], *Allah made it obligatory for the Muslims to fight in Jihad against the evil of the enemy who transgress against Islam...though you dislike it means, 'Fighting is difficult and heavy on your hearts.' Indeed, fighting is as the Ayah describes it, as it includes being killed, wounded, striving against the enemies and enduring the hardship of travel. Allah then said: ...and it may be that you dislike a thing which is good for you, meaning, fighting is followed by victory, dominance over the enemy, taking over their lands, money and offspring. Allah continues: ...and that you like a thing which is bad for you.*
>
> *This Ayah is general in meaning. Hence, one might covet something, yet in reality it is not good or beneficial for him, such as refraining from joining the Jihad, for it might lead to the enemy taking over the land and the government.*[31]

Al-Qurtubi provided a similar explanation:

> *This means that fighting is obligatory and refers to the obligation of jihad...What is meant by fighting is fighting the enemies among the unbelievers.*[32]

---

[31] *Tafsir Ibn Kathir*, Vol. 1, pp. 596-597.

[32] *Tafsir Al-Qurtubi*, p. 544.

Al-Qurtubi pointed out:

> *It may be that you hate something when it is good for you and it may be that you love something when it is bad for you....in other words: "You do hate the hardship in jihad but it is good for you in that you conquer, have victory, take booty and are rewarded and whoever dies dies a martyr. You do love peace and not fighting but it is evil for you since you will be overcome and abased and your authority lost." This is absolutely true and it happened in Andalusia when they abandoned jihad and avoided fighting and many fled. The enemy took the land and captured, killed and enslaved the Muslims. We belong to Allah and to Him we return!*[33]

The explanation from the *Tafsir Al-Jalalayn*:

> *Fighting against the unbelievers is prescribed and hereby made obligatory for you even if it is hateful to you...So you may dislike fighting, but it is good for you: either through winning victory and booty or by gaining martyrdom and its reward...Allah knows what is good for you and you do not know that. So hasten to what He commands you.*[34]

From the *Tafsir Ibn 'Abbas*:

> *...(but it may happen that ye hate a thing) fighting in the way of Allah (which is good for you) in that you obtain martyrdom and spoils, (and it may happen that ye love a thing) abstaining from fighting in the way of Allah (which is bad for you) in that you will not obtain martyrdom or spoils. (And Allah knoweth) that fighting in His way is*

---

33 Ibid., p. 546.

34 *Tafsir Al-Jalalayn*, p. 79.

better for you, (ye know not) that abstention from fighting in His way is bad for you.[35]

And finally, from the modern *Tafsir Ahsanul-Bayan*:

> *...jihad, which appears unpleasant, leads ultimately to conquest and domination, honor and wealth. On the other hand, things that you like (sitting comfortably at home instead of going out for jihad) may be quite fraught with dangers like dishonor, slavery and humiliation at the hands of the enemies.*[36]

Once again we must ask. Did ISNA not know what the authoritative scholars said about 2:216? Were they engaging in *tafsir* by personal opinion, which Muhammad condemned? Or could there be another explanation?

Hurt no one so that no one may hurt you

On many Muslim websites Muhammad is quoted as saying, "Hurt no one so that no one may hurt you," or similar wording. And you might see this used as support for the claim that Islam is concerned about human rights, or even as an example of the Golden Rule being a part of Islam.[37] But this statement was made during Muhammad's Farewell Speech in February 632. Here is the section of his speech that included this statement:

> *He who has a pledge let him return it to him who entrusted him with it; all usury is abolished, but you have*

---

35 *Tafsir Ibn 'Abbas*, p. 44.

36 *Tafsir Ahsanul-Bayan*, Vol. 1, p. 191.

37 For example, see the Muslim website at http://muslima61.hubpages.com/hub/Lessons-from-the-Holy-Quran-that-we-should-apply-to-our-Daily-Lives. Accessed July 30, 2012.

your capital. Wrong not and you shall not be wronged. God has decreed that there is to be no usury and the usury of 'Abbas b. 'Abdu'l-Muttalib is abolished, all of it.[38]

When mentioning this section of Muhammad's speech, the translator's note in *The History of al-Tabari: The Last Years of the Prophet* directs us to 2:279 of the Koran.[39] To understand the full context of this statement, here are Verses 2:278-279:

> *O you who believe! Be afraid of Allah and give up what remains (due to you) from Riba (from now onward), if you are (really) believers. And if you do not do it, then take a notice of war from Allah and His Messenger but if you repent, you shall have your capital sums. Deal not unjustly (by asking more than your capital sums), and you shall not be dealt with unjustly (by receiving less than your capital sums).*

Ibn Kathir explained that these verses talked about the prohibition of *Riba* (usury, interest) in Islam. He wrote that one should not deal unjustly "by taking the *Riba*," and as a consequence one's capital would not be diminished, meaning one would not be treated unjustly.[40]

Al-Qurtubi also said that these verses dealt with the prohibition of usury, and

---

[38] Muhammad Ibn Ishaq, *The Life of Muhammad (Sirat Rasul Allah)*, trans. Alfred Guillaume, (Karachi: Oxford University Press, 2007), p. 651. Similar wording is found in Abu Ja'far Muhammad b. Jarir al-Tabari, *The History of al-Tabari: The Last Years of the Prophet*, Vol. IX, trans. and annotated Ismail K. Poonawala (Albany, New York: State University of New York Press, 1990), p. 112.

[39] *The History of al-Tabari: The Last Years of the Prophet*, p. 112, n. 761.

[40] *Tafsir Ibn Kathir*, Vol. 2, pp. 78-80.

> *...Allah returns to usurers their capital and tells them not to wrong others by taking usury "and that they will not be wronged" by their capital being retained so that they lose it.*[41]

The *Tafsir Al-Jalalayn*, *Tafsir Ibn 'Abbas*, and *Al-Wahidi's Asbab al-Nuzul* also agreed that these verses pertained to the prohibition of usury and the fact that asking for *Riba* would be unjust; and if you did not ask for *Riba*, you would not be treated unjustly by getting back less than your capital.[42]

It is interesting to note that the *Tafsir Ahsanul-Bayan* explained these verses the same way, pointing out:

> *You wrong the borrower if you take more than the money loaned. Similarly, if you are not given back the money you have loaned, you will be wronged.*[43]

So we can see from the *tafsirs* that Muhammad was talking about loans and usury, not human rights or a Golden Rule.

Do not throw yourselves into destruction

This is another statement you might come across. It is based on the following verse of the Koran:

Chapter 2, Verse 195

> *And spend in the Cause of Allah (i.e. Jihad of all kinds) and do not throw yourselves into destruction (by not*

---

41 *Tafsir Al-Qurtubi*, p. 725; see pp. 709-729 for an in-depth explanation.

42 *Tafsir Al-Jalalayn*, p. 107; *Tafsir Ibn 'Abbas*, p. 59; and *Al-Wahidi's Asbab al-Nuzul*, pp. 41-42.

43 *Tafsir Ahsanul-Bayan*, Vol. 1, p. 258.

spending your wealth in the Cause of Allah), and do good. Truly, Allah loves Al-Muhsinun (the good-doers).

The parenthetical explanations provided in the above verse from *The Noble Qur'an* give us a head start in understanding this verse. But in other translations of the Koran, you would find the verse presented simply as:

Spend your wealth for the cause of Allah, and be not cast by your own hands to ruin; and do good. Lo! Allah loveth the beneficent.[44]

OR

And spend [freely] in God's cause, and let not your own hands throw you into destruction; and persevere in doing good: behold, God loves the doers of good.[45]

Translations of 2:195 like these latter two allow Muslims and non-Muslims to explain that this verse prohibits suicide and/or suicide bombing, and addresses the importance of spending money for the sake of Allah without having to fight. But what do the *tafsirs* say about this verse?

Ibn Kathir stated that this verse

...includes the order to spend in Allah's cause, in the various areas and ways that involve obedience and drawing closer to Allah. It especially applies to spending in fighting the enemies and on what strengthens the Muslims against the enemy. Allah states that those who

---

[44] *The Meaning of the Glorious Koran*, trans. Marmaduke Pickthall (1930; rpt. New York: Alfred A. Knopf, 1992), p. 48.

[45] *The Message of the Qur'an*, trans. Muhammad Asad, (Bristol, England: The Book Foundation, 2003), p. 52. During the 2006 time period thousands of copies of this translation of the Koran were distributed at no charge by the Council on American-Islamic Relations (CAIR).

refrain from spending in this regard will face utter and certain demise and destruction...[46]

Ibn Kathir pointed out that "destruction" also referred to Muslim warriors staying with their families and estates and "abandoning *Jihad*."[47]

The *Tafsir Al-Jalalayn* explained:

> *Spend in the Way of Allah in obedience to Him on jihad and other things...The destruction referred to is brought about by refusing to spend in jihad or abandoning it because that will make the enemy stronger against you.*[48]

The *Tafsir Ahsanul-Bayan* explained the meaning of *destruction*:

> *Scholars have interpreted it in different ways: "refraining from spending in the way of Allah" or "refraining from fighting in the way of Allah (jihad)" or "committing sin upon sin." In fact, all these things lead to ruin and disaster. Giving up jihad or refraining from spending in the cause of jihad will surely make your enemy stronger, and make you weaker. Either way, the result is disaster.*[49]

The strong connection between this verse and participation in *jihad* is also emphasized in a number of *hadiths*, e.g.:

> *It was reported from Aslam Abu 'Imran, who said: "We went on a military expedition from Al-Madinah headed for Constantinople, and 'Abdur-Rahman bin Khalid bin Al-*

---

46 *Tafsir Ibn Kathir*, Vol. 1, p. 538.

47 Ibid., p. 537.

48 *Tafsir Al-Jalalayn*, p. 70.

49 *Tafsir Ahsanul-Bayan*, Vol. 1, pp. 172-173.

Walid was (commander) over the group. The Romans had gathered before the wall of the city (ready to fight). So a man went to attack the enemy. Thereupon the people said: 'Stop, stop! None has the right to be worshipped but Allah! He is throwing himself into destruction!' Thus Abu Ayyub said: 'This Verse was revealed about us, the people of the Ansar, when Allah granted victory to His Prophet and gave Islam dominance, we said: "Come, let us stay with our wealth (and properties) and improve it." Thereupon, Allah, the Mighty and Sublime, revealed: "And spend in the cause of Allah, and do not throw yourselves into destruction." So, to "throw oneself into destruction" means: To stay with our wealth and improve it, and abandon Jihad.'"[50]

So we see that the verse of the Koran admonishing Muslims not to throw themselves into destruction has nothing to do with suicide or suicide bombers, but rather emphasizes the importance of staying involved with *Jihad*.

---

[50] *Sunan Abu Dawud*, Vol. 3, No. 2512, pp. 211-212. This was also reported in *Al-Wahidi's Asbab al-Nuzul*, p. 24. A similar version of this *hadith* was reported in *Jami' At-Tirmidhi*, Vol. 5, No. 2972, pp. 294-295; the comment on p. 295 about this *hadith* pointed out:

> *This Hadith proves that a person showing courage, bravery and boldness, making the enemies fearful and scared, breaking through the rows of the enemy, is correct...Being engaged for the betterment of one's wealth and business by giving up Jihad and military expedition is to provide opportunity to the enemy to overcome; therefore it leads to destruction, devastation and helplessness, which is totally wrong.*

A much shorter version of this *hadith*, also focusing on the importance of *jihad*, was reported in Muhammad bin Ismail bin Al-Mughirah Al-Bukhari, *Sahih Al-Bukhari*, trans. Muhammad Muhsin Khan, Vol. 6 (Riyadh, Kingdom of Saudi Arabia: Darussalam, 1997), Book 65, No. 4516, pp. 46-47.

These five examples show us that verses of the Koran can be misconstrued by non-Muslims and Muslims alike. But we see that by relying on the *tafsirs*, we can learn the true meaning of the verses in the Koran.

As Iyas ibn Mu'awiya pointed out, it is the light from the *tafsirs* that keeps us from being led astray:

> *Iyas ibn Mu'awiya said, "The metaphor of those who recited the Qur'an without knowing its tafsir is that of some people to whom a letter comes from their king at night when they have no lamp. They are alarmed, not knowing what the letter contains. The metaphor of the one who knows the tafsir is that of a man who brings them a lamp so that they can read what the letter says."*[51]

---

51 *Tafsir Al-Qurtubi*, pp. 27-28.

2

The *Hadiths* and *Sira*

Now that we realize how important the *tafsirs* are to understanding the Koran and Islam, we need to learn what information the scholars relied on to explain the meanings and contexts of the verses in the Koran. The answer is the *Sunnah*, the examples, ways, and teachings of Muhammad that have become rules to be followed by Muslims. There are two sources for the *Sunnah*:

1. The *Hadiths*[52] (*ahadith*)

2. The *Sira*[53] (the authoritative biography of Muhammad)

The *Hadiths*

The *hadiths* are reports about the examples, ways, and teachings of Muhammad believed to have come from those who were with him and observed and heard them. They are second only to the Koran in importance to Islam. And the Koran cannot be understood without relying on the *hadiths*.[54]

---

52 Pronounced "hadeeths."

53 Pronounced "seerah."

54 *Tafsir Ahsanul-Bayan*, Vol. 1, p. 73; *Tafsir Ibn Kathir*, Vol. 1, p. 29; and *Tafsir Al-Qurtubi*, pp. 40-42.

There are numerous *hadith* collections, with varying degrees of reliability. But there are two collections considered to be the most reliable (*sahih/saheeh*).

The first is *Sahih Al-Bukhari*, collected by Muhammad bin Ismail al-Bukhari (810-870) and considered the most reliable collection of *hadiths*:

> *The authenticity of Al-Bukhari's work is such that the religious learned scholars of Islam said concerning him: "The most authentic book after the Book of Allah (i.e. Al-Qur'an) is Sahih Al-Bukhari."* [55]

It was said that Al-Bukhari collected over 300,000 *hadiths* and personally memorized 200,000 of them. However, during this time *hadiths* were being forged to please various rulers. So after praying over each *hadith*, Bukhari chose approximately 2,230 *hadiths* of which he had no doubt about their authenticity. In his multi-volume work he repeated many of the *hadiths* in different sections, resulting in a total of approximately 7,275 *hadiths* in his collection.[56]

The next most reliable *hadith* collection is *Sahih Muslim*, collected by Abu'l Hussain 'Asakir-ud-Din Muslim bin Hajjaj al-Qushayri al-Naisaburi (821-875). Muslim was a student of Al-Bukhari. Muslim collected 300,000 *hadiths* and, after a thorough examination of each of them, retained only 4,000 as authentic.[57]

The two *Sahihs* and four other *hadith* collections make up the authoritative "Six Books of *Hadith*," or "The Sound Six."[58] Here are the other four *hadith* collections:

---

55 *Sahih Al-Bukhari*, Vol. 1, p. 18.

56 Ibid., pp. 18-19.

57 *Sahih Muslim*, Vol. 1, p. xi.

58 A searchable data base for some of these *hadith* collections, and for a Koran, is at the website of the University of Southern California Center for

Sunan Ibn Majah - Muhammad Bin Yazeed Ibn Majah Al-Qazwini (831-895)

Sunan An-Nasa'i - Abu Abdur Rahman Ahmad bin Shu'aib bin 'Ali An-Nasa'i (836-925)

Sunan Abu Dawud - Abu Dawud Sulaiman bin Al-Ash'ath bin Ishaq (824-897)

Jami' At-Tirmidhi - Abu 'Eisa Mohammad Ibn 'Eisa at-Tirmidhi (827-901)

Although designated as the "Six Books," the English translations of these collections total 39 volumes. It should be noted that Muhammad died in 632, and these *hadith* collections were put together over 200 years later.

So what does a *hadith* look like? It starts off with a sequential list of the names of the narrators going back to who first reported the *hadith.* Since the list named a chain of narrators over a 200 year time period, it could include a large number of names. However, the list is usually shortened in English translations, e.g.:

> *It was narrated from Musawir Al-Himyari from his mother that she heard Umm Salamah say: "I heard the Messenger of Allah say: 'Any woman who dies when her husband is pleased with her, will enter Paradise.'"*[59]

Muslim-Jewish Engagement, at the Religious Texts tab: http://cmje.org/. Although this website purportedly uses the same translations of *Sahih Al-Bukhari* and *Sahih Muslim* as used in this book, the numbering systems of, and some of the wording in the *hadiths*, are different at the website. There is also a different translation of *Al-Muwatta of Imam Malik ibn Anas* than used in this book. And the website has only a partial translation of *Sunan Abu Dawud*, also written by a different translator than the volumes used in this book.

[59] Muhammad Bin Yazeed Ibn Majah Al-Qazwini, *Sunan Ibn Majah*, trans. Nasiruddin al-Khattab, Vol. 3 (Riyadh, Kingdom of Saudi Arabia: Darussalam, 2007), No. 1854, p. 64.

And English translations generally just mention the original narrator:

> *Narrated Abu Hurairah: Allah's Messenger said, "The Hour will not be established until you fight against the Jews, and the stone behind which a Jew will be hiding will say, 'O Muslim! There is a Jew hiding behind me, so kill him.'"*[60]

The *Sira*

The second source for the *Sunnah* is the authoritative biography of Muhammad, known as the *Sira*. It is titled *The Life of Muhammad (Sirat Rasul Allah)* and was written by Muhammad Ibn Ishaq (704-773) over 100 years after Muhammad's death.

So now when being told that "it's not in the Koran," implying that it is not a part of Islam, you can respond by mentioning the existence of the authoritative *hadiths* and *Sira*, which are second only to the Koran in importance to Islam, and are key to understanding Islam.

---

60 *Sahih Al-Bukhari*, Vol. 4, Book 56, No. 2926, p. 113. For a similarly worded *hadith* (narrated by 'Abdullah bin 'Umar), see *Sahih Al-Bukhari*, Vol. 4, Book 56, No. 2925, p. 113. This was also reported in *Sahih Muslim,* Vol. 8, No. 2921, p. 348; *Jami At-Tirmidhi*, Vol. 4, No. 2236, p. 283; and *Tafsir Ibn Kathir*, Vol. 3, p. 34. A variation of this is also found in *Sunan Ibn Majah*, Vol. 5, No. 4077, p. 268.

3

Doctrine of Abrogation

Muhammad said: *The Qur'an does not contradict itself. Rather, it testifies to the truth of itself.*[61]

Introduction

Understanding the Doctrine of Abrogation is fundamental to understanding the Koran and Islam. In order to understand abrogation, we must first get a basic understanding of the Koran. The Koran is the sacred book of Islam, and it is considered by Muslims to be the infallible, pure word of Allah, eternal and perfect, and the Koran in Arabic is an exact copy of the book that Allah has beside him in Paradise. The verses of the Koran were delivered through the angel Gabriel to the final prophet Muhammad in a series of "revelations." Muhammad started receiving such "revelations" in 610 and they continued until his death in 632.

The Koran has 114 chapters (*suras/soorahs*). However, they are not arranged in chronological order. With the exception of the first chapter, they are rather arranged generally by the length of the chapter, with the shortest chapters coming at the end. For example, the first chapter, *Al-Fatihah*, has only seven verses, while the second, third, and fourth chapters have 286, 200, and 176 verses, respectively. Translations of the Koran usually indicate whether a chapter was "revealed" in Mecca (*Makkah*) or in Medina. In the Koran you will also find that the chapters of the earlier "revelations" from Mecca are interspersed among chapters of the later "revelations" from Medina.

---

61 *Tafsir Ibn Kathir*, Vol. 2, p. 526.

Mecca vs Medina

There is an important significance to where a verse or chapter was "revealed." While in Mecca, the religion of Islam was just starting and it was generally not well received. Perhaps as a result of this, the verses of the Koran "revealed" in Mecca were generally more peaceful and accommodating toward non-Muslims than the verses later "revealed" in Medina. The verses from Medina have a general tendency to be more belligerent and intolerant, and more inclined to make sharp differentiations between Muslims (believers) and non-Muslims (disbelievers).

This can lead to a conflict between the message of a Meccan verse and that of a Medinan verse addressing the same general topic. But how can there be such a conflict if the Koran is the infallible, eternal, "revealed" word of Allah? This was covered in a Medinan verse in the Koran that introduced the concept of "abrogation":[62]

Chapter 2, Verse 106

> *Whatever a Verse (revelation) do We abrogate or cause to be forgotten, We bring a better one or similar to it. Know you not that Allah is Able to do all things?*

Abrogation therefore means that if there is a conflict between the messages of two "revelations" in the Koran, then the most recent "revelation" is the one to be followed. Consequently, a "revelation" made in Medina would supersede a similar, earlier "revelation" made in Mecca if there was a conflict between the two.

But the same chronological approach is taken when it comes to Medinan verses considered as a group. Let's look at how the doctrine of abrogation was applied to verses that were all "revealed" in Medina.

---

[62] A basis for abrogation is also found in 16:101:

> *And when We change a Verse (of the Qur'an) in place of another - and Allah knows best what He sends down - they (the disbelievers) say: "You (O Muhammad) are but a Muftari! (forger, liar)." Nay, but most of them know not.*

Banning Alcoholic Drinks - all Medinan Verses[63]

At the time of the emigration to Medina, the Muslims were consuming alcohol and gambling. In response came the following verse of the Koran:

Chapter 2, Verse 219

> *They ask you (O Muhammad) concerning alcoholic drink and gambling. Say: "In them is a great sin, and (some) benefits for men, but the sin of them is greater than their benefit"...*

But some of the Muslims continued drinking and gambling in Medina even after this verse was "revealed." They rationalized that Allah had not strictly prohibited it.

However, one day one of the Emigrants (from Mecca) led a group in prayer while he was intoxicated, and he mixed up some verses from Chapter 109 of the Koran. Here is what he said:

> *Say, 'O disbelievers! I do not worship that which you worship, but we worship that which you worship.'*

This was a significant error, because here is what he should have said:

Chapter 109, Verses 2-3

> *I worship not that which you worship, nor will you worship that which I worship.*

There were also times when some of the Muslims were so intoxicated they forgot how many cycles of prayers they had completed.

---

63 This section is based on *Tafsir Ibn Kathir*, Vol. 1, pp. 604-607, Vol. 2, pp. 466-468, and Vol. 3, pp. 256-263; *Tafsir Ahsanul-Bayan*, Vol. 1, pp. 458-459, and 650-651; and *Al-Wahidi's Asbab al-Nuzul*, pp. 73, and 99-100.

This then led to the next "revelation":

Chapter 4, Verse 43

> *O you who believe! Approach not As-Salat (the prayers) when you are in a drunken state until you know (the meaning) of what you utter...*

As a result, some of the Muslims would drink well before time so they could be sober when attending prayer. But, even after this "revelation," when it was time for prayer Muhammad would have someone announce:

> *Those in a drunken state are not to approach the prayer.*

But this didn't seem to work, because Muslims were not always sober when it came time for prayers, and disputes were occurring between intoxicated Muslims.

This eventually led to the complete prohibition of alcoholic drinks for Muslims in the following verses:

Chapter 5, Verses 90-91

> *O you who believe! Intoxicants (all kinds of alcoholic drinks) and gambling...are abominations of Shaitan's (Satan's) handiwork. So avoid (strictly all) that (abominations) in order that you may be successful. Shaitan wants only to excite enmity and hatred between you with intoxicants and gambling, and hinder you from the remembrance of Allah and from As-Salat (the prayer). So will you not then abstain?*

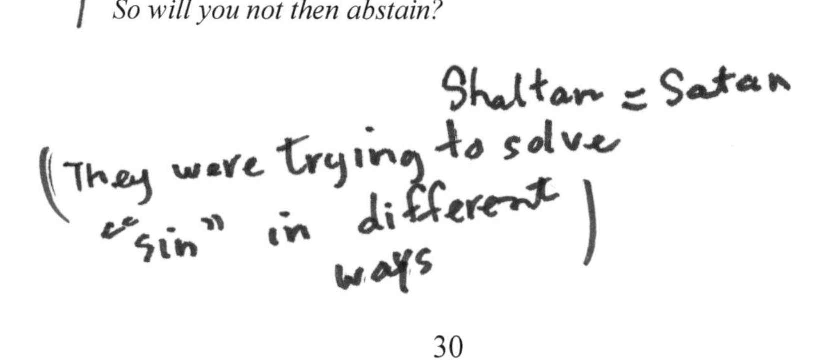

Other Examples

Now let's take a more serious look at the significance of the Doctrine of Abrogation. You might hear someone mentioning these tolerant sounding verses:

1. Chapter 4, Verse 90

   Except those who join a group, between you and whom there is a treaty (of peace), or those who approach you with their breasts restraining from fighting you as well as fighting their own people. Had Allah willed, indeed He would have given them power over you, and they would have fought you. So if they withdraw from you, and fight not against you, and offer you peace, then Allah has opened no way for you against them.

2. Chapter 6, Verse 159

   Verily, those who divide their religion and break up into sects (all kinds of religious sects), you (O Muhammad) have no concern with them in the least. Their affair is only with Allah, Who then will tell them what they used to do.

3. Chapter 86, verse 17

   So give a respite to the disbelievers; and leave them for a while.[64]

---

[64] This verse is not as benign toward disbelievers as it sounds. Ibn Kathir explained this verse by pointing out that one should not be in haste concerning the disbelievers because one will eventually "see what befalls them of torment, punishment and destruction." See *Tafsir Ibn Kathir*, Vol. 10, pp. 442-443.

A similar explanation was provided in the modern *Tafsir Ahsanul-Bayan*:

However, these three verses were abrogated by the Medinan *Verse of the Sword*:[65]

Chapter 9, Verse 5

> *Then when the Sacred Months (the 1st, 7th, 11th, and 12th months of the Islamic calendar) have passed, then kill the Mushrikun wherever you find them, and capture them and besiege them, and lie in wait for them in every ambush. But if they repent [by rejecting Shirk* [[66]] *(polytheism) and accept Islamic Monotheism] and perform As-Salat (the prayers), and give Zakat (obligatory charity), then leave their way free. Verily, Allah is Oft-Forgiving, Most Merciful.*

One might come across another tolerant sounding verse:

Chapter 2, Verse 109

> *Many of the people of the Scripture (Jews and Christians) wish that if they could turn you away as disbelievers after you have believed, out of envy from their ownselves, even after the truth (that Muhammad is Allah's Messenger) has*

> *Do not hasten for their punishment, for Allah gives respite to disbelievers and leads them on gradually to their destruction.*

Tafsir Ahsanul-Bayan (Part 30), p. 146.

[65] *Tafsir Al-Jalalayn*, pp. 206, 324 and 1317, where 9:5 is also referred to as the *Verse of the Sword*; and *Tafsir Ibn Kathir*, Vol. 2, p. 539. Ibn Kathir also referred to 9:5 as the *Verse of the Sword* - see *Tafsir Ibn Kathir*, Vol. 4, pp. 375 and 377.

[66] *Shirk* means polytheism, worshipping others along with Allah, and/or ascribing partners to Allah (including ascribing a Son to him). For a further discussion about *Shirk*, see Chapter 8, *Three Religions with the Same God?*.

> *become manifest to them. But forgive and overlook, till Allah brings His Command. Verily, Allah is able to do all things.*

But, Ibn Kathir and Al-Qurtubi pointed out that this verse had been abrogated not only by the *Verse of the Sword*, but by a second verse:[67]

Chapter 9, Verse 29

> *Fight against those who believe not in Allah, nor in the Last Day, nor forbid that which has been forbidden by Allah and His Messenger (Muhammad), and those who acknowledge not the religion of truth (i.e. Islam) among the people of the Scripture (Jews and Christians), until they pay the Jizyah with willing submission, and feel themselves subdued.*

We will take a closer look at the meanings of 9:5 and 9:29 in Chapter 5, *The Religion of Peace*.

These are but a few examples of the abrogation of verses. However, they show the importance of the *tafsirs* and the significance of the concept of abrogation when it comes to truly understanding Islam. Unless otherwise indicated, the verses mentioned in this book have not been abrogated.

> *So you should not see contradiction in the Qu'ran, for all of it is from Allah.*
>
> Abdullah Ibn 'Abbas, Muhammad's cousin and an authoritative commentator on the Koran.[68]

---

[67] *Tafsir Ibn Kathir*, Vol. 1, pp. 333-334; and *Tafsir Al-Qurtubi*, p. 328. Abrogation of 2:109 by 9:29 was also pointed out in *The Noble Qur'an*, p. 32, n. 1.

[68] *Sahih Al-Bukhari*, Vol. 6, Book 65, p. 293.

4

The Significance of Muhammad

Every saying and action of the Prophet is Shari'ah. (Islamic Law). So acceptance and obedience of the Prophet is one of the fundamentals of Islam.[69]

The Life of Muhammad

Without Muhammad, there would be no Koran and no Islam. Every verse of the Koran is a "revelation" Muhammad said he received from Allah. What do these "revelations" tell us about Muhammad? In 4:80 the Koran states that Muhammad speaks for Allah:

He who obeys the Messenger (Muhammad), has indeed obeyed Allah...[70]

And lest there be any confusion about this relationship, Muhammad himself said,

Whoever obeys me, he obeys Allah, and whoever disobeys me, he disobeys Allah...[71]

---

69 *Sunan Ibn Majah*, Vol. 4, p. 106, Comment "a."

70 There are numerous verses in the Koran commanding Muslims to obey Allah and Muhammad: e.g. 3:32, 3:132, 4:13, 4:59, 4:69, 5:92, 8:1, 8:20, 8:46, 9:71, 24:52, 24:54, 47:33, 48:17, 49:14, and 64:12.

71 *Sahih Al-Bukhari*, Vol. 9, Book 93, No. 7137, p. 160; and Vol. 4, Book 56, No. 2957, p. 131. This statement by Muhammad was also reported in *Sahih Muslim*, Vol. 6, No. 1835, p. 248.

And the Koran specifically commands Muslims to obey Muhammad: Chapter 59, Verse 7

> *...And whatsoever the Messenger (Muhammad) gives you, take it; and whatsoever he forbids you, abstain (from it). And fear Allah; verily, Allah is Severe in punishment.*

And in 33:21 the Koran states that Muhammad is considered the timeless standard by which Muslims should conduct themselves:

> *Indeed in the Messenger of Allah (Muhammad) you have a good example to follow for him who hopes for (the Meeting with) Allah and the Last Day, and remembers Allah much.*

And this too was reinforced by Muhammad stating,

> *Whoever obeys me will enter Paradise, and whoever disobeys me is the one who refuses (to enter it).*[72]

Muhammad is known as, inter alia, the Prophet of Allah, the Apostle, and Allah's Messenger. But who was Muhammad?

He was born Muhammad bin 'Abdullah (son of 'Abdullah) in Mecca in 570. His father died before he was born, and his mother died when he was 6 years old. Muhammad then lived with his grandfather for two years until his grandfather died. His uncle, Abu Talib, then became his guardian.

Abu Talib was a successful Meccan businessman, and he initially employed Muhammad as a camel driver in his commercial caravans. Muhammad started working his way up in his uncle's business and continued accompanying the caravans.

---

[72] *Sahih Al-Bukhari*, Vol. 9, Book 96, No. 7280, p. 235.

Muhammad met Khadija, who was a wealthy Meccan widow and businesswoman.[73] She hired him and he eventually became her business partner. They were married in 595 when he was 25 and she was 40. By his late 30's Muhammad was living a life of material comfort. He and Khadija had seven children; but of these, only the four daughters lived to become Muslims and emigrate to Medina. The three boys died at young ages.

It was in 610 when Muhammad, who was 40 years old, claimed to have received his first "revelation" from Allah while he was in a cave (the Cave of *Hira*) outside of Mecca.[74] He started quietly preaching about these "revelations" to his family and close friends. Khadija became the first Muslim. The second Muslim was Muhammad's ten year old cousin, Ali bin Abi Talib. But the number of Muslims grew slowly.

For the first 3 years, Muhammad kept his preaching about Islam somewhat concealed. There was even a verse of the Koran "revealed" about this:

Chapter 17, Verse 110

> *Say (O Muhammad): Invoke Allah or invoke the Most Gracious (Allah), by whatever name you invoke Him (it is the same), for to Him belong the Best Names. And offer your Salat (prayer) neither aloud nor in a low voice, but follow a way between.*

And the small number of additional Muslims who joined him prayed away from the view of their fellow tribe members.

---

[73] It has been claimed that Khadija was an example of how well women were treated in early Islam. This is not accurate because before meeting Muhammad, and well before the advent of Islam, Khadija was already a wealthy Meccan businesswoman and a much sought-after widow.

[74] The cave was located on Mt. Nur, about two miles from Mecca. It was described as four yards long and 1.75 yards wide. See *Al-Wahidi's Asbab al-Nuzur*, p. 2, n. 4.

But in 613 Muhammad received a "revelation" telling him to start openly preaching Islam in Mecca:

Chapter 15, Verse 94

> *Therefore proclaim openly (Allah's Message - Islamic Monotheism) that which you are commanded, and turn away from Al-Mushrikun (polytheists, idolaters, and disbelievers).*

For many years Mecca had been a destination for pilgrims because it was the location of the Ka'bah, a sacred building housing numerous pagan tribal gods. Providing food and lodging for these pilgrims was a lucrative business for many Meccans. But now Muhammad was going around preaching that there was only one god. Consequently, resistance to this new religion started building among the Meccans, and the Muslims started being harassed and ill-treated.

In 615 some of the Muslims actually emigrated to Abyssinia (Ethiopia) for safety. Muhammad remained in Mecca under the protection of Abu Talib. However, Muslims without the protection of a powerful Meccan individual or tribe were harassed, and even at times beaten, by some of the other Meccans.[75] And even though Muhammad was protected by his uncle, he was still harassed. There were reports that a sheep's uterus used to be thrown at him at times while he was praying, and that one was even thrown into his cooking pot.[76] And once the entrails of a camel were placed on Muhammad's back while he was prostrated in prayer; they were removed by his daughter Fatima.[77]

---

75 *The Life of Muhammad.* pp. 143-145.

76 Ibid., p. 191.

77 *Sahih Al-Bukhari*, Vol. 1, Book 4, No. 240, p. 182. This was also related in *Sahih Muslim*, Vol. 6, Nos. 1794-1794R1, pp. 212-213.

In 619 both Khadija and Abu Talib, died. Even though Muhammad had requested it, Abu Talib refused to convert to Islam on his death bad.[78] Fortunately for Muhammad, he was able to find protection from another powerful Meccan named Al-Mut'im b. 'Adi.

For a number of years Muhammad had been going amongst the pilgrims preaching Islam, with no success. However, in 620 he met with a group of six men from Medina who were making a pilgrimage to Mecca. He converted this group to Islam, and the religion started to grow in Medina. These early Muslim converts in Medina became known as the *Ansar* (Helpers). They also provided a new base of support for Muhammad.

In 621, twelve of the *Ansar* came to Mecca and met with Muhammad. They took an oath of allegiance to Muhammad and a pledge to accept and practice Islam. This became known as the First Pledge of al-'Aqabah. However, there was no consideration of fighting or providing protection for Muhammad. Therefore this first pledge was known as the "Pledge of Women." And Islam continued to grow in Medina.

In June 622, 70-73 males and two females of the *Ansar* joined other (non-Muslim) Medinans in a pilgrimage to Mecca. These *Ansar* secretly met with Muhammad. The men took an oath of allegiance to Muhammad and swore to protect him as they would their wives and children if he came to Medina. This oath included a pledge to wage war against all of mankind, and it became known as the Second Pledge of al-'Aqabah.[79]

---

[78] Muhammad later claimed to have interceded for Abu Talib with Allah. Muhammad said that Abu Talib was "in a shallow fire, and had it not been for me, he would have been in the bottom of the (Hell) Fire." See *Sahih Al-Bukhari*, Vol. 5, Book 63, No. 3883, p. 130.

[79] Al-Tabari wrote:

> *When they gathered to take the oath of allegiance to the Messenger of God, al-'Abbas b. 'Ubadah b. Nadlah al-Ansari, the brother of the Banu Salim b. 'Awf, said, "People of the Khazraj, do you know what you are pledging yourselves to in swearing allegiance to this man?" "Yes," they said. He*

Prior to this, Muhammad had not been given permission by Allah to fight or to shed blood. After this second pledge, verses of the Koran were soon "revealed" to Muhammad that allowed the Muslims to start fighting. For example:

> *continued, "In swearing allegiance to him you are pledging yourselves to wage war against all mankind..."*

See Abu Ja'far Muhammad b. Jarir al-Tabari, *The History of al-Tabari: Muhammad at Mecca*, Vol. VI, trans. and annotated W. Montgomery Watt and M. V. McDonald (Albany, New York: State University of New York Press, 1988), p. 134. This was reported with slightly different wording in *The Life of Muhammad*, p. 204. This oath also meant that the *Ansar* would have to sever their ties with the Jews of Medina:

> *O Messenger of God, there are ties between us and other people which we shall have to sever (meaning the Jews). If we do this and God gives you victory, will you perhaps return to your own people and leave us?" The Messenger of God smiled and then said, "Rather, blood is blood, and blood shed without retaliation is blood shed without retaliation. You are of me and I am of you. I shall fight whomever you fight and make peace with whomever you make peace with."*

The History of al-Tabari: Muhammad at Mecca, p. 133. For another version of this see *The Life of Muhammad*, pp. 203-204.

The *Ansar* would later say

> *We are those who have given the Bai'a (pledge) to Muhammad for Jihad (i.e. holy fighting) as long as we live.*

See *Sahih Al-Bukhari*, Vol. 5, Book 63, No. 3796, p. 86. Another *hadith* mentioned the Emigrants (from Mecca) as having also given that pledge. See *Sahih Al-Bukhari*, Vol. 4, Book 56, No. 2834, p. 71.

1. Chapter 2, Verse 193

> *And fight them until there is no more Fitnah (disbelief and worshipping of others along with Allah) and (all and every kind of) worship is for Allah (Alone)...*

2. Chapter 22, Verse 39

> *Permission to fight (against disbelievers) is given to those (believers) who are fought against, because they have been wronged; and surely, Allah is able to give them (believers) victory.*

Ibn 'Abbas, a cousin of Muhammad's, said that when 22:39 was revealed, he knew "there would be fighting" because this verse was the first one "that was revealed concerning fighting."[80]

622

In July 622 the Muslims started leaving Mecca for Medina.[81] There were about 70 Muslim males and their families who emigrated from Mecca. They became known as the *Muhajirun* (Emigrants). Muhammad emigrated to Medina in September of that year, accompanied by Abu Bakr, his close companion and father-in-law. This emigration was known as the *Hijra*, and it was so significant for Islam that the year 622 became the first year of the Muslim calendar.

In early 623 Muhammad started sending out Muslim raiding parties to intercept and attack Meccan caravans, most of the time with no success. However, matters eventually started to favor the Muslims. In March 624

---

[80] Abu Abdur Rahman Ahmad bin Shu'aib bin 'Ali An-Nasa'i, *Sunan An-Nasa'i*, trans. Nasiruddin al-Khattab, Vol. 4 (Riyadh, Kingdom of Saudi Arabia: Darussalam, 2007), No. 3087, p. 15. See *The Life of Muhammad*, pp. 212-213, for further details. Abu Bakr also said that when this verse was revealed, "I knew at that point that there will be fighting." See *Al-Wahidi's Asbab al-Nuzul*, p. 159.

[81] Medina was originally known as *Yathrib*. Muhammad renamed it *Madinat al-Nabi* (City of the Prophet).

the Muslims set out to attack a Meccan caravan. The caravan avoided them and the Muslims ended up fighting with, and defeating, a much larger relief force from Mecca. This was known as the Battle of Badr, and Muhammad said that angels had assisted them in fighting against the Meccans. Afterwards, Muhammad received a "revelation" allowing the plunder from this battle, and all future plunder, to be divided among the Muslim warriors. And Chapter 8 of the Koran, *Al-Anfal* (The Spoils of War), was "revealed" to Muhammad about events that happened during this battle.

As the *Chronology* section of this book shows, over the next few years there were numerous battles and raids by the Muslims against their non-Muslim neighbors. The military strength of the Muslims grew, as did the number of converts to Islam. In January 630, less than eight years after the *Hijra*, Muhammad returned with an army of 10,000 Muslim warriors and conquered Mecca. For a discussion about reasons for this exponential growth in Muslim military power, see Footnotes 838 and 839.

Over the next two years there were numerous battles as the Muslims consolidated their hold on the Arabian peninsula. Muhammad continued to live in Medina and received "revelations" until his death. He died in Medina on June 7, 632. On his death bed he gave one last command:

> *It has been narrated by 'Umar b. Al-Khattab that he heard the Messenger of Allah (may peace be upon him) saying: I will expel the Jews and Christians from the Arabian Peninsula and will not leave any but Muslims.*[82]

---

[82] *Sahih Muslim*, Vol. 5, No. 1767, p. 189; *Sunan Abu Dawud*, Vol. 3, No. 3030, p. 517; *Jami' At-Tirmidhi*, Vol. 3, Nos. 1606-1607, p. 368; and *The Sealed Nectar*, p. 554 (where it is stated that Muhammad said this four days before his death). For reports that Muhammad actually mentioned expelling non-Muslims in general, see *Sahih Al-Bukhari*, Vol. 4, Book 56, No. 3053, pp. 179-180, and Vol. 5, Book 64, No. 4431, pp. 438-439; *The Life of Muhammad*, p. 689; and *The History of al-Tabari: The Last Years of the Prophet*, p. 175.

In the following sections we will learn more about Muhammad, his teachings, and his relationship to the Muslims around him.

The Wives of Muhammad

It is generally accepted that Muhammad consummated marriages with eleven women during his life. During the time of his first marriage, he had only one wife, Khadija. During the last three years of his life, he had nine wives at one time. Here are his wives in order of marriage:

1. **Khadija bint Khuwaylid b. Asad**

    Khadija was Muhammad's first wife. She was a widow and already a wealthy businesswoman when Muhammad went to work for her. When they married in 595 Muhammad was 25 and Khadija was 40. They had seven children:

    Three sons: Al-Qasim, Al-Tayyib, and Al-Tahir

    Four daughters: Ruqayyah, Zaynab, Umm Kulthum, and Fatima

    Their three sons died as young children. The four daughters all lived to become Muslims and emigrate to Medina. Khadija was the first person to accept Islam. She died in 619.

2. **Sawdah bint Zam'ah b. Qays**

    Married to Muhammad in 619 after Khadija's death.

3. **Aisha bint Abi Bakr al-Siddiq**

Aisha

> Muhammad, at about age 50, married Aisha in April 620, when she was only six years old, and he consummated the marriage in May 623, when she was nine.[83] She was his

---

[83] *Sahih Al-Bukhari*, Vol. 5, Book 63, No. 3896, p. 140 (statement by "Hisham's father"); Vol. 7, Book 67, No. 5133, p. 57 (statement by Aisha); and Vol. 7, Book 67, No. 5158, p. 69 (statement by 'Urwa). Also see *Sunan Ibn Majah*, Vol. 3, No. 1877, p. 77 (statement by 'Abdullah that Aisha was seven when she married Muhammad and nine when she consummated the marriage).

There are additional statements about this from Aisha in *Sahih Muslim*, Vol. 4, Nos. 1422-1422R3, pp. 353-355; *Sunan Abu Dawud*, Vol. 2, No. 2121, p. 540; *Sunan An-Nasa'i*, Vol. 4, Nos. 3257-3260, pp. 118-119, and Nos. 3380-3381, pp. 181-182; and Abu Ja'far Muhammad b. Jarir al-Tabari, *The History of al-Tabari: The Foundation of the Community*, Vol. VII, trans. M. V. McDonald and annotated W. Montgomery Watt (Albany, New York: State University of New York Press, 1987), pp. 6-7.

A 1979 award-winning biography of Muhammad stated that he married Aisha when she was six and he consummated the marriage when she was nine - see *The Sealed Nectar*, pp. 176-177, and 562. These ages for Aisha were also stated in *The Life of Muhammad*, p. 792, n. 918 (where the respective ages were seven, and "nine or ten"; and in a 2004 book about Muhammad's wives: *The Honorable Wives of the Prophet*, ed. Abdul Ahad (Riyadh, Kingdom of Saudi Arabia: Darussalam, 2004), p. 42.

The comment for *Sunan An-Nasa'i Hadith* No. 3380 pointed out that, "Due to climatic conditions and her own physical wholesomeness," Aisha "had reached puberty at the age of nine years." - see *Sunan An-Nasa'i*, Vol. 4, comment to *Hadith* No. 3380, p. 181. With regard to *Hadiths* 3257-3260 in this same volume, reporting that Aisha said her marriage was consummated when she was nine, the comments noted:

> *Some individuals, who ostensibly claim to be researchers, deny the aforementioned narrations concerning the age of 'Aishah. These narrations are, however, authentic. It is the statement of 'Aishah herself, which her various pupils have transmitted from her. A great majority of her pupils cannot make the same mistake.*

Sunan An-Nasa'i, Vol. 4, Comments, p. 119.

favorite wife. Aisha talked about the day her marriage was consummated in Medina:

> *The Messenger of God came to our house and men and women of the Ansar gathered around him. My mother came to me while I was being swung on a swing between two branches and got me down. Jumaymah, my nurse, took over and wiped my face with some water and started leading me. When I was at the door, she stopped so I could catch my breath. I was then brought [in] while the Messenger of God was sitting on a bed in our house. [My mother] made me sit on his lap and said, "These are your relatives. May God bless you with them and bless them with you!" Then the men and women got up and left. The Messenger of God consummated his marriage with me in my house when I was nine years old.*[84]

4. **Hafsa bint 'Umar b. al-Khattab** 625

Married to Muhammad in February 625.

The translator of the *Sahih Muslim* collection wrote that Aisha

> *was a precocious girl and was developing both in mind and body with rapidity peculiar to such rare personalities.*

Sahih Muslim, Vol. 4, p. 354, n. 1.

[84] *The History of al-Tabari: The Last Years of the Prophet*, pp. 130-131. For similar narrations from Aisha, see *Sahih Al-Bukhari*, Vol. 5, Book 63, No. 3894, pp. 139-140; *Sunan Abu Dawud*, Vol. 5, Nos. 4933-4937, pp. 327-328; *Sunan Ibn Majah*, Vol. 3, No. 1876, p. 76, where at the time Aisha was "with some of my friends"; and *Sahih Muslim*, Vol. 4, No. 1422, p. 354, where Aisha said she was playing on the swing "along with my playmates."

5. **Zaynab bint Khuzaymah**

Married to Muhammad in March 625 and died eight months later.

6. **Hind bint Abi Umayyah (Umm Salamah)**

Married to Muhammad in March 626.

7. **Zaynab bint Jahsh**

Married to Muhammad in April 627.

8. **Juwayriyyah bint al-Harith**

Juwayriyyah, whose first name had been Barrah, was 20 years old and among the captives taken when the Muslims defeated the Bani Al-Mustaliq tribe in December 627. Juwayriyyah had been married to Musafih bin Safwan, who was killed in the battle, and she was the daughter of Al-Harith bin Abu Dirar, the leader of the Bani Al-Mustaliq. She was originally given to one of the Muslim warriors. But because of her status, she was then given to Muhammad, who married her and changed her first name to Juwayriyyah.

9. **Ramlah bint Abi Sufyan (Umm Habibah)**

Married to Muhammad in May 628.

10. **Safiyyah bint Huyayy**

Safiyyah was among the captives taken when the Muslims conquered Khaybar in May 628.[85] Muhammad married her after ordering the torture and beheading of her husband, Kinanah b. al-Rabi'. Kinanah had refused to reveal the location of the rest of the treasure of the Bani al-Nadir, the Jewish tribe that had been expelled from Medina in August 625, and some of whom had subsequently settled in Khaybar.[86] Safiyyah's father had also been killed during the battle.

---

[85] Like Juwayriyyah, Safiyyah had originally been given to another Muslim warrior when the war plunder was divided. Muhammad bought her from that warrior for seven slaves - see *Sunan Ibn Majah*, Vol. 3, No. 2272 and Comments, p. 298. This purchase price was also mentioned in *Sahih Muslim*, Vol. 4, No. 1365R4, p. 360; and Sa'd Yusuf Abu 'Aziz, *Men and Women Around the Messenger*, trans. Suleman Fulani (Riyadh, Kingdom of Saudi Arabia: Darussalam, 2009), p. 587. For a general reference that Muhammad bought Safiyyah from another Muslim, see *The History of al-Tabari: The Last Years of the Prophet*, p. 135, n. 899.

[86] When Kinanah b. al-Rabi' refused to reveal the location, Muhammad

> *gave orders to al-Zubayr b. al-'Awwam, 'Torture him until you extract what he has,' so he kindled a fire with flint and steel on his chest until he was nearly dead. Then the apostle delivered him to Muhammad b. Maslama and he struck off his head, in revenge for his brother Mahmud.*

See *The Life of Muhammad*, p. 515. This was also related in Abu Ja'far Muhammad b. Jarir al-Tabari, *The History of al-Tabari: The Victory of Islam*, Vol. VIII, trans. and annotated Michael Fishbein (Albany, New York: State University of New York Press, 1997), pp. 122-123. However, in a modern biography of Muhammad it was stated that Kinanah b. al-Rabi' was simply "killed" for refusing to reveal the location of a bag of jewels and money - see *The Sealed Nectar*, p. 439.

11. **Maymunah bint al-Harith**

Married to Muhammad in March 629.

These were the wives of Muhammad. And it was reported that Muhammad had the strength and stamina to have sexual relations with all of his wives in one day:

> *Narrated Qatada: Anas bin Malik said, "The Prophet used to visit all his wives in a round, during the day and night and they were eleven in number." I asked Anas, "Had the Prophet the strength for it?" Anas replied, "We used to say that the Prophet was given the strength of thirty (men)." And Sa'id said on the authority of Qatada that Anas had told him about nine wives only (not eleven).*[87]

But Muhammad usually tried to spend equal amounts of time, in terms of nights, with each of his wives. However, a verse of the Koran was later "revealed" to him allowing him the option of spending more time, or no time, with a particular wife, because Allah knew that Muhammad liked some wives more than others; and this verse also allowed him to accept or reject any other woman who offered herself to him: [88]

Chapter 33, Verse 51

> *You (O Muhammad) can postpone (the turn of) whom you will of them (your wives), and you may receive whom you will. And whomsoever you desire of those whom you have set aside (her turn temporarily), it is no sin on you (to*

---

[87] *Sahih Al-Bukhari*, Vol. 1, Book 5, No. 268, p. 195. For a shorter narration about this in which Anas specified that there were only nine wives and that this was done during one night, see *Sahih Al-Bukhari*, Vol. 1, Book 5, No. 284, p. 202; and Vol. 7, Book 67, No. 5068, p. 22.

[88] *Tafsir Ibn Kathir*, Vol. 8, pp. 17-20; *Tafsir Ahsanul-Bayan*, Vol. 4, pp. 403-404; *Tafsir Al-Jalalayn*, pp. 907-908; and *Tafsir Ibn'Abbas*, p. 551.

receive her again); that is better that they may be comforted and not grieved, and may all be pleased with what you give them. Allah knows what is in your hearts, And Allah is Ever All-Knowing, Most Forbearing.

As a result of this "revelation," Muhammad's wife Aisha made an interesting observation:

I said (to the Prophet), "I feel that your Lord hastens in fulfilling your wishes and desires."[89]

During the last three years of Muhammad's life he had nine wives at one time. But the Koran states that a Muslim man can only have up to four wives at a time. This is found in 4:3:[90]

And if you fear that you shall not be able to deal justly with the orphan girls then marry (other) women of your choice, two or three, or four;...

However, 33:50 was later "revealed," and it provided a lengthy exemption from this limitation of four wives, but only for Muhammad:[91]

O Prophet (Muhammad)! Verily, We have made lawful for you your wives, to whom you have paid their Mahr (bridal money given by the husband to his wife at the time

---

[89] *Sahih Al-Bukhari*, Vol. 6, Book 65, No. 4788, p. 268. A similarly worded observation by Aisha was reported in *Sahih Al-Bukhari*, Vol. 7, Book 67, No. 5113, p. 45; *Sunan Ibn Majah*, Vol. 3, No. 2000, p. 143; *Sunan An-Nasa'i*, Vol. 4, No. 3201, p. 83; and *Tafsir Ibn Kathir*, Vol. 7, p. 722, and Vol. 8, p. 18.

[90] *Tafsir Ibn Kathir*, Vol. 2, pp. 374-375; *Tafsir Al-Jalalayn*, p. 174; *Tafsir Ahsanul-Bayan*, Vol. 1, p. 418; and *Tafsir Ibn 'Abbas*, p. 99.

[91] *Tafsir Ibn Kathir*, Vol. 7, p. 724; *Tafsir Al-Jalalayn*, p. 907; *Tafsir Ahsanul-Bayan*, Vol. 4, pp. 401-402; and *Tafsir Ibn'Abbas*, p. 551. For commentary on 33:50 see Chapter 11, *Whom Your Right Hands Possess*.

of marriage), and those (slaves) whom your right hand possesses - whom Allah has given to you, and the daughters of your 'Amm (paternal uncles) and the daughters of your 'Ammat (paternal aunts) and the daughters of your Khal (maternal uncles) and the daughters of your Khalat (maternal aunts) who migrated (from Makkah) with you, and a believing woman if she offers herself to the Prophet, and the Prophet wishes to marry her - a privilege for you only, not for the (rest of) the believers. Indeed We know what We have enjoined upon them about their wives and those (slaves) whom their right hands possess, in order that there should be no difficulty on you. And Allah is Ever Oft-Forgiving, Most Merciful.

The "Slave Concubines" of Muhammad[92]

Muhammad had at least two slave concubines:

1. **Mariyah bint Sham'un (Qibtiyyah),[93] the Copt**

   Mariyah was a Coptic Christian given to Muhammad by al-Muqawis, the ruler of Egypt. She bore Muhammad a son named Ibrahim, who died as a young child in January 632.[94] Mariyah was the female slave mentioned in the

---

[92] This is the description used in *The History of al-Tabari: The Last Years of the Prophet*, p. 141. Ibn Hisham said he had been told that Mariyah was Muhammad's "concubine" - see *The Life of Muhammad*, p. 711, n. 129. Mariyah and Rayhanah were referred to as Muhammad's "slave girls" in the *Tafsir Ahsanul-Bayan*, Vol. 4, p. 402.

[93] In listing "slave girls" owned by Muhammad, Ibn Kathir identified Mariyah as Mariyah Al-Qibtiyyah - see *Tafsir Ibn Kathir*, Vol. 7, p. 720.

[94] Muhammad said, "There is a wet-nurse for him in Paradise." See *Sahih Al-Bukhari*, Vol. 2, Book 23, No. 1382, p. 266.

following *hadith* where two of Muhammad's wives were angry that he had intercourse with a female slave. This resulted in the "revelation" of 66:1 of the Koran, a portion of which is mentioned at the end of the *hadith*:

> *It was narrated from Anas, that the Messenger of Allah had a female slave with whom he had intercourse, but 'Aishah and Hafsah would not leave him alone until he said that she was forbidden for him. Then Allah, the Mighty and Sublime, revealed: "O Prophet! Why do you forbid (for yourself) that which Allah has allowed to you, until the end of the Verse.*[95]

The *Tafsir Al-Jalalayn* noted that Hafsa was angry because while she was away, Muhammad had slept with Mariyah in Hafsa's bed.[96]

2. **Rayhanah bint Zayd al-Quraziyyah (Rayhanah bint 'Amr b. Khunafah)**

Rayhanah was among the captives when the Muslims defeated the Bani Al-Qurayzah, and she was chosen by

---

[95] *Sunan An-Nasa'i*, Vol. 4, No. 3411, pp. 204-205. Here is 66:1:

> *O Prophet! Why do you forbid (for yourself) that which Allah has allowed to you, seeking to please your wives? And Allah is Oft-Forgiving, Most Merciful.*

Technically, 33:50 not only exempted Muhammad from the restriction on having only four wives, but also made Mariyah "lawful" for him because she was his slave.

[96] *Tafsir Al-Jalalayn*, p. 1220. A variation of this *hadith* reported that Hafsa actually found Muhammad and Mariyah in her house engaged in "an intimate moment." See *Al-Wahidi's Asbab al-Nuzul*, p. 237.

627 - 632 + Muhammad 632

Muhammad. He freed her after she accepted Islam and married her in 627.[97] She died soon after his return from the Farewell Pilgrimage in February 632.

In one source it was reported that Muhammad also had

> *two more slave girls. Jamilah, a captive, and another one, a bondwoman granted to him by Zainab bint Jahsh.*[98]

And Ibn Ishaq wrote that on one occasion Muhammad had been given "four slave girls," one of whom was Mariyah.[99]

How the Muslims viewed Muhammad

Muhammad was treated as if he had divine qualities:

1. *...By Allah, whenever Allah's Messenger spitted, the spittle would fall in the hand of one of them (i.e., the Prophet's companions) who would rub it on his face and skin; if he ordered them they would carry out his orders immediately; if he performed ablution, they would struggle to take the remaining water; and when they*

---

[97] *The History of al-Tabari: The Last Years of the Prophet*, p. 137, n. 909. However, Ibn Ishaq did not indicate that Muhammad freed Rayhanah; Ibn Ishaq wrote that Rayhanah "remained with him until she died, in his power." See *The Life of Muhammad*, p. 466. That she was Muhammad's "captive" instead of a freed woman was also pointed out in *The Sealed Nectar*, p. 565. In listing "slave girls" owned by Muhammad, Ibn Kathir identified Rayhanah as Rayhanah bint Sham'un An-Nadariyyah - *Tafsir Ibn Kathir*, Vol. 7, p. 720.

[98] *The Sealed Nectar*, p. 565.

[99] *The Life of Muhammad*, p. 653.

spoke to him, they would lower their voices and would not look at his face constantly out of respect...[100]

2. *Narrated Abu Juhaifa: I came to the Prophet while he was inside a red leather tent and I saw Bilal taking the remaining water of the ablution of the Prophet, and the people were taking of that water and rubbing it on their faces; and whoever could not get anything of it, would share the moisture of the hand of his companion (and then rub it on his face).*[101]

3. Umm Salama, one of Muhammad's wives, would dip some of Muhammad's hair into a vessel of water, which would then be used for bathing, or drank, by a sick person seeking to be healed.[102]

Lying about Muhammad

Muhammad said that those who intentionally lied about him would go to the Fires of Hell:

---

[100] *Sahih Al-Bukhari*, Vol. 3, Book 54, No. 2731-2732, p. 531. A shorter version of this, focusing on the spittle, was reported in *Sahih Al-Bukhari*, Vol. 1, Book 4, Chapter 70, p. 183. Muhammad's wife Aisha even sought the "blessing from the saliva" of Muhammad by using his *Siwak* after he cleaned his teeth - see *Sunan Abu Dawud*, Vol. 1, No. 52, and Comments, p. 54. The *Siwak* is a toothbrush made from a stick by flaring one end - a "toothstick."

[101] *Sahih Al-Bukhari*, Vol. 7, Book 77, No. 5859, p. 407. There was a report that drinking the remainder of Muhammad's ablution water might have had curative powers - *Sahih Al-Bukhari*, Vol. 4, Book 61, No. 3541, p. 456.

[102] Ibid., Vol. 7, Book 77, No. 5896, p. 422, and n.1.

> *Narrated 'Ali: The Prophet said, "Do not tell a lie against me for whoever tells a lie against me (intentionally) then he will surely enter Hell-fire."*[103]

But there was a fear that even an unintentional misstatement about Muhammad would be seen as intentional, with the same dire consequences:

> *Narrated Anas: The fact which stops me from narrating a great number of Ahadith to you is that the Prophet said: "Whoever tells a lie against me intentionally, then (surely) let him occupy his seat in Hell-fire."*[104]

The concern that an unintentional lie about Muhammad would be treated as intentional could be based on the following *hadiths*:

1. *It was narrated that Abu Qatadah said: "While he was on this pulpit, I heard the Messenger of Allah saying: 'Beware of narrating too many Ahadith from me. Whoever attributes something to me, let him speak the truth faithfully. Whoever attributes to me something that I did not say, let him take his place in Hell.'"*[105]

2. *It was narrated that Abu Hurairah said: "The Messenger*

---

[103] Ibid., Vol. 1, Book 3, No. 106, p. 118. For additional examples of narrators reporting the same statement from Muhammad, see *Sahih Al-Bukhari*, Vol. 1, Book 3, Nos. 107, 109, and 110, pp. 118-119; Vol. 2, Book 23, No. 1291, pp. 220-221; and *Jami' At-Tirmidhi*, Vol. 5, Nos. 2661-2662, pp. 61-62.

[104] *Sahih Al-Bukhari*, Vol. 1, Book 3, No. 108, p. 119. Az-Zubair, another of Muhammad's companions, expressed the same reason for not providing narratives about Muhammad - see *Sunan Abu Dawud*, Vol. 4, No. 3651, p. 212.

[105] *Sunan Ibn Majah*, Vol. 1, No. 35, p. 96.

of Allah said: 'Whoever attributes to me something that I have not said, let him take his place in Hell.'"[106]

3. *...Ibn 'Abbas who said: "Allah's Messenger, Allah bless him and give him peace, said: 'Avoid reporting anything from me other than what you know, for whoever lies about me shall be in hell fire: and whoever lies about the Qur'an shall enter hell fire.'"*[107]

Those Who Criticize or Revile Muhammad

Uttering irreverent words about Muhammad is blasphemy:

Chapter 9, Verse 74

> *They swear by Allah that they said nothing (bad), but really they said the word of disbelief, and they disbelieved after accepting Islam...*

The modern *Tafsir Ahsanul-Bayan* explained this section of 9:74:

> *...We also learn from this verse that uttering irreverent words about the Messenger of Allah is blasphemy and heresy. It puts a person outside the pale of Islam.*[108]

And the Koran said that those who "annoy" Muhammad would be cursed by Allah:

---

106 Ibid., No. 34, p. 96.

107 *Al-Wahidi's Asbab al-Nuzul*, p. 2. For additional *hadiths* about the dire consequences of telling a lie about Muhammad, intentional or not, see *Jami' At-Tirmidhi*, Vol. 5, Nos. 2659-2660, pp. 59-60.

108 *Tafsir Ahsanul-Bayan*, Vol. 2, p. 383.

Chapter 33, Verse 57

> *Verily, those who annoy Allah and His Messenger, Allah has cursed them in this world and in the Hereafter, and has prepared for them a humiliating torment.*

Ibn Kathir explained this verse:

> *Here, Allah warns and threatens those who annoy Him by going against His commands and doing that which He has forbidden, and who persist in doing so, and those who annoy His Messenger by accusing him of having faults or shortcomings - Allah forbid...The Ayah appears to be general in meaning and to apply to all those who annoy him* [Muhammad] *in any way, because whoever annoys him annoys Allah, just as whoever obeys him obeys Allah.*[109]

Annoying Allah included attributing a son to him, and annoying Muhammad included denying that Muhammad was the Messenger of Allah; and there was a belief among some Muslim scholars that 33:57 was directed against Christians and Jews.[110]

Muhammad did not like to be criticized or reviled. As his power grew, he killed a number of those who had criticized or even mocked him (details of these killings are in the Chronology section). This was best summarized in a letter written after the Muslim conquest of Mecca. It was sent to the poet Ka'b bin Zuhair, who used to satirize Muhammad, from his brother:

> *Allah's Messenger killed some men in Makkah who used to satirize and harm him, and the poets who survived fled in all directions for their lives. So, if you want to save*

---

109 *Tafsir Ibn Kathir*, Vol. 8, pp. 42-43.

110 *Tafsir Al-Jalalayn*, p. 910; *Tafsir Ibn 'Abbas*, p. 552; and *Tafsir Ahsanul-Bayan*, Vol. 4, p. 412.

your skin, hasten to Allah's Messenger. He never kills those who come to him repenting. If you refuse to do as I say, it is up to you to try to save your skin by any means.[111]

After further correspondence between the brothers, Ka'b travelled to Medina, converted to Islam, and was forgiven by Muhammad.

Muhammad said there was no punishment for the killing of anyone who reviled and/or criticized him:

1. *It was narrated that 'Ikrimah said: "Ibn 'Abbas told us that a blind man had a female slave who had borne him a child (Umm Walad* [[112]]*) who reviled the Prophet and disparaged him, and he told her not to do that, but she did not stop, and he rebuked her, but she paid no heed. One night she started to disparage and revile the Prophet, so he took a dagger and put it in her stomach and pressed on it and killed her. There fell between her legs a child who was smeared with the blood that was there. The next morning mention of that was made to the Prophet and he assembled the people and said: 'By Allah, I adjure the man who did this, to stand up.' The blind man stood up and came through the people, trembling, and he came and sat before the Prophet. He said: 'O Messenger of Allah, I am the one who did it. She used to revile you and disparage you, and I told her not to do it, but she did not stop, and I rebuked her, but she paid no heed. I have two sons from her who are like two pearls, and she was good to me. Last night she started to revile you and disparage you, and I took a dagger and placed it on her stomach and I pressed on it until I*

---

[111] *The Sealed Nectar*, p. 521.

[112] *Umm* is the Arabic word for mother or "mother of." *Umm Walad* is a concubine who has born a child to her master.

killed her.' The Prophet said: 'Bear witness that no retaliation is due for her blood.'"[113]

2. *It was narrated from 'Ali that a Jewish woman used to revile and disparage the Prophet. A man strangled her until she died, and the Messenger of Allah declared that no recompense was payable for her blood.*[114]

And then there was the case of Uqba bin Abu Mu'ayt. He had initially listened to Muhammad preaching in Mecca. However, after being soundly criticized for doing so, Uqba spat in Muhammad's face,[115] and then continued to mistreat Muhammad.[116] And, in the incident mentioned earlier, Uqba had even thrown the entrails of a camel onto Muhammad's back while he was prostrated in prayer.[117] However, during the later battle of Badr in 624, Uqba was captured by the Muslims. After the battle was over, Muhammad ordered that Uqba be killed. Uqba said, "But who will look after my children, O Muhammad?" Muhammad replied, "Hell," and Uqba was killed.[118]

The tradition of treating harshly those who reviled Muhammad was continued. Soon after Muhammad's death, two singing women appeared before Al-Muhajir, the Muslim governor of the Yemen. One of them sang

---

113 *Sunan Abu Dawud*, Vol. 5, No. 4361, pp. 20-21. This narration was also reported in *Sunan An-Nasa'i*, Vol. 5, No. 4075, pp. 66-67; in this *hadith* Muhammad said, "I bear witness that her blood is permissible."

114 *Sunan Abu Dawud*, Vol. 5, No. 4362, p. 21.

115 *The Life of Muhammad*, p. 164.

116 Ibid., p. 191.

117 *Sahih Al-Bukhari*, Vol. 1, Book 4, No. 240, p. 182; and *Sahih Muslim*, Vol. 6, No. 1794R1, p. 213. Also see *Sunan Abu Dawud*, Vol. 3, No. 2686 and Comments, pp. 307-308.

118 *The Life of Muhammad*, p. 308.

a song reviling Muhammad, and Al-Muhajir had her hand cut off and a front tooth pulled out. Abu Bakr, then the Caliph, wrote to Al-Muhajir:

> *I have learned what you did regarding the woman who sang and piped with abuse of the Apostle of God. If you had not beaten me to (punishing her), I would have ordered you to kill her, for the punishment (for abuse) of prophets is not like (other) punishments. So whoever does (something like) that among those claiming to be Muslims is (actually) an apostate; or among those claiming to be at peace with the Muslims is (actually) at war (with them) and a traitor...Now then: I have learned that you cut off the hand of a woman because she sang satirizing the Muslims, and that you pulled her front tooth. If she was among those who claim (to have embraced) Islam, then (it is) good discipline and a reprimand, and not mutilation.*[119]

Stoning Adulterers

One might hear that stoning someone to death for committing adultery is not a part of Islam because it is not mentioned in the Koran. This is partially correct: stoning is not mentioned in the Koran. The original punishment for adultery was to be found in Chapter 4, Verse 15:

> *And those of your women who commit illegal sexual intercourse, take the evidence of four witnesses from amongst you against them; and if they testify, confine them (i.e. women) to houses until death comes to them or Allah ordains for them some (other) way.*

[119] Abu Ja'far Muhammad b. Jarir al-Tabari, *The History of al-Tabari: The Conquest of Arabia*, Vol. X, trans. and annotated Fred M. Donner (Albany, New York: State University of New York Press, 1993), pp. 191-192.

Ibn Kathir explained this verse in a section titled *The Adulteress is Confined to her House; A Command Later Abrogated*:

> *At the beginning of Islam, the ruling was that if a woman commits adultery as stipulated by sufficient proof, she was confined to her home, without leave, until she died...'Some other way' mentioned here is the abrogation of this ruling that came later. Ibn Abbas said, "The early ruling was confinement, until Allah sent down Surat an-Nur (chapter 24) which abrogated that ruling with the ruling of flogging (for fornication) or stoning to death (for adultery)." Similar was reported from 'Ikrimah, Sa'id bin Jubayr, Al-Hasan, 'Ata' Al-Khurasani, Abu Salih, Qatadah, Zayd bin Aslam and Ad-Dahhak, and this is a matter that is agreed upon.*[120]

The *Tafsir Al-Jalalayn*, *Tafsir Ibn 'Abbas*, and the modern *Tafsir Ahsanul-Bayan* all pointed out that this verse was later abrogated by the command that stoning was the penalty for married women or married people who committed adultery.[121]

The *Tafsir Al-Jalalayn* also noted that there was a *hadith* which clarified the new penalty of stoning that had resulted from the phrase *or Allah ordains for them some (other) way.*[122] Here is that *hadith*:

> *'Ubada b. As-Samit reported: Allah's Messenger (SAW) saying: Receive (teaching) from me, receive (teaching) from me. Allah has ordained a way for those (women). When an unmarried male commits adultery with an unmarried female (they should receive) one hundred*

---

120 *Tafsir Ibn Kathir*, Vol. 2, p. 400.

121 *Tafsir Al-Jalalayn*, p. 180; *Tafsir Ibn 'Abbas*, p. 101; and *Tafsir Ahsanul-Bayan*, Vol. 1, p. 430.

122 *Tafsir Al-Jalalayn*, p. 180.

lashes and banishment for one year. And in case of married male committing adultery with a married female, they shall receive one hundred lashes and be stoned to death.[123]

Flogging as a penalty[124] was codified in Chapter 24, Verse 2 of the Koran:

> *The fornicatress and the fornicator, flog each of them with a hundred stripes. Let not pity withhold you in their case, in a punishment prescribed by Allah, if you believe in Allah and the Last Day. And let a party of the believers witness their punishment.*

Ibn Kathir noted that flogging applied only to someone who was an unwed virgin; if the person was married, the punishment was stoning, based on the actions and examples of Muhammad (the *Sunnah*).[125] This was also pointed out in the *Tafsir al-Jalalayn* and the *Tafsir Ahsanul-Bayan.*[126]

It is interesting to note that there had been a claim that a verse about stoning had actually been "revealed" to Muhammad. And it was further claimed that this verse had been left out when the Koran was compiled after Muhammad's death. The claim came from 'Umar, the second Caliph after Muhammad's death, and he made this claim from the pulpit of the mosque in Medina sometime after Muhammad's death:

---

[123] *Sahih Muslim*, Vol. 5, No. 1690, p. 131. A similar *hadith* is found in *Sunan Abu Dawud*, Vol. 5, No. 4415, pp. 50-51; and *Sunan Ibn Majah*, Vol. 3, No. 2550, p. 462. *SAW* is the abbreviation for *Sallallahu 'Alaihe wa Sallam*. This is translated as, "May the peace and blessings of Allah be upon him."

[124] For some requirements and restrictions pertaining to the penalty of flogging, see *Sahih Muslim*, Vol. 5, p. 144, n. 1.

[125] *Tafsir Ibn Kathir*, Vol. 7, pp. 18-19.

[126] *Tafsir Al-Jalalayn*, p. 749, and *Tafsir Ahsanul-Bayan*, Vol. 3, pp. 664-665.

> *Allah sent Muhammad with the Truth and revealed the Book (the Qur'an) to him, and among what Allah revealed, was the Verse of the Rajm (the stoning to death) of married person* [sic] *(male and female) who commits illegal sexual intercourse, and we did recite this Verse and understood and memorized it. Allah's messenger did carry out the punishment of stoning and so did we after him. I am afraid that after a long time has passed, somebody will say, 'By Allah, we do not find the Verse of the Rajm in Allah's Book,' and thus they will go astray by leaving an obligation which Allah has revealed.*[127]

But 'Umar had tried to get the verse included in the Koran. During Muhammad's lifetime the "revelations" had not been collected into one book. However, after Muhammad died there were no more "revelations." Then there came the realization that, while many of the "revealed" verses had been written down by scribes (Muhammad was reportedly illiterate), others of the verses had only been memorized by one or more of the Muslims who had reportedly heard them from Muhammad. And in the Wars of Apostasy after Muhammad's death, some of these Muslims were getting killed in battle. Consequently, Abu Bakr, the first Caliph, commanded that all of the "revelations," whether written down or only memorized, be collected in order to be put into one book. He was assisted

---

[127] *Sahih Al-Bukhari*, Vol. 8, Book 86, No. 6830, p. 431. This concern of 'Umar's was also reported in *Sahih Al-Bukhari*, Vol. 8, Book 86, No. 6829, pp. 428-429; and Vol. 9, Book 96, No. 7323, p. 261; *Sahih Muslim*, Vol. 5, No. 1691, pp. 132-133; *Jami' At-Tirmidhi*, Vol. 3, No. 1432, p. 216; *Sunan Abu Dawud*, Vol. 5, No. 4418, pp. 52-53; *Sunan Ibn Majah*, Vol. 3, No. 2553, p. 464; *Tafsir Ibn Kathir*, Vol. 7, pp. 19-20; and *The Life of Muhammad*, p. 684.

'Umar was the fortieth person to embrace Islam - see *Al-Wahidi's Asbab al-Nuzul*, p. 116.

by 'Umar, who required that each "revelation" had to be "certified by two witnesses" before it would be accepted as part of the Koran.[128]

Zayd Ibn Thabit was put in charge of the compilation, and he adhered to 'Umar's requirement of two witnesses. This created a problem for 'Umar in terms of the Verse of the Rajm:

> *And verily, 'Umar brought Zayd ayat al-rajm (the "stoning verse") to include in the codex, but Zayd did not include it because 'Umar was the only witness.*[129]

But there appeared to have actually been a second witness, Muhammad's wife Aisha. Here is what she said about the "stoning verse":

> *It was narrated that 'Aishah said: "The Verse of stoning and of breastfeeding an adult ten times was revealed, and the paper was with me under my pillow. When the Messenger of Allah died, we were preoccupied with his death, and a tame sheep came in and ate it."*[130]

Now in property matters, the Koran requires the testimony of two women to equal that of one man (2:282). This was a standard certain to be upheld in compiling the Koran. Consequently, if we accept the claims of 'Umar and Aisha that there really had been a "stoning verse," we would still only have at best one and one-half witnesses, and so fail to meet 'Umar's requirement of two witnesses. Perhaps this is why there is no "stoning verse" in the Koran.

---

128 For an interesting overview of how the Koran was compiled see Jalal-al-Din 'Abd al-Rahman al-Suyuti, *The Perfect Guide to the Sciences of the Qur'an*, trans. Hamid Algar, et al. (Reading, UK: Garnet Publishing, 2011), pp. 137-153.

129 Ibid., p. 140.

130 *Sunan Ibn Majah*, Vol. 3, No. 1944, pp. 113-114.

There have been contemporary Muslim claims that although Muhammad had ordered stoning, it was later abrogated by 24:2 of the Koran and replaced by flogging; consequently, according to these claims stoning was no longer a part of Islam after the "revelation" of 24:2.

However, this goes against the *tafsir* commentaries mentioned above. Also, the Muslim scholar 'Allama Bad-ud-Din 'Aini specifically said that Muhammad was "awarded the punishment of stoning after the revelation" of Chapter 24 of the Koran.[131] The fact that stoning was not abrogated by 24:2 is also supported by the following considerations:

1. Chapter 24 was among the earlier chapters to be "revealed" in Medina.[132]

2. There were two specific occasions when Muhammad said that adulterers had to be stoned: 1) During the Conquest of Mecca in January 630[133] ; and 2) During his Farewell Pilgrimage to Mecca in February 632, shortly before his death on June 7th.[134]

3. And, according to 'Umar, the second Caliph, stoning continued to be a part of Islam:

---

131 *Sahih Muslim*, Vol. 5, p. 141, n. 1. The translator also made the following observation in that same footnote:

> *...the punishment* [flogging] *prescribed in the Qur'an related to unmarried persons and the punishment of stoning is prescribed by the Holy Prophet (may peace be upon him) for married persons.*

132 For a brief commentary about when Chapter 24 was possibly "revealed" see *Sahih Muslim*, Vol. 5, p. 141, n. 1.

133 *Sahih Al-Bukhari*, Vol. 5, Book 64, No. 4303, pp. 360-361.

134 *The Life of Muhammad*, p. 652.

> *'Umar bin Al-Khattab said: "The Messenger of Allah stoned, Abu Bakr* [the first Caliph] *stoned, and I stoned..."*[135]

'Umar followed the *Sunnah*. So let's see how Muhammad approached stoning:

1. *It was narrated from 'Aishah that the Messenger of Allah said: "It is not permissible to shed the blood of a Muslim except in three cases: A adulterer who had been married, who should be stoned to death..."*[136]

2. *Narrated 'Abdullah bin 'Umar: The Jews brought to the Prophet a man and a woman from among them who had committed illegal sexual intercourse. The Prophet said to them, "How do you usually punish the one amongst you who has committed illegal sexual intercourse?" They replied, "We blacken their faces with coal and beat them." He said, "Don't you find the order of Ar-Rajm (i.e. stoning to death) in the Taurat (Torah)?" They replied, "We do not find anything in it." 'Abdullah bin Salam (after hearing this conversation) said to them, "You have told a lie! Bring here the Taurat and recite it if you are truthful." (So the Jews brought the Taurat). And the religious teacher who was teaching it to them, put his hand over the Verse of Ar-Rajm and started reading what was written above and below the place hidden with his hand, but he did not read the Verse of Ar-Rajm. 'Abdullah bin Salam removed his (i.e. the teacher's) hand from the Verse of Ar-Rajm and said, "What is this?" So when the Jews saw the Verse, they said, "This is the Verse of Ar-Rajm." So, the Prophet ordered that both the adulterer and the adulteress be stoned to death, and*

---

[135] *Jami' At-Tirmidhi*, Vol. 3, No. 1431, p. 215. The translator of *Sahih Muslim* also pointed out that 'Umar had ordered stonings for those engaging in "temporary marriages." See *Sahih Muslim*, Vol. 4, p. 346, n.1. For more about "temporary marriages," see Chapter 10, *Sharia Law and Women.*

[136] *Sunan An-Nasa'i*, Vol. 5, No. 4053, pp. 56-57.

they were stoned to death near the place where biers used to be placed near the mosque. I saw her companion (i.e. the adulterer) falling over her so as to protect her from the stones.[137]

3. Muhammad said: *I am the first to revive the order of God and His book and to practice it* [stoning].[138]

4. *Narrated Abu Hurairah and Zaid bin Khalid Al-Juhani: A bedouin came to Allah's Messenger and said, "O Allah's Messenger! I ask you by Allah to judge my case according to Allah's Laws." His opponent, who was more learned than he, said, "Yes, judge between us according to Allah's Laws, and allow me to speak." Allah's Messenger said, "Speak." He (i.e. the bedouin or the other man) said, "My son was working as a labourer for this (man) and he committed illegal sexual intercourse with his wife. The people told me that it was obligatory that my son should be stoned to death. So, in lieu of that I ransomed my son by paying one hundred sheep and a slave girl. Then I asked the religious scholars about it, and they informed me that my son must be lashed one hundred lashes, and be exiled for one year, and the wife of this (man) must be stoned to death." Allah's Messenger*

---

137 *Sahih Al-Bukhari*, Vol. 6, Book 65, No. 4556, pp. 72-73. This was also reported in *Sahih Muslim*, Vol. 5, No. 1699, p. 139; *Sunan Abu Dawud*, Vol. 5, No. 4446, pp. 68-69; *The Life of Muhammad*, pp. 266-267; and *Al-Wahidi's Asbab al-Nuzul*, p. 94. Another *hadith* stated that the location for this stoning was the *Balat*, "a tiled courtyard opposite the gate of the Prophet's Mosque." See *Sahih Al-Bukhari*, Vol. 8, Book 86, No. 6819, p. 423. In this *hadith*, Ibn 'Umar stated

> *Both of them were stoned at the Balat and I saw the Jew sheltering the Jewess.*

138 *The Life of Muhammad*, p. 267. A similar statement by Muhammad was reported in *Sahih Muslim*, Vol. 5, No. 1700, p. 140; *Sunan Ibn Majah*, Vol. 3, No. 2558, pp. 466-467; and *Sunan Abu Dawud*, Vol. 5, Nos. 4447-4448, pp. 69-71. In these four *hadiths*, a Jew, who had committed adultery and had already been flogged and had his face blackened with coal, was then stoned to death because of Muhammad's statement.

said, "By Him in Whose Hands my soul is, I will judge between you according to Allah's Laws. The slave-girl and the sheep are to be returned to you, your son is to receive a hundred lashes and be exiled for one year. You, O Unais, go to the wife of this (man) and if she confesses her guilt, stone her to death." Unais went to that woman next morning and she confessed. Allah's Messenger ordered that she be stoned to death.[139]

5. *Narrated Abu Hurairah: A man came to Allah's Messenger while he was in the mosque, and he called him, saying, "O Allah's Messenger! I have committed illegal sexual intercourse." The Prophet turned his face to the other side, but the man repeated his statement four times, and after he bore witness against himself four times, the Prophet called him, saying, "Are you mad?" The man said, "No." the Prophet said, "Are you married?" The man said, "Yes." Then the Prophet said, "Take him away and stone him to death." Jabir bin 'Abdullah said, "I was among the ones who participated in stoning him and we stoned him at the Musalla. When the stones troubled him, he fled, but we overtook him at Al-Harra and stoned him to death."*[140] (man)

6. *Narrated Ibn 'Abbas: When Ma'iz bin Malik came to the Prophet (in order to confess), the Prophet said to him, "Probably you have only kissed (the lady), or winked, or looked at her?" He said, "No, O Allah's Messenger!" The Prophet said, using no euphemism, "Did you had* [sic] *sexual intercourse with her?" The narrator added: At that, (i.e., after his confession) the Prophet ordered that he be stoned (to death).*[141]

---

[139] *Sahih Al-Bukhari*, Vol. 3, Book 54, Nos. 2724-2725, pp. 522-523.

[140] Ibid., Vol. 8, Book 86, Nos. 6815-6816, pp. 421-422. The *Musalla* is an area designated for prayer. It can be of various sizes.

[141] Ibid., No. 6824, p. 426. For more detailed accounts about Ma'iz bin Malik and his stoning, see *Sahih Muslim*, Vol. 5, Nos. 1691R2-1695R1, pp. 133-137; *Jami' At-Tirmidhi*, Vol. 3, Nos. 1427-1428, pp. 211-212; *Sunan Ibn Majah*,

7. *'Imran b. Husain reported that a woman from Juhaina came to Allah's Apostle (SAW) and she had become pregnant as a result of adultery. She said: Allah's Apostle, I have done something for which (prescribed punishment) must be imposed upon me, so impose that. Allah's Apostle (SAW) called her master and said: Treat her well, and when she delivers bring her to me. He did accordingly. Then Allah's Apostle (SAW) judged her and her clothes were tied around her and then he commanded her to be stoned to death. He then prayed over her (dead body).*[142]

8. *'Abdullah b. Buraida reported on the authority of his father...There came to the Holy Prophet a woman from Ghamid and said: Allah's Messenger, I have committed adultery, so purify me. He (the Holy Prophet) turned her away. On the following day she said: Allah's Messenger, why do you turn me away? Perhaps you turn me away as you turned away Ma'iz. By Allah, I have become pregnant. He said: Well, if you insist upon it, then go away until you give birth to (the child). When she delivered she came with the child (wrapped) in a rag and said: Here is the child whom I have given birth to. He said: Go away and suckle him until you wean him. When she had weaned him, she came to him (the Holy Prophet) with the child who was holding a piece of bread in his hand. She said: Allah's Apostle, here is he as I have weaned him and he eats food. He (the Holy Prophet) entrusted the child to one of the Muslims and then pronounced punishment. And she was put in a ditch up to her chest and he commanded people to stone her.*[143]

Vol. 3, No. 2554, pp. 464-465; and *Sunan Abu Dawud*, Vol. 5, Nos. 4419-4427, pp. 53-58, and No. 4431, p. 60.

142 *Sahih Muslim*, Vol. 5, No. 1696, p. 138.

143 Ibid., No. 1695R1, p. 137. In this *hadith* we find that as the woman was being stoned,

> *Khalid b. Walid came forward with a stone which he flung at her head, and there spurted blood on the face of Khalid and so*

9. *Narrated Ash-Sha'bi: When 'Ali stoned a lady to death on a Friday, he (Ali) said, "I have stoned her according to the Sunna (legal way) of Allah's Messenger."*[144]

Simply put, stoning is *Sunnah* and part of Islam:

> *...Ibn 'Abbas said, "He who disbelieves in stoning (the adulterer to death) will have inadvertently disbelieved in the Qur'an, for Allah said, 'O People of the Scripture! Now has come to you Our Messenger explaining to you much of that which you used to hide from the Scripture, and stoning was among the things that they used to hide."*[145]

And the modern *Tafsir Ahsanul-Bayan* explained it this way:

> *Now the punishment of adultery has been fixed, which is stoning to death. That punishment also remained in force during the times of the Rightly-Guided caliphs (successors of the Messenger of Allah) and that remained the unanimous opinion of all the jurists and scholars afterwards. Only the Kharijites, and other new groups of innovators reject this law. The reason why all of them refuse this punitive law can be traced their* [sic] *denial of*

> *he abused her. Allah's Apostle (SAW) heard his (Khalid's) curse that he hurled upon her. Thereupon he (the Holy Prophet) said: Khalid, be gentle. By him in Whose hand is my life, she has repented...he prayed over her and she was buried.*

A similar narration was reported in *Sunan Abu Dawud*, Vol. 5, No. 4442, pp. 66-67.

144 *Sahih Al-Bukhari*, Vol. 8, Book 86, No. 6812, p. 420.

145 *Tafsir Ibn Kathir*, Vol. 3, pp. 131-132.

> *the authority of hadeeths. The law that prescribes stoning the adultery* [sic] *to death is supported by authentic hadeeths, and their narrators are numerous, and hence, scholars grade those hadeeths as mutawatir* [frequently reported]. *A Muslim has, therefore, no choice except to acknowledge and accept it.* [my emphasis][146]

Muhammad and Slaves[147]

Despite claims to the contrary, during the time of Muhammad the Muslims possessed, bought, and sold slaves. In the Koran there are numerous verses acknowledging and accepting the Muslim possession of slaves, e.g.:

1. Stating how Muslims should act around or treat their slaves (slavery was an accepted condition): 2:221, 16:71, 24:31, 24:58, 30:28, and 33:55.

2. Freeing a slave, but only in atonement for one's misdeed (not because slavery was wrong): 2:178, 4:92, 5:89, and 58:3.

And Muhammad adhered to these teachings. For example, after the defeat of the Jewish Bani Qurayzah tribe, Muhammad divided up that tribe's "property, wives, and children" among the Muslims; but some of the women he sent to Najd to be sold for horses and weapons.[148] During one battle Muhammad "got some prisoners as spoils of war," and he distributed them among his Muslim warriors.[149] Muhammad and the Muslims saw no

---

[146] *Tafsir Ahsanul-Bayan*, Vol. 3, p. 665.

[147] Also see Chapter 11, *Whom Your Right Hands Possess*, which deals exclusively with the treatment of non-Muslim women captured in battle.

[148] *The Life of Muhammad*, p. 466. This is also mentioned in *The Sealed Nectar*, p. 378; and *Sahih Muslim*, Vol. 5, No. 1766, pp. 186-187.

[149] *Sunan An-Nasa'i*, Vol. 3, No. 1955, p. 83.

problem with selling their slave women, even if they had fathered children by those women.[150] And Muhammad said that the "blood money" for the killing of a fetus was a male or female slave.[151]

There are a number of authoritative reports in which Muhammad is personally involved in possessing, buying, selling, or giving away slaves:

1. *It was narrated from Anas that the Prophet bought Safiyyah* [a wife of Muhammad] *for seven slaves.*[152]

2. *It was narrated that 'Abdul-Majid bin Wahb said: "Adda' bin Khalid bin Hawdhah said to me: 'Shall I not read to you a letter that the Messenger of Allah wrote to me?' I said: 'Yes.' So he took out a letter. In it was: 'This is what 'Adda' bin Khalid bin Hawdhah bought [from] Muhammad the Messenger of Allah. He bought from him a slave' - or - 'a female slave, having no ailments, nor being a runaway, nor having any malicious behavior. Sold by a Muslim to a Muslim.'"*[153]

3. *They* [the Muslims] *took several captives from the people of Mina' which is on the shore, a mixed lot among them. They were sold as slaves and families were separated. The apostle arrived as they were weeping and inquired the reason. When he was told he said, 'Sell them only in lots', meaning the mothers with the children.*[154]

---

150 *Sunan Ibn Majah*, Vol. 3, No. 2517, p. 440.

151 Ibid., No. 2639, p. 518.

152 Ibid., No. 2272, p. 298. This purchase price was also mentioned in *Sahih Muslim*, Vol. 4, No. 1365R4, p. 360; and *Men and Women Around the Messenger*, p. 587. For a general reference that Muhammad bought Safiyyah from another Muslim, see *The History of al-Tabari: The Last Years of the Prophet*, p. 135, n. 899.

153 *Sunan Ibn Majah*, Vol. 3, No. 2251, p. 285.

154 *The Life of Muhammad*, p. 791, n. 914.

4. *The Prophet sent Ibn Abi Hadrad in this party with Abu Qatadah. The party consisted of sixteen men, and they were away fifteen nights. Their shares [of booty] were twelve camels [for each man]...When the people fled in various directions, they took four women, including one young woman who was very beautiful. She fell to Abu Qatadah. Then Mahmiyah b. al-Jaz' spoke of her to the Messenger of God, and the Messenger of God asked Abu Qatadah about her. Abu Qatadah said, "I purchased her from the spoils." The Messenger of God said, "Give her to me." So he gave her to him, and the Messenger of God gave her to Mahmiyah b. Jaz' al-Zubaydi.*[155]

5. *It was narrated that Jabir said: "A slave came and gave his pledge to the Prophet, pledging to emigrate, and the Prophet did not realize that he was a slave. Then his master came looking for him, and the Prophet said: 'Sell him to me,' and he bought him in exchange for two black slaves. Then after that he did not accept the pledge from anyone until he had asked whether he was a slave.*[156]

6. *Asma' reported: I performed the household duties of Zubair and he had a horse; I used to look after it. Nothing was more burdensome for me than looking after the horse. I used to bring grass for it and looked after it, then I got a servant as Allah's Apostle (may peace be upon him) had some prisoners of war in his possession. He gave me a female servant. She (the female servant) then began to look after the horse and thus relieved me of this burden.*[157]

---

155 *The History of al-Tabari: The Victory of Islam*, pp. 150-151.

156 *Sunan Ibn Majah*, Vol. 4, No. 2869, p. 107. This narration was also reported in *Sunan An-Nasa'i*, Vol. 5, No. 4189, p. 126.

157 *Sahih Muslim*, Vol. 6, No. 2182R1, pp. 446-447. Asma' was a daughter of Abu Bakr and married to Zubair.

7. *Then they brought Umm Qirfah's daughter and 'Abdallah b. Mas'adah to the Messenger of God...The Messenger of God asked Salamah* [who had captured the daughter originally] *for her, and Salamah gave her to him. He then gave her to his maternal uncle, Hazn b. Abi Wahb, and she bore him 'Abd al Rahman b. Hazn.*[158]

8. Muhammad gave Hassan b. Thabit, "Sirin a Copt slave -girl, and she bare him 'Abdu'l-Rahman."[159]

9. Muhammad gave his foster-sister a gift of a male and a female slave.[160]

10. After the defeat of the Jews at Khaybar, Muhammad had the women of Khaybar "distributed among the Muslims."[161]

11. After the Hawazin tribe was defeated, Muhammad gave Ali, 'Umar, and 'Uthman (all later caliphs) each a woman from among those captured. 'Umar then gave his to his son.[162]

12. *It was narrated from 'Imran bin Husain that a man had six slaves, and he did not have any other wealth apart from them, and he set them free when he died. The Messenger of Allah divided them into groups, set two free and left four as slaves.*[163]

---

158 *The History of al-Tabari: The Victory of Islam*, pp. 96-97. The same story is related in *The Life of Muhammad*, p. 665; but in this source it appeared that Salamah asked Muhammad for her, and Hazn appeared to be the uncle of Salamah, not Muhammad.

159 *The Life of Muhammad*, p. 499.

160 Ibid., p. 576.

161 Ibid., p. 511.

162 Ibid., p. 593.

163 *Sunan Ibn Majah*, Vol. 3, No. 2345, p. 340. For other reports that Muhammad sold slaves who were supposed to have been freed after their owners

13. *Anas reported that a man was charged with fornication with the slave-girl of Allah's Messenger (may peace be upon him). Thereupon Allah's Messenger (may peace be upon him) said to Ali: Go and strike his neck. Ali came to him and found him in a well cooling his body. Ali said to him: Come out, and as he took hold of his hand and brought him out, he found that his sexual organ had been cut. Hadrat Ali refrained from striking his neck. He came to Allah's Apostle (may peace be upon him) and said: Allah's Messenger, he has not even the sexual organ.*[164]

14. Muhammad tried to get the Bani Salamah tribe to join him in attacking the Byzantines at Tabuk. He told their leader,

> *O Abu Wahb, would you not like to have scores of Byzantine women and men as concubines and servants?*[165]

15. After a raid Muhammad enslaved a captive named Yasar; he put Yasar in charge of his "milch-camels."[166]

---

died (known as *Mudabbar*), see *Sahih Al-Bukhari*, Vol. 3, Book 34, No. 2231, p. 240; *Sahih Muslim*, Vol. 5, No. 1668, p. 107; and *Sunan Ibn Majah*, Vol. 3, Nos. 2512-2513, pp. 438-439.

For a report that Muhammad sold *Mudabbar* while their masters were still alive, see *Sahih Al-Bukhari*, Vol. 3, Book 34, No. 2230, p. 240; *Sahih Muslim*, Vol. 5, Nos. 997-997R3, p. 108 (the slave was a Coptic Christian and Muhammad sold him for 800 dirhams); and *Sunan An-Nasa'i*, Vol. 3, No. 2547, pp. 370-371. With regard to the slave sold for 800 dirhams, the slave was named Ya'qub, and his master was an *Ansar* named Abu (Madhkur) - see *Sunan An-Nasa'i*, Vol. 5, Nos. 4656-4657, pp. 344-345.

164 *Sahih Muslim*, Vol. 8, No. 2771, p. 281. *Hadrat* is an honorific title.

165 *Al-Wahidi's Asbab al-Nuzul*, p. 122.

166 *The Life of Muhammad*, p. 677.

Muhammad even had a black slave guarding him:

> *Narrated 'Umar: I went to (the house of the Prophet) and behold, Allah's Messenger was staying in a Mashruba (attic room) and a black slave of Allah's Messenger was at the top of its stairs. I said to him, "Tell (the Prophet) that here is 'Umar bin Al-Khattab (asking for permission to enter)." Then he admitted me.*[167]

'Umar said he was not admitted on another occasion:

> *I went to the upper room and asked a black slave of the Prophet to ask for his permission to see me, and the boy went in and then came out saying, 'I mentioned you to him and he remained silent.' I then went out...*[168]

And Muhammad also had at least one "black slave-girl."[169]

One Muslim website mentioned by name 39 male slaves that Muhammad had; according to this site, Muhammad freed only a few shortly after he acquired them.[170] However, according to *The Sealed Nectar*, the award-winning modern biography of Muhammad, he did not free his slaves until the day before he died.[171]

---

[167] *Sahih Al-Bukhari*, Vol. 9, Book 95, No. 7263, p. 227.

[168] *Tafsir Ibn Kathir*, Vol. 10, p. 62. For a similar narration in which 'Umar has multiple dealings with Muhammad's slave, see *Sahih Al-Bukhari*, Vol. 7, Book 67, No. 5191, p. 85.

[169] *Sunan Abu Dawud*, Vol. 1, No. 332, p. 212.

[170] http://www.al-islam.org/hayat-al-qulub-vol2-allamah-muhammad-baqir-al-majlisi/58.htm. Accessed on July 31, 2012. This website referred to Muhammad's male slaves as "clients."

[171] *The Sealed Nectar*, p. 555.

Cutting Off a Thief's Hand

In Chapter 5, Verse 38, the Koran states that amputation of the right hand is the punishment for theft:

> *And (as for) the male thief and the female thief, cut off (from the wrist joint) their (right) hands as a recompense for that which they committed, a punishment by way of example from Allah. And Allah is All-Powerful, All-Wise.*

Muhammad followed this command of the Koran and said he would even cut off the hand of one of his daughters if she was a thief:

> *Narrated 'Urwa bin Az-Zubair: A lady committed theft during the lifetime of Allah's Messenger in the Ghazwa of Al-Fath (i.e. the conquest of Mecca). Her folk went to Usama bin Zaid to intercede for her (with the Prophet). When Usama interceded for her with Allah's Messenger, the colour of the face of Allah's Messenger changed and he said, "Do you intercede with me in a matter involving one of the legal punishments prescribed by Allah?" Usama said, "O Allah's Messenger! Ask Allah's Forgiveness for me." So in the afternoon, Allah's Messenger got up and addressed the people. He praised Allah as He deserved and then said, "Amma ba'du (then after)! The nations before you were destroyed because if a noble amongst them stole, they used to excuse him, and if a poor person amongst them stole, they would apply (Allah's) Legal Punishment to him. By Him in whose Hand Muhammad's soul is, if Fatima, the daughter of Muhammad stole, I would cut her hand." Then Allah's Messenger gave his order in the case of that woman and her hand was cut off.*[172]

---

[172] *Sahih Al-Bukhari*, Vol. 5, Book 64, No. 4304, pp. 361-362. This story was also reported by Aisha - see *Sahih Al-Bukhari*, Vol. 4, Book 60, No. 3475, p. 427; and *Sunan Abu Dawud*, Vol. 5, No. 4373, pp. 27-28.

But Muhammad decided that there had to be a minimum value to the stolen item before the thief's hand was cut off:

1. *Narrated 'Aishah: The Prophet said, 'The hand should be cut off for stealing something that is worth a quarter of a Dinar or more.*[173]

2. *Narrated Ibn 'Umar: The Prophet cut off the hand of a thief for stealing a shield that was worth three Dirham.*[174]

3. *Narrated Abu Hurairah: Allah's Messenger said, "Allah curses the thief who steals an egg (or a helmet) for which his hand is to be cut off, or steals a rope, for which his hand is to be cut off."*[175]

And Muhammad set an example for what could be done with the hand that was cut off:

> *It was narrated that Ibn Muhairiz said, "I asked Fadalah bin 'Ubaid about hanging the hand (of the thief) from his neck, and he said: 'It is Sunnah. The Messenger of Allah cut off a man's hand then hung it from his neck.'"*[176]

And once the matter had been presented to Muhammad, the victim could not change his mind:

---

173 *Sahih Al-Bukhari*, Vol. 8, Book 86, No. 6789, p. 410.

174 Ibid., No. 6796, p. 412.

175 Ibid., No. 6799, p. 413.

176 *Sunan Ibn Majah*, Vol. 3, No. 2587, p. 483. On the same page, the commentary noted, "This narration is Weak but the matter and the standard of punishment is correct..." This *hadith* was also reported in *Sunan Abu Dawud*, Vol. 5, No. 4411, p. 49.

> *It was narrated from Safwan bin Umayyah that a man stole his Burdah* [cloak], *so he brought him before the Prophet, who ordered that his hand be cut off. He said: "O Messenger of Allah, I will let him have it." He said: "O Abu Wahb! Why didn't you do that before you brought him to me?" And the Messenger of Allah had (the man's) hand cut off.*[177]

And Muhammad set the example for the progressive punishment of thieves:

> *It was narrated that Jabir bin 'Abdullah said: "A thief was brought to the Messenger of Allah and he said: 'Kill him.' They said: 'O Messenger of Allah, he only stole.' He said: 'Cut off (his hand).' So his hand was cut off. Then he was brought a second time and he said: 'Kill him.' They said: 'O Messenger of Allah, he only stole.' He said: "Cut off (his foot).' So his foot was cut off. He was brought to him a third time and he said: 'Kill him.' They said: 'O Messenger of Allah, he only stole.' He said: 'Cut off (his other hand).' Then he was brought to him a fourth time and he said: 'Kill him.' They said: 'O Messenger of Allah, he only stole.' He said: 'Cut off (his other foot).' He was brought to him a fifth time and he said: 'Kill him.'" Jabir said: "So we took him to an animal pen and attacked him. He lay down on his back then waved his arms and legs (in the air), and the camels ran away. Then they attacked him a second time and he did the same thing, then they attacked him a third time, and we threw stones at him and killed him, then we threw him into a well and threw stones on top of him."*[178]

---

177 *Sunan An-Nasa'i*, Vol. 5, No. 4883, p. 462.

178 Ibid., No. 4981, pp. 499-500. A similar narration is reported in *Sunan Abu Dawud*, Vol. 5, No. 4410, p. 48.

And even Muhammad's wife Aisha ordered this punishment. On one occasion a slave belonging to another person stole one of Aisha's cloaks. The slave was questioned and confessed. Aisha then ordered that his hand be cut off.[179]

Muhammad and Violence in General

Keeping in mind that Muhammad speaks for Allah and is the timeless standard of good conduct for Muslims, let's look at what he said and did in terms of violence in general:

1. *Narrated Abu Hurairah: Allah's Messenger said, "I have been sent with the shortest expressions bearing the widest meanings, and I have been made victorious with terror (cast in the hearts of the enemy), and while I was sleeping, the keys of the treasures of the world were brought to me and put in my hand."*[180]

2. *It was narrated that Jabir bin 'Abdullah said: "The Messenger of Allah said: 'I have been given five things that were not given to anyone before me: I have been supported with fear being struck into the hearts of my enemy for a distance of one month's travel...*[181]

3. *Narrated Ibn 'Umar that the Prophet said, "My livelihood is under the shade of my spear, and he who disobeys my orders will be humiliated by paying Jizya."*[182]

---

179 Malik ibn Anas ibn Malik ibn Abi 'Amir al-Asbahi, *Al-Muwatta of Imam Malik ibn Anas: The First Formulation of Islamic Law*, trans. Aisha Abdurrahman Bewley (Inverness, Scotland: Madinah Press, 2004), 41.7.25.

180 *Sahih Al-Bukhari*, Vol. 4, Book 56, No. 2977, p. 140.

181 *Sunan An-Nasa'i*, Vol. 1, No. 432, p. 254.

182 *Sahih Al-Bukhari*, Vol. 4, Book 56, Chapter 88, p. 108. The footnote for this *hadith* pointed out that *Under the shade of my spear* meant "from war booty."

4. *...Imam Ahmad narrated that Ibn 'Umar said that the Messenger of Allah said, I was sent with the sword just before the Last Hour, so that Allah is worshipped alone without partners. My sustenance was provided for me from under the shadow of my spear. Those who oppose my command were humiliated and made inferior, and whoever imitates a people, he is one of them.*[183]

5. *Narrated Abu Qilaba: Anas said, "Some people of 'Uki or 'Uraina tribe came to Al-Madina and its climate did not suit them. So the Prophet ordered them to go to the herd of (milch) camels and to drink their milk and urine (as a medicine). So they went as directed and after they became healthy, they killed the shepherd of the Prophet and drove away all the camels. The news reached the Prophet early in the morning and he sent (men) in their pursuit and they were captured and brought at noon. He then ordered to cut* [off] *their hands and feet (and it was done), and their eyes were branded with heated pieces of iron. They were put in Al-Harra* [a place of stony ground in Medina] *and when they asked for water, no water was given them." Abu Qilaba added, "Those people committed theft, murder, became disbelievers after embracing Islam (Murtadin) and fought against Allah and His Messenger."*[184]

---

183 *Tafsir Ibn Kathir*, Vol. 1, pp. 321-322.

184 *Sahih Al-Bukhari*, Vol. 1, Book 4, No. 233, pp. 178-179. A similar narration is found in *Sahih Al-Bukhari*, Vol. 4, Book 56, No. 3018, pp. 160-161; and Vol. 7, Book 76, No. 5727, pp. 344-345; *Sahih Muslim*, Vol. 5, Nos. 1671-1671R7, pp. 112-114; *Jami' At-Tirmidhi*, Vol. 1, Nos. 72-73, pp. 98-100; *Sunan Ibn Majah*, Vol. 3, Nos. 2578-2579, p. 479; *Sunan An-Nasa'i*, Vol. 1, Nos. 306-307, pp. 188-189; *Sunan Abu Dawud*, Vol. 5, Nos. 4364-4370, pp. 22-26; *Al-Wahidi's Asbab al-Nuzul*, p. 93; and *The Life of Muhammad*, pp. 677-678.

In another *hadith* Anas reported something else he saw at *Al-Harra*:

I saw one of them licking the earth with his tongue till he died.

See *Sahih Al-Bukhari*, Vol. 7, Book 76, No. 5685, p. 328. Anas also reported that he saw one of them "biting at the ground out of thirst, until they died." See *Sunan*

6. *It was narrated from Mu'awiyah bin Qurrah that his father said: "The Messenger of Allah sent me to a man who had married his father's wife after he died, to strike his neck (execute him) and confiscate his wealth."*[185]

7. *Narrated Abu Hurairah: I heard Allah's Messenger saying, 'By Him, in Whose Hand my soul is! Were it not for some men who dislike to be left behind and for whom I do not have means of conveyance, I would not stay away (from any Holy Battle). I would love to be martyred in Allah's Cause and come back to life and then get martyred and then come back to life and then get martyred and come back to life and then get martyred.'"*[186]

8. *It has been narrated on the authority of Abu Huraira that*

Abu Dawud, Vol. 5, No. 4367, p. 24. Chapter 5, Verse 33 of the Koran was "revealed" in relationship to this incident.

185 *Sunan Ibn Majah*, Vol. 3, No. 2608, pp. 494-495; also see No. 2607, p. 494. Similar narrations were reported in *Sunan Abu Dawud*, Vol. 5, Nos. 4456-4457, pp. 75-76. Such a woman was considered *Mahram*, an unmarriageable relative, and such a marriage is strictly prohibited in 4:22 of the Koran.

186 *Sahih Al-Bukhari*, Vol. 9, Book 94, No. 7226, p. 210. In another *hadith* Muhammad explained what was meant by *Allah's Cause*:

> *Narrated Abu Musa: A man came to the Prophet and asked, "O Allah's Messenger! What kind of fighting is in Allah's Cause? (I ask this), for some of us fight because of being enraged and angry and some for the sake of their pride and haughtiness." The Prophet raised his head (as the questioner was standing) and said, "He who fights that Allah's Word (i.e. Allah's Religion of Islamic Monotheism) should be superior, fights in Allah's Cause."*

Sahih Al-Bukhari, Vol. 1, Book 3, No. 123, p. 128. For similar *hadiths*, see *Sahih Muslim*, Vol. 6, Nos. 1904-1904R1, p. 286. Fighting in Allah's Cause is *Al-Jihad*; see n. 30 for further information.

the Messenger of Allah (may peace be upon him) said: One who died but did not fight in the way of Allah nor did he express any desire (or determination) for Jihad died the death of a hypocrite.[187]

9. *It was reported from Anas, who said: "The Prophet used to attack at the time of the Subh (Fajr) prayer. He used to listen; if he heard the Adhan, he would not attack, otherwise he would attack."*[188]

10. Muhammad was involved in the beheading of 600-900 captured males of the Jewish Bani Qurayzah tribe. He

> *sent for them and struck off their heads...as they were brought out to him in batches...This went on until the apostle* [Muhammad] *made an end of them.*

Muhammad then "divided" their wives, children, and property among the Muslims, and sold other of the women "for horses and weapons."[189]

11. When Kinanah bin al-Rabi of the Jewish Bani al-Nadir tribe would not reveal where his conquered tribe's treasures were hidden, Muhammad ordered one of his soldiers, "Torture him until you extract what he has," so a fire was built on Kinanah's chest until

---

187 *Sahih Muslim*, Vol. 6, No. 1910, p. 289. Muhammad also said that meeting Allah in such a state indicated the Muslim had "a defect" or "a deficiency." See, respectively, *Jami' At-Tirmidhi*, Vol. 3, No. 1666, p. 412; and *Sunan Ibn Majah*, Vol. 4, No. 2763, p. 47.

188 *Sunan Abu Dawud*, Vol. 3, No. 2634, p. 274. The *Adhan* is the Muslim call to prayer.

189 *The Life of Muhammad*, pp. 464 and 466.

Kinanah nearly died. Kinanah's head was then cut off by one of the Muslims.[190]

Muhammad Forgetting Verses from the Koran and Prayers

On occasion, Muhammad would forget verses from the Koran:

> *Narrated 'Aishah: Allah's Messenger heard a man reciting the Qur'an at night, and said, "May Allah bestow his Mercy on him, as he has reminded me of such and such Verses of such and such Surah, which I was caused to forget.*[191]

---

[190] Ibid., p. 515. This was also related in *The History of al-Tabari: The Victory of Islam*, pp. 122-123.

It is interesting to note that Ibn Hisham, who edited *The Life of Muhammad*, had written that in his editing he left out

> *...things which it is disgraceful to discuss; matters which would distress certain people...But God willing I shall give a full account of everything else so far as it is known and trustworthy tradition is available.*

The Life of Muhammad, p. 691, n. 10. If it is not considered disgraceful or distressing to mention the beheading of hundreds of war captives and the torture of another captive, one can only wonder about the nature of the disgraceful, distressing events that were actually left out of *The Life of Muhammad*! As was previously noted, a modern biography of Muhammad took Ibn Hisham's approach by stating that Kinanah was simply "killed" for refusing to reveal the location of a bag of jewels and money - see *The Sealed Nectar*, p. 439.

[191] *Sahih Al-Bukhari*, Vol. 6, Book 66, No. 5038, p. 449; on the same page a similar *hadith* was narrated by Hisham (No. 5037).

And there were times when Muhammad would forgetfully increase or decrease the number of *rak'a*[192] in a particular prayer, e.g.:

1. *Narrated Ibn Mas'ud that Allah's Prophet led them in the Zuhr Salat (prayer) and he offered either more or less Rak'a, and it was said to him, "O Allah's Messenger! Has the Salat (prayer) been reduced, or have you forgotten?" He asked, "What is that?" They said, "You have offered so many Rak'a." So he performed with them two more prostrations and said, "These two prostrations are to be performed by the person who does not know whether he has offered more or less (Rak'a) in which case he should seek to follow what is right. And then complete the rest [of the Salat (prayer)] and perform two extra prostrations.*[193]

2. *It was narrated that 'Abdullah said, "The Messenger of Allah prayed, and he added or omitted something." (One of the narrators) Ibrahim said: "The confusion stems from me. (i.e., he was not sure which it was)." "It was said to him: 'O Messenger of Allah! Has something been added to the prayer?' He said: 'I am only human, I forget just as you forget. If anyone of you forgets, let him perform two prostrations when he is sitting (at the end).' Then the Prophet turned and prostrated twice."*[194]

3. *It was narrated that Mu'awiyah bin Hudaij that* [sic] *the*

---

[192] *Rak'a* is the basic cycle of prayer which includes standing, bowing and prostration. The number of *rak'as* in each of the five daily prayers varies from two to four - see Dr. Mamdouh N. Mohamed, *Salaat: The Islamic Prayer from A to Z* (Fairfax, VA: B 200 Inc., 2005), pp. 137 and 140.

[193] *Sahih Al-Bukhari*, Vol. 8, Book 83, No. 6671, p. 351. For *hadiths* from other narrators about Muhammad forgetting the number of *rak'a*, see *Sahih Al-Bukhari*, Vol. 8, Book 78, No. 6051, pp. 52-53; Vol. 8, Book 83, No. 6670, p. 350-351; and Vol. 9, Book 95, No. 7249, p. 222.

[194] *Sunan Ibn Majah*, Vol. 2, No. 1203, p. 223.

Messenger of Allah prayed one day and said the Taslim when there was still a Rak'ah left of the prayer. A man caught up with him and said: 'You forgot a Rak'ah of the prayer!' So he came back into the Masjid [mosque] *and told Bilal to call the Iqamah for prayer, then he led the people in praying one Rak'ah...*[195]

Digging Up the Graves of Non-Muslims to Build His Mosque

When Muhammad emigrated to Medina, the first mosque was built on land that had been used as a cemetery by non-Muslims. Muhammad ordered that their graves be dug up:

> *Narrated Anas: The Prophet came to Al-Madina and ordered a mosque to be built and said, "O Bani Najjar! Suggest to me the price (of your land)." They said, "We do not want its price except from Allah" (i.e., they wished for a reward from Allah for giving up their land free). So, the Prophet ordered the graves of the Mushrikun to be dug out and the land to be levelled, and the date-palm trees to be cut down. The cut date-palms were fixed in the direction of the Qiblah of the mosque.*[196]

Here is how this mosque (the "Prophet's *Masjid*") was described:

> *The location was that of the graves of the polytheists. The ground was cleared of weeds, shrubs, palm trees and*

---

[195] *Sunan An-Nasa'i*, Vol. 1, No. 665, p. 391. For further examples see *Sunan An-Nasa'i*, Vol. 2, Nos. 1223-38, pp. 215-222; Nos. 1243-45, pp. 225-227; Nos. 1255-60, pp. 230-232; and No. 1262, p. 234.

[196] *Sahih Al-Bukhari*, Vol. 3, Book 29, No. 1868, p. 68. For a longer narration of the same *hadith*, see *Sahih Al-Bukhari*, Vol. 5, Book 63, No. 3932, pp. 167-168. This *hadith* was also reported in *Sunan Ibn Majah*, Vol. 1, No. 742, pp. 486-487 (where it was designated *the Prophet's Mosque*); and *Sunan An-Nasa'i*, Vol. 1, No. 703, pp. 415-416.

rubbish. The graves of the polytheists dug up and then levelled and the trees planted around. The Qiblah (the direction in which the Muslims turn their faces in prayer) was constructed to face Jerusalem! Two beams were also erected to hold the ceiling up. It was square in form, each side measuring approximately 100 yards, facing towards the north and having three gates on each of the remaining sides. Nearby, rooms reserved for the Prophet's household were built of stones and adobe bricks with ceilings of palm leaves. To the north of the Masjid, a place was reserved for the Muslims who had neither family nor home.[197]

How Muhammad Used the Mosque

Once a mosque was built, it served a number of purposes for Muhammad:

Mosques play an extremely significant and fundamental role in the building of the Islamic society. The Messenger of Allah used the mosque for a myriad of purposes - as the capital of the Islamic state, as a command center for military expeditions, as a consultation chamber for state affairs, as a public treasury, as an Islamic court, as the first Islamic university, as a Civil secretariat, as a state guest house, and for many other constructive purposes.[198]

---

197 *The Sealed Nectar*, p. 227. With regard to the *Qiblah*, the Muslims originally faced Jerusalem when they prayed. However, after emigrating to Medina, the *Qiblah* was changed to Mecca (see the entry for February 624 in the *Chronology* for further details).

198 *Sunan Ibn Majah*, Vol. 1, Comment "e," p. 483.

Muhammad's Statements about Homosexuality

To put it plainly, Muhammad cursed gays and lesbians:

1. *Ibn 'Abbas said that the Messenger of Allah said, "Whoever you catch committing the act of the people of Lut (homosexuality), then kill both parties to the act."*[199]

2. *It was narrated from Abu Hurairah that the Messenger of Allah cursed women who imitate men and men who imitate women.*[200]

3. *Narrated Ibn 'Abbas: The Prophet cursed the effeminate men and those women who assume the similitude (manners) of men. He also said, "Turn them out of your houses." He turned such and such person out, and 'Umar also turned out such and such person.*[201]

4. *Ibn 'Umar narrated that the Messenger of Allah said: "Three types of men will not enter Paradise, a son who is undutiful to his parents, a cuckold (a man who agrees to his wife committing adultery), and a woman who imitates men."*[202]

---

[199] *Tafsir Ibn Kathir* Vol. 2, p. 402. This was also reported in *Sunan Abu Dawud*, Vol. 5, Nos. 4462-4463, pp. 78-79. Similar such statements from Muhammad were also reported in *Sunan Ibn Majah*, Vol. 3, Nos. 2561-2562, p. 469.

[200] *Sunan Ibn Majah*, Vol. 3, No. 1903, p. 93. This statement by Muhammad was also reported by Ibn 'Abbas in the next *hadith*, No. 1904, on the same page, and also in *Sahih Al-Bukhari*, Vol. 7, Book 77, Nos. 5885-5886, p. 418.

[201] *Sahih Al-Bukhari*, Vol. 8, Book 86, No. 6834, p. 436. 'Umar was a father-in-law of Muhammad, one of his close Companions, and he became the second Caliph after Muhammad's death.

[202] Muhammad ibn Sulayman at-Tamimi, *The Book of Major Sins*, trans. Dr. Ibraheem as-Selek (Riyadh, Kingdom of Saudi Arabia: International Islamic Publishing House, 2007), p. 107.

Muhammad also ordered his wives not to allow "effeminate men" into their houses.[203] And Muhammad said that on the Day of Resurrection, Allah would not look upon "the woman who imitates men in her outward appearance."[204]

Muslims Can't Inherit from Non-Muslims and Vice-versa

1. *Narrated Usama bin Zaid: The Prophet said, "A Muslim cannot be the heir of a disbeliever, nor can a disbeliever be the heir of a Muslim."*[205]

2. *It was reported from 'Abdullah bin 'Amr who said, "The Messenger of Allah said: 'The people of two religions do not inherit (each other) at all.'"*[206]

A Reminder

Now that we know more about Muhammad, let's remind ourselves how he is viewed by Muslims of our day:

1. *The Messenger of Allah is the perfect role model for his Ummah* [Muslim community/nation], *and all his actions represent the highest standard of conduct, so that the people should emulate and follow his example.*[207]

---

[203] *Sahih Al-Bukhari*, Vol. 7, Book 77, No. 5887, p. 419.

[204] *Sunan An-Nasa'i* Vol. 3, No. 2563, p. 380.

[205] *Sahih Al-Bukhari*, Vol. 8, Book 85, No. 6764, pp. 399-400.

[206] *Sunan Abu Dawud*, Vol. 3, No. 2911, p. 442.

[207] *Jami' At-Tirmidhi*, Vol. 4, Comments, p. 102.

2. *There is then the great Messenger of Allah whose moral visible attributes, aspects of perfection, talents, virtues, noble manners and praiseworthy deeds, entitle him to occupy the innermost cells of our hearts, and become the dearest target that the self yearns for. Those were the attributes and qualities on whose basis the Prophet wanted to build a new society, the most wonderful and the most honorable society ever known in history.*[208]

3. *...he is a paragon worth emulating in all matters, be it worship or social, economic or political affairs. He ought to be followed in all walks of life.*[209]

And this high praise might have partially resulted from what Muhammad said there was *no room for* in Islam:

> [Muhammad] *went out and gave a sermon to people in which he said: 'How come some people have forbidden sleeping with women, eating, wearing perfume, sleeping and the desires of this world? I am not commanding you to be priests or monks, for there is no room in my religion for abstention from eating meat and sleeping with women, nor is there room for adoption of monasteries. The wandering of my community consists of fasting and its monasticism is Jihad...'*[210]

---

208 *The Sealed Nectar*, pp. 235-236.

209 *Tafsir Ahsanul-Bayan*, Vol. 4, Commentary, p. 374.

210 *Al-Wahidi's Asbab al-Nuzul*, p. 99.

5

The Religion of Peace

Abu 'Ubayda said, "Every ayat [verse] *which obviates fighting is Makkan and abrogated by the command to fight.*[211]

Introduction

With the concept and significance of abrogation in mind, let's take a look at Chapter Nine of the Koran. It is titled *At-Taubah* (The Repentance), although it is also known as *Al-Bara'ah* (The Immunity). This was the last complete chapter of the Koran to be "revealed" to Muhammad,[212] and Ibn 'Abbas said it was meant to "humiliate" the non-believers,[213] meaning non-Muslims. Consequently, we can consider it the final word on the matters is covers. Let's look at some of those matters:

Chapter 9, Verse 5 - The "Verse of the Sword"[214]

Then when the Sacred Months (the 1st, 7th, 11th, and 12th months of the Islamic calendar) have passed, then kill the Mushrikun wherever you find them, and capture them and

211 *Tafsir Al-Qurtubi*, pp. 328-329.

212 *Sahih Al-Bukhari*, Vol. 5, Book 64, No. 4364, p. 396; *Sahih Muslim*, Vol. 5, No. 1618R2, p. 70; *Tafsir Ibn Kathir*, Vol. 4, pp. 369-370; *The Perfect Guide to the Sciences of the Qur'an*, pp. 5, 45-46, 49, and 51; *Al-Wahidi's Asbab al-Nuzul*, p. 4; and *Tafsir Al-Jalalayn*, p. 397.

213 *Sahih Muslim*, Vol. 8, No. 3031, p. 404.

214 Muslim scholars actually refer to 9:5 as the Verse (*Ayah*) of the Sword. For example, see *Tafsir Ibn Kathir*, Vol. 4, pp. 375 and 377.

> *besiege them, and lie in wait for them in every ambush. But if they repent [by rejecting Shirk (polytheism) and accept Islamic Monotheism] and perform As-Salat (the prayers), and give Zakat (obligatory charity), then leave their way free. Verily, Allah is Oft-Forgiving, Most Merciful.*

Let's look at what this verse means. The Sacred Months were the four months each year during which fighting was prohibited - the 1st, 7th, 11th, 12th months of the Islamic calendar.[215] But after they had passed, the Muslims were commanded to kill the *Mushrikun*, who are defined as

> *Polytheists, pagans, idolaters, and disbelievers in the Oneness of Allah and His Messenger Muhammad.*[216]

A *Mushrikun* is in essence any non-Muslim. And they were to be killed *wherever you find them*. For Ibn Kathir, this meant "on the earth in general, except for the Sacred Area..."[217]

But on the other hand, in the *Tafsir Al-Jalalayn*, there were no restrictions to *wherever you find them;* this phrase meant "whether they be in the Haram or outside it."[218]

The *Tafsir Ibn 'Abbas* went one step further, explaining that *wherever you find them* meant

---

215 However, in the early days of Islam a significant exception was made to the prohibition of fighting during the Sacred Months. See the *Chronology* entry for December 623 AD, the Expedition of Nakhlah.

216 *The Noble Qur'an*, Glossary, p. 866.

217 *Tafsir Ibn Kathir*, Vol. 4, pp. 376. The Sacred Area is considered Mecca and Medina, and is also known as the *Haram*.

218 *Tafsir Al-Jalalayn*, p. 398.

> *whether in the Sacred Precinct or outside it, during the sacred months or at any other time...*[219]

And what about *capture them*? Ibn Kathir explained that this meant "executing some and keeping some as prisoners."[220] The modern *Tafsir Ahsanul-Bayan* noted that *capture them* meant one of two options: "take them as prisoners or kill them."[221]

Then we come to the command to *besiege them, and lie in wait for them in every ambush.* The *Tafsir Ibn 'Abbas* said that this meant to besiege them "in their homes."[222] The *Tafsir Al-Jalalayn* said this meant

> *besiege them in citadels and fortresses until they either fight or become Muslim*[223]

The *Tafsir Ahsanul-Bayan* had a similar explanation:

> *That is, do not wait until you get a chance to take action against them, but besiege them wherever they are, in their forts and in their places of refuge, and lie in wait for them everywhere until they find it impossible to move without your permission.*[224]

And Ibn Kathir explained that this meant

---

219 *Tafsir Ibn 'Abbas*, p. 229.

220 *Tafsir Ibn Kathir*, Vol. 4, p. 376.

221 *Tafsir Ahsanul-Bayan*, Vol. 2, p. 326.

222 *Tafsir Ibn 'Abbas*, p. 229.

223 *Tafsir Al-Jalalayn*, p. 398.

224 *Tafsir Ahsanul-Bayan*, Vol. 2, p. 326.

do not wait until you find them. Rather, seek and besiege them in their areas and forts, gather intelligence about them in the various roads and fairways so that what is made wide looks ever smaller to them. This way, they will have no choice, but to die or embrace Islam.[225]

So 9:5 commands Muslims to aggressively seek-out and attack non-Muslims, and to kill some, and to capture some. And the only way non-Muslims could save themselves would be to convert to Islam. But what happens if Jews and Christians do not want to convert to Islam, and would rather not fight to the death? That will be found later in Chapter 9, Verse 29.

It is interesting to note that the following verses in the Koran were specifically abrogated by the *Verse of the Sword*: 2:109, 4:90 (starting with *If Allah willed*), 5:13, 6:159, 8:61, 10:41, 15:85, and 86:17.[226] Although generally speaking, any verse in the Koran advocating good relations with *Mushrikun* would be abrogated.

Chapter 9, Verse 12

But if they violate their oaths after their covenant, and attack your religion with disapproval and criticism then fight (you) the leaders of disbelief (chiefs of Quraish pagans of Makkah) - for surely, their oaths are nothing to them - so that they may stop (evil actions).

The significant section of this verse is *attack your religion with disapproval and criticism*. Ibn Kathir explained that:

---

[225] *Tafsir Ibn Kathir*, Vol. 4, p. 376.

[226] Ibid., Vol. 1, pp. 333-334; *Tafsir Al-Qurtubi*, p. 328; *Tafsir Al-Jalalayn*, pp. 206, 241, 324, 392, 449, 557, and 1317.

with disapproval and criticism, it is because of this that one who curses the Messenger, peace be upon him, or attacks the religion of Islam by way of criticism and disapproval, they are to be fought.[227]

In the *Tafsir Ibn 'Abbas*, attacking the religion meant to "defame the Religion of Islam."[228]

Here is how the *Tafsir Ahsanul-Bayan* explained this verse:

The meaning is that if they break their pledge and discredit and refute your religion, then never accept their oaths, but fight these leaders of disbelief, so that they may desist from disbelief. Any breach of such calls for the death penalty. [my emphasis][229]

And Ibn Kathir pointed out that

this Ayah [verse] *is general, even though the specific reason behind revealing it was the idolators of Quraysh. So this Ayah generally applies to them and others as well, Allah knows best.*[230]

So this verse of the Koran orders Muslims to fight anyone who criticizes and/or defames Islam or Muhammad.

---

227 *Tafsir Ibn Kathir*, Vol. 4, p. 383.

228 *Tafsir Ibn 'Abbas*, p. 230.

229 *Tafsir Ahsanul-Bayan*, Vol. 2, p. 331.

230 *Tafsir Ibn Kathir*, Vol. 4, pp. 383-384.

Chapter 9, Verse 23

> *O you who believe! Take not as Auliya' (supporters and helpers) your fathers and your brothers if they prefer disbelief to Belief. And whoever of you does so, then he is one of the Zalimun (wrongdoers).*

Ibn Kathir succinctly explained this verse:

> *Allah commands shunning the disbelievers, even if they are one's parents or children, and prohibits taking them as supporters if they choose disbelief instead of faith.*[231]

The *Tafsir Ahsanul-Bayan* pointed out:

> *The contents of this verse are the same as those of many other verses of the Qur'an...They are repeated here again because they are especially important in the context of jihad and hijra (Emigration). Love of father and brothers often overcomes a man and prevents him from leaving home and fighting in the cause of Allah. Hence, Allah cautions the believers: Let the love of blood-ties not overcome you in the way of Allah. If your fathers and brothers are disbelievers, they can never be your friends. If you love them, you will wrong yourselves.* [my emphasis][232]

Just one of many verses in the Koran commanding Muslims not to be friends with non-Muslims. For examples of other such verses, see the explanation for 5:51 of the Koran in the next chapter of this book, *Religion of Peace, Redux*.

---

231 Ibid., p. 394.

232 *Tafsir Ahsanul-Bayan*, Vol. 2, p. 339. The following verses were listed in this commentary as "the same as" 9:23: 3:28, 3:118, 5:51, and 58:22.

Chapter 9, Verse 29

> *Fight against those who believe not in Allah, nor in the Last Day, nor forbid that which has been forbidden by Allah and His Messenger (Muhammad), and those who acknowledge not the religion of truth (i.e. Islam) among the people of the Scripture (Jews and Christians), until they pay the Jizyah with willing submission, and feel themselves subdued.*

In a paragraph titled *The Order to fight People of the Scriptures until They give the Jizyah*, Ibn Kathir explained the meaning of this verse:

> *Therefore, when People of the Scriptures disbelieved in Muhammad, they had no beneficial faith in any Messenger or what the Messengers brought. Rather, they followed their religions because this conformed with their ideas, lusts and ways of their forefathers, not because they are Allah's Law and religion. Had they been true believers in their religions, that faith would have directed them to believe in Muhammad...Allah commanded His Messenger to fight the People of the Scriptures, Jews and Christians...*[233]

So had the Jews and Christians been "true believers" in their own religions, they would have become Muslim! As a consequence of the lack of this true belief, the Muslims were therefore commanded by Allah to fight against the Jews and Christians *until they pay the Jizyah with willing submission, and feel themselves subdued.* The *Jizyah* is a

> *Head tax imposed by Islam on all non-Muslims* [*Dhimmis*] *living under the protection of an Islamic government.*[234]

---

233 *Tafsir Ibn Kathir*, Vol. 4, pp. 404-405.

234 *The Noble Qur'an*, Glossary, p. 862.

But what about having to pay it *with willing submission* and with a sense of feeling *subdued*?

In a paragraph titled *Paying Jizyah is a Sign of Kufr* [unbelief] *and Disgrace*, Ibn Kathir explained that if the Jews and Christians chose not to embrace Islam, they would have to pay the *Jizyah* "in defeat and subservience," and feel "disgraced, humiliated, and belittled." Ibn Kathir continued

> *Therefore, Muslims are not allowed to honor the people of Dhimmah* [those who are *Dhimmis*] *or elevate them above Muslims, for they are miserable, disgraced and humiliated.*[235]

This was affirmed in the *Tafsir Al-Jalalayn* when the *Jizyah* section of 9:29 was being discussed:

> *...until they pay the jizya with their own hands - meaning the Jews and the Christians who must pay it in submission or directly with their actual hands - in a state of complete abasement - humble and subject to the judgements* [sic] *of Islam.*[236]

The *Tafsir Ibn 'Abbas* reiterated that the people to be fought were the Jews and Christians, until they paid "the tribute" and were "abased."[237]

This was also noted in the modern *Tafsir Ahsanul-Bayan*:

> *The command to fight the pagans was already given. Now Allah commands the believers to fight the Jews and*

---

235 *Tafsir Ibn Kathir*, Vol. 4, pp. 405-406.

236 *Tafsir Al-Jalalayn*, pp. 404-406.

237 *Tafsir Ibn 'Abbas*, p. 231.

Christians (if they do not accept Islam) until they pay the jizya and live under the rule of the Muslims.[238]

So Muslims are specifically commanded to fight the Jews and Christians. Fortunately for Jews and Christians, we find that 9:29 abrogated 9:5 in that, instead of only the two options for non-Muslims mentioned in 9:5 (conversion or death), Jews and Christians now had a third option: live as *Dhimmis* and pay the *Jizyah.*

Chapter 9, Verse 30

And the Jews say: 'Uzair (Ezra) is the son of Allah, and the Christians say: Messiah is the son of Allah. That is their saying with their mouths, resembling the saying of those who disbelieved aforetime. Allah's curse be on them, how they are deluded away from the truth!

In a paragraph titled *Fighting the Jews and Christians is legislated because They are Idolators and Disbelievers*, Ibn Kathir explained the meaning of this verse:

*Allah the Exalted encourages the believers to fight the polytheists, disbelieving Jews and Christians, who uttered this terrible statement and utter lies against Allah, the Exalted. As for the Jews, they claimed that 'Uzayr was the son of God, Allah is free of what they attribute to Him. As for the misguidance of Christians over 'Isa [*Jesus*], it is obvious. This is why Allah declared both groups to be liars.*[239]

---

238 *Tafsir Ahsanul-Bayan*, Vol. 2, pp. 345-346.

239 *Tafsir Ibn Kathir*, Vol. 4, p. 408.

The *Tafsir Ibn 'Abbas* stated that Allah cursed the Jews and Christians because of their lies.[240] The *Tafsir Al-Jalalayn* said that Allah cursed the Jews and Christians because they had "turned aside from the truth when the proof has been established!"[241]

So this verse tells Muslims that Allah curses the Jews and Christians because they are liars.

Chapter 9, Verse 32

> *They (the disbelievers, the Jews and the Christians) want to extinguish Allah's Light (with which Muhammad has been sent - Islamic Monotheism) with their mouths, but Allah will not allow except that His Light should be perfected even though the Kafirun (disbelievers) hate (it).*

In a section titled *People of the Scriptures try to extinguish the Light of Islam*, Ibn Kathir explained this verse:

> *Allah says, the disbelieving idolators and People of the Scriptures want to, extinguish the Light of Allah. They try through argument and lies to extinguish the guidance and religion of truth that the Messenger of Allah was sent with.*[242]

The *Tafsir Ibn 'Abbas* also pointed out that the Jews and Christians used lies to "thwart" Islam.[243]

---

240 *Tafsir Ibn 'Abbas*, p. 233.

241 *Tafsir Al-Jalalayn*, p. 406.

242 *Tafsir Ibn Kathir*, Vol. 4, p. 411.

243 *Tafsir Ibn 'Abbas*, p. 234.

The *Tafsir Ahsanul-Bayan* explained the verse:

> *The Jews and the Christians would love to blot out the guidance and the right religion that Allah has sent through His Messenger by their subtle arguments. But this they cannot do...The religion of Allah shall triumph and prevail over all other religions...*[244]

So according to this verse, the Jews and Christians are hostile to Islam, the religion of truth, and use lies in an attempt to "blot" it out. Nevertheless, Islam will be triumphant.

Chapter 9, Verse 33

> *It is He Who has sent His Messenger (Muhammad) with guidance and the religion of truth (Islam), to make it superior over all religions even though the Mushrikun (polytheists, pagans, idolaters, disbelievers in the Oneness of Allah) hate (it).*[245]

Under a section titled *Islam is the Religion That will dominate over all Other Religions*, Ibn Kathir provided a *hadith* to explain this verse:

> *Imam Ahmad recorded from Tamim Ad-Dari that he said, I heard the Messenger of Allah saying, "This matter (Islam) will keep spreading as far as the night and day reach, until Allah will not leave a house made of mud or hair, but will make this religion enter it, while bringing might to a mighty person (a Muslim) and humiliation to a disgrace person (who rejects Islam). Might with which*

---

244 *Tafsir Ahsanul-Bayan*, Vol. 2, p. 348.

245 The statement that Allah had sent Muhammad to make Islam superior over all other religions is also found in, for example, 48:28 of the Koran. See Chapter 8, *Three Religions with the Same God?* for explanations of 48:28.

Allah elevates Islam (and its people) and disgrace with which Allah humiliates disbelief (and its people)."[246]

Ibn Kathir then added,

> *Tamim Ad-Dari [who was a Christian before Islam] used to say, "I have come to know the meaning of this Hadith in my own people. Those who became Muslims among them acquired goodness, honor and might. Disgrace, humiliation and Jizyah befell those who remained disbelievers."*[247]

The *Tafsir Ahsanul-Bayan* provided a more contemporary explanation:

> *When the Muslims practiced Islam faithfully and completely, they were a dominant power in the world, and if they practice it now as their earlier generations did, they would again be entrusted with ruling the world, because Allah has promised the Party of Allah domination and power.*[248]

So Islam is to be superior over all other religions, whether non-Muslims like it or not.

Chapter 9, Verse 63

> *Know they not that whoever opposes and shows hostility to Allah and His Messenger, certainly for him will be the fire of Hell to abide therein. That is the extreme disgrace.*

---

246 *Tafsir Ibn Kathir*, Vol. 4, pp. 412-413.

247 Ibid., p. 413.

248 *Tafsir Ahsanul-Bayan*, Vol. 2, p. 349.

Ibn Kathir wrote that this verse

> *means, have they not come to know and realize that those who defy, oppose, wage war and reject Allah, thus becoming on one side while Allah and His Messenger on another side, certainly for him will be the fire of Hell to abide therein, in a humiliating torment, That is the extreme disgrace, that is the greatest disgrace and the tremendous misery.*[249]

So those who disagree with and/or show hostility toward Allah and Muhammad are destined for the Fires of Hell.

Chapter 9, Verse 73

> *O Prophet (Muhammad)! Strive hard against the disbelievers and the hypocrites, and be harsh against them, their abode is Hell, - and worst indeed is that destination.*

Ibn Kathir explained this verse in a section titled *The Order for Jihad against the Disbelievers and Hypocrites*:

> *Allah commanded His Messenger to strive hard against the disbelievers and the hypocrites and to be harsh against them...Ibn 'Abbas said, "Allah commanded the Prophet to fight the disbelievers with the sword, to strive against the hypocrites with the tongue and annulled lenient treatment of them." Ad-Dahhak commented, "Perform Jihad against the disbelievers with the sword and be harsh with the hypocrites with words, and this is the Jihad performed against them." Similar was said by Muqatil and Ar-Rabi'...In combining these statements, we*

249 *Tafsir Ibn Kathir*, Vol. 4, p. 461.

could say that Allah causes punishment of the disbelievers and hypocrites with all of these methods in various conditions and situations, and Allah knows best.[250]

The *Tafsir Al-Jalalayn* explained that this verse meant:

O Prophet, do jihad against the unbelievers with the sword and against the hypocrites with the tongue and evidence and be harsh with them through rebuke and hatred.[251]

And there was a similar explanation in the *Tafsir Ibn 'Abbas*:

(O Prophet! Strive against the disbelievers) with the sword (and the hypocrites) with words! (Be harsh) be tough (with them) with both parties with words and actions.[252]

The *Tafsir Ahsanul-Bayan* pointed out:

Allah commands His Messenger and all the believers to fight the disbelievers and hypocrites, and to be stern with them...The intended meaning is that Muslims should take stern action against the enemy. It does not mean harshness and rudeness of speech, because that is against the character of the Messenger of Allah...The command to fight them and deal sternly with them are matters relating to this world. Their punishment in Hell is a thing relating to the Hereafter.[253]

---

250 *Tafsir Ibn Kathir*, Vol. 4, pp. 474-475.

251 *Tafsir Al-Jalalayn*, p. 419.

252 *Tafsir Ibn 'Abbas*, p. 240.

253 *Tafsir Ahsanul-Bayan*, Vol. 2, pp. 381-382.

These Islamic scholars interpret this verse as a command to fight against disbelievers with the sword. And after reading this verse, it is interesting to note that 5:17 of the Koran specifically states that Christians are disbelievers (see the explanations for 5:17 in the next chapter, *Religion of Peace, Redux*).

Chapter 9, Verse 111

> *Verily, Allah has purchased of the believers their lives and their properties for (the price) that theirs shall be Paradise. They fight in Allah's Cause, so they kill (others) and are killed. It is a promise in truth which is binding on Him in the Taurat (Torah) and the Injil (Gospel) and the Qur'an. And who is truer to his covenant than Allah? Then rejoice in the bargain which you have concluded. That is the supreme success.*

In a section titled *Allah has purchased the Souls and Wealth of the Mujahidin in Return for Paradise*, Ibn Kathir explained that in this verse

> *Allah states that He has compensated His believing servants for their lives and wealth - if they give them up in His cause - with Paradise.*[254]

This promise of Paradise in exchange for dying while fighting in Allah's Cause was also noted in the *Tafsir Al-Jalalayn*, *Tafsir Ibn 'Abbas*, and *Al-Wahidi's Asbab al-Nuzul*.[255]

The *Tafsir Ahsanul-Bayan* further explained:

---

[254] *Tafsir Ibn Kathir*, Vol. 4, p. 520. *Mujahidin* are those Muslim warriors engaging in *jihad*, fighting for the Cause of Allah.

[255] *Tafsir Al-Jalalayn*, p. 431; *Tafsir Ibn 'Abbas*, p. 246; and *Al-Wahidi's Asbab al-Nuzul*, pp. 129-130.

> *This is a special favor of Allah for the believers. He gave them Paradise in exchange for their lives and property...These words have been addressed to the Muslims. But the Muslims can only rejoice in it if they agree to this bargain, meaning when they do not shrink back from sacrificing their lives and wealth in the cause of Allah.*[256]

So for Muslims there is one guaranteed way to get to Paradise: die while fighting in Allah's Cause.

Chapter 9, Verse 123

> *O you who believe! Fight those of the disbelievers who are close to you, and let them find harshness in you; and know that Allah is with those who are Al-Muttaqun (the pious* [believers of Islamic Monotheism]*).*

In a section titled *The Order for Jihad against the Disbelievers, the Closest, then the Farthest Areas*, Ibn Kathir explained that

> *Allah commands the believers to fight the disbelievers, the closest in area to the Islamic state, then the farthest. This is why the Messenger of Allah started fighting the idolators in the Arabian Peninsula. When he finished with them, and Allah gave him control over Makkah, Al-Madinah, At-Ta'if, Yemen, Yamamah, Hajr, Khaybar, Hadramawt and other Arab provinces, and the various Arab tribes entered Islam in large crowds, he then started fighting the People of the Scriptures.*[257]

---

256 *Tafsir Ahsanul-Bayan*, Vol. 2, p. 414.

257 *Tafsir Ibn Kathir*, Vol. 4, p. 546.

The admonition to fight the closest disbelievers first, and then the disbelievers farther away, was also noted in the *Tafsir Al-Jalalayn.*[258]

And the modern *Tafsir Ahsanul-Bayan* pointed out:

> *The verse sets an important rule for strategy for jihad: Muslims should fight those disbelievers first who are close, followed by those who are further, then the next, and so on, in the same order. This is what the Messenger of Allah did.*[259]

The *Tafsir Ahsanul-Bayan* also pointed out that when dealing with disbelievers, "the Muslims should not be soft or lenient, but harsh to them."[260]

Ibn Kathir further explained that:

> *The complete believer is he who is kind to his believing brother, and harsh with his disbelieving enemy.*[261]

So here we have another verse in the Koran telling Muslims to fight and be harsh with non-Muslims.

Summary

Chapter Nine is commonly considered to be the last chapter of the Koran to be revealed. Consequently, according to the Doctrine of Abrogation,

---

258 *Tafsir Al-Jalalayn*, p. 435.

259 *Tafsir Ahsanul-Bayan*, Vol. 2, p. 425.

260 Ibid., p. 426.

261 *Tafsir Ibn Kathir*, Vol. 4, p. 548.

Chapter Nine provided the final word on particular matters. So what does this chapter teach Muslims?

This chapter is meant to "humiliate" non-Muslims. Islam is to be made superior over all other religions. Jews and Christians are liars and Allah has cursed them because of that. And they use their lies to try to "extinguish" Islam. Muslims are not to take non-Muslims as friends; rather they are to be harsh toward non-Muslims. Muslims are to fight non-Muslims until the latter are killed or convert to Islam. The Muslims are to start with those non-Muslims closest to them, and then spread out. If the non-Muslims are Christians or Jews, they have the option of becoming a second-class citizen living under Muslim protection and paying a tax, feeling "disgraced, humiliated, and belittled." Anyone who criticizes, opposes, and/or defames Islam is to be fought, and they will be condemned to the Fires of Hell. And Muslims who die fighting in Allah's Cause are guaranteed to go to Paradise.

6

The Religion of Peace, Redux

Introduction

Chapter Five of the Koran is titled *Al-Ma'idah* (The Table). Some scholars believed that it was the next-to-the-last chapter to be revealed.[262] However, there were other reports that it was the last chapter to be revealed.[263] Aisha, Muhammad's favorite wife, also said that Chapter Five was the last chapter to be revealed. Regarding this chapter, she stated

> *Therefore, whatever permissible matters you find in it, then consider (treat) them permissible. And whatever impermissible matters you find in it, then consider (treat) them impermissible.*[264]

It is interesting to note that Aisha was considered very knowledgeable and to be "a scholar of Islamic jurisprudence."[265]

---

262 *The Perfect Guide to the Sciences of the Qur'an*, p. 5, and *Tafsir Al-Jalalayn*, p. 397.

263 *Tafsir Ibn Kathir*, Vol. 3, pp. 71 and 308.

264 Ibid., p. 71. A similar report is in *The Perfect Guide to the Sciences of the Qur'an*, p. 51.

265 *The Honorable Wives of the Prophet*, pp. 50-52.

So let's take a look at Chapter Five, keeping in mind that if it is the next-to-the-last chapter, is anything abrogated by Chapter Nine, and if it is the last chapter, does it abrogate anything in Chapter Nine?

Chapter 5, Verse 3

This verse starts out with a lengthy description of food forbidden to Muslims and the prohibition against the use of divining arrows. It ends by saying that someone forced by severe hunger could eat forbidden food. For our purposes, the significance of this verse is found in this section:

> *...This day, I have perfected your religion for you, completed My Favour upon you, and have chosen for you Islam as your religion...*

Ibn Kathir explained that this section meant Allah

> *has completed their religion* [Islam] *for them, and they, thus do not need any other religion or any other Prophet except Muhammad. This is why Allah made Muhammad the Final Prophet and sent him to all humans and Jinn. Therefore, the permissible is what he allows, the impermissible is what he prohibits, the Law is what he legislates and everything that he conveys is true and authentic and does not contain lies or contradictions.*[266]

The *Tafsir Al-Jalalayn* pointed out that this verse meant Islam had been perfected "by finalising its rulings and obligations..."[267]

The *Tafsir Ibn 'Abbas* explained that Allah had "elucidated" to the Muslims

---

266 *Tafsir Ibn Kathir*, Vol. 3, p. 93.

267 *Tafsir Al-Jalalayn*, p. 236.

the prescriptions of your religion: the lawful and the unlawful, the commands and the prohibitions...[268]

So this verse tells Muslims that their religion has been perfected and completed, and they have no need for any other religion or prophet.

Chapter 5, Verse 17

Surely, in disbelief are they who say that Allah is the Messiah, son of Maryam (Mary)...

The significant portion of this verse is found in the first sentence. According to Ibn Kathir, this verse meant that "Christians are disbelievers" because Christians believe that Jesus is the Son of God.[269] And because of this, Ibn Kathir wrote of the Christians

may Allah's continued curses be upon them until the Day of Resurrection.[270]

---

268 *Tafsir Ibn 'Abbas*, p. 133.

269 *Tafsir Ibn Kathir*, Vol. 3, p. 133. That Christians are disbelievers is also stated in 5:72-73 of the Koran.

270 *Tafsir Ibn Kathir*, Vol. 3, p. 134. It is interesting to note that in his writings Ibn Kathir repeatedly called for Allah to curse the Christians and (especially) the Jews (e.g., *Tafsir Ibn Kathir*, Vol. 1, pp. 285, 320, 327, and 350; Vol. 2, pp. 171, 195, 214, and 477; and Vol. 3, pp. 18, 25, 26, 38, 149, 204, 221, 222, 238, and 246). Ibn Kathir also repeatedly called the Jews and Christians "the enemies of Islam" (e.g. *Tafsir Ibn Kathir*, Vol. 3, pp. 179, 200, 204, 209, and 224). His attitude toward Jews and Christians is significant because, as was previously noted, Ibn Kathir's *tafsir*

is the most popular interpretation of the Qur'an in the Arabic language, and the majority of the Muslims consider it to be the best source based on Qur'an and Sunnah.

The *Tafsir Ahsanul-Bayan* noted that the purpose of this verse was to refute the Christian belief in the divinity of Jesus:

> *Today, the concept of the Trinity (or three hypostases) is the most fundamental pillar of Christian faith. The Qur'an refutes it, and declares that imputing divine attributes to a Messenger of Allah* [Jesus] *is sheer heresy and outright blasphemy. This is the error of Christians.*[271]

Therefore, Christians are heretical, blasphemous, and automatically included when verses of the Koran demand intolerance and hostility toward disbelievers.

Chapter 5, Verse 32

> *Because of that, We ordained for the Children of Israel that if anyone killed a person not in retaliation of murder, or to spread mischief in the land - it would be as if he killed all mankind, and if anyone saved a life, it would be as if he saved the life of all mankind. And indeed, there came to them Our Messengers with clear proofs, evidences, and signs, even then after that many of them continued to exceed the limits (e.g. by doing oppression unjustly and exceeding beyond the limits set by Allah by committing the major sins) in the land.*

On June 4, 2009, President Barack Obama was in Cairo, Egypt giving a speech to the Muslim world in which he spent much of the time speaking inaccurately about Islam. During his speech he said that violent extremism was "irreconcilable" with Islam because:

Tafsir Ibn Kathir, Vol. 1, p. 5. Could his attitude toward Jews and Christians be a factor in that popularity?

[271] *Tafsir Ahsanul-Bayan*, Vol. 1, p. 586.

The Holy Koran teaches that whoever kills an innocent is as -- it is as if he has killed all mankind. And the Holy Koran also says whoever saves a person, it is as if he has saved all mankind.

President Obama was referring to 5:32, and he was engaging in *tafsir*. According to his interpretation, 5:32 was issuing a general admonition against the killing of innocents and a general praise for the saving of lives. However, authoritative Islamic scholars are of a somewhat different opinion.

This verse starts out *Because of that*. This refers to the preceding five verses that dealt with Cain (*Qabil)* killing Abel (*Habil*). 5:32 then states *We ordained for the Children of Israel*, which means this verse was not general in nature, but originally directed toward the Jews (although some Islamic scholars claim it is now general).

Ibn Kathir then explained the first part of what had been ordained:

The Ayah states, whoever kills a soul without justification - such as in retaliation for murder or causing mischief on earth - will be as if he has killed all mankind, because there is no difference between one life or another.[272]

It is easy to see that someone who had committed murder would probably not be considered one of the innocents mentioned in President Obama's speech. But, as Ibn Kathir noted, this verse also states that it is justified to kill someone for *causing mischief on earth*. What is *mischief*?

Ibn Kathir agreed with a number of Muslim scholars who said,

"Do not make mischief on the earth," means, "Do not commit acts of disobedience on the earth. Their mischief is disobeying Allah, because whoever disobeys Allah on

---

272 *Tafsir Ibn Kathir*, Vol. 3, p. 158.

the earth, or commands that Allah be disobeyed, he has committed mischief on the earth."[273]

Ibn Kathir added that

> *taking the disbelievers as friends is one of the categories of mischief on the earth..In this way Allah severed the loyalty between the believers and the disbelievers.*[274]

The *Tafsir Al-Jalalayn* used the word *corruption* instead of *mischief*, and *corruption* was defined as including *unbelief*.[275]

So disobeying, or not believing in Allah is committing *mischief in the land*. Consequently, any non-Muslim is, by definition, committing *mischief in the land* and could be justifiably killed. And taking disbelievers as friends is also committing *mischief*. As we found in 5:17, Christians are specified as disbelievers. So according to 5:32, a Muslim could be killed for taking a Christian as a friend.

Now let's look at the section of 5:32 that mentions saving a life:

> *...if anyone saved a life, it would be as if he saved the life of all mankind.*

A common Western understanding of this idea would be some positive action that prevents another person from dying as a result of, for example, disease, an accident, or a violent act. However, Ibn Kathir referred to Ibn 'Abbas, a Muslim scholar who viewed it differently:

> *Saving life in this case occurs by not killing a soul that Allah has forbidden. So this is the meaning of saving the*

---

273 Ibid., Vol. 1, pp. 131-132.

274 Ibid., p. 132.

275 *Tafsir Al-Jalalayn*, p. 248.

> *life of all mankind, for whoever forbids killing a soul without justification, the lives of all people will be saved from him.*[276]

So according to this interpretation, simply refraining from killing anybody without justification means you are saving peoples' lives.

And Ibn Kathir pointed out another Muslim scholar whose interpretation of this verse was quite different from that presented by President Obama:

> *Sa'id bin Jubayr said, "He who allows himself to shed the blood of a Muslim, is like he who allows shedding the blood of all people. He who forbids shedding the blood of one Muslim, is like he who forbids shedding the blood of all people.*[277]

So with 5:32 telling Muslims it is justifiable to kill non-Muslims because they are, by definition, committing *mischief in the land*, this verse is hardly proof that violent extremism is "irreconcilable" with Islam. It's also a good thing President Obama stopped at 5:32 for that claim. Let's look at the next verse.

---

276 *Tafsir Ibn Kathir*, Vol. 3, p. 159.

277 Ibid. A similar interpretation about the unity of Muslims was made in the modern *Tafsir Ahsanul-Bayan* when discussing the statement *do not kill yourselves*, found in 4:29:

> *This may also mean suicide... and killing a Muslim, the latter because the Muslims as a whole are like a single body, and hence killing him is like killing oneself.*

Tafsir Ahsanul-Bayan, Vol. 1, p. 447. 4:29 is further discussed in Chapter 15, *Suicide or Paradise?*.

Chapter 5, Verse 33

> *The recompense of those who wage war against Allah and His Messenger and do mischief in the land is only that they shall be killed or crucified or their hands and their feet be cut off from opposite sides, or be exiled from the land. That is their disgrace in this world, and a great torment is theirs in the Hereafter.*

According to Ibn Kathir, to *wage war against* Allah and Muhammad meant to

> *oppose and contradict, and it includes disbelief, blocking roads and spreading fear in the fairways.*[278]

In the *Tafsir Al-Jalalayn* we find that simply engaging in "fighting the Muslims" meant one was waging war against Allah and Muhammad.[279]

And with 5:33 we see that punishment for committing *mischief in the land* goes beyond simply being killed; those committing *mischief* could be crucified, have their hands and feet cut off, or be exiled.

Ibn Kathir said that this verse was

> *general in meaning and includes the idolators and all others who commit the types of crimes the Ayah mentioned.*[280]

The *Tafsir Ahsanul-Bayan* also noted that this verse was "general in scope and application," and explained:

---

278 *Tafsir Ibn Kathir*, Vol. 3, p. 161. We previously saw in 9:12 of the Koran that criticizing Islam was the same as waging war against Islam.

279 *Tafsir Al-Jalalayn*, p. 248.

280 *Tafsir Ibn Kathir*, Vol. 3, p. 162.

> *This verse is called Ayat-ul-Muharaba (Verse of Waging War). This is general in scope and application. That is, it applies to both Muslims and non-Muslims. Muharaba means an organized and armed group of men waging war in or near the borders of a Muslim country, killing and pillaging, kidnapping and dishonoring them.* [my emphasis] *The verse lists four punishments for such men but the ruler (imam) of the time has the right to give whatever of the four punishments he deems proper, according to his discretion.*[281]

So according to this verse, those who oppose, criticize, dishonor, or even disbelieve in Islam are waging war against Allah and Muhammad, and can face brutal repercussions.

Chapter 5, Verse 51

> *O you who believe! Take not the Jews and the Christians as Auliya' (friends, protectors, helpers), they are but Auliya' of each other. And if any amongst you takes them as Auliya', then surely, he is one of them. Verily, Allah guides not those people who are the Zalimun (polytheists and wrongdoers and unjust).*

In a section titled *The Prohibition of Taking the Jews, Christians and Enemies of Islam as Friends*, Ibn Kathir explained this verse by pointing out that

> *Allah forbids His believing servants from having Jews and Christians as friends, because they are the enemies of Islam and its people, may Allah curse them. Allah then states that they are friends of each other and He gives a*

---

281 *Tafsir Ahsanul-Bayan*, Vol. 1, p. 600.

warning threat to those who do this, And if any among you befriends them, then surely he is one of them.[282]

The *Tafsir Al-Jalalayn* explained that this verse meant Muslims were not to join Jews and Christians "in mutual friendship and love," or "in their unbelief."[283]

The *Tafsir Ibn 'Abbas* stated that Muslims who take Jews and Christians as friends are "not included in Allah's protection and safety."[284]

The modern *Tafsir Ahsanul-Bayan* agreed with these interpretations:

> *The verse forbids Muslims to keep intimate relations with them and take them as protectors and helpers, because they are the enemies of Allah, the Muslims, and Islam. It should be noted that those who take them as protectors and helpers will be considered among them .*[285]

Allah's command could not be more unambiguous.

---

282 *Tafsir Ibn Kathir*, Vol. 3, p. 204. For examples of other verses in the Koran which prohibit Muslims from taking non-Muslims in general as friends, and/or show a hostile attitude toward non-Muslims, see 2:105, 2:193, 2:221, 3:28, 3:118, 4:89, 4:101 (*the disbelievers are ever to you open enemies*), 4:139-140, 4:144, 8:12-13, 8:22, 8:39, 8:59-60, 8:73, 9:5, 9:23, 9:29, 9:30, 9:73, 9:123, 13:18, 13:41, 21:44, 47:4, 47:35, 58:22, 60:1, 60:10, 60:13, 66:9, and 68:35 . And 48:29 is quite clear:

> *Muhammad is the Messenger of Allah. And those who are with him are severe against disbelievers, and merciful among themselves.*

283 *Tafsir Al-Jalalayn*, p. 256.

284 *Tafsir Ibn 'Abbas*, p. 143.

285 *Tafsir Ahsanul-Bayan*, Vol. 1, p. 616.

Chapter 5, Verse 55

> *Verily, your Wali (Protector or Helper) is none other than Allah, His Messenger, and the believers - those who perform As-Salat (the prayers), and give Zakat (obligatory charity), and they are Raki'un (those who bow down or submit themselves with obedience to Allah in prayer).*

Ibn Kathir explained that this verse meant:

> *the Jews are not your friends. Rather, your allegiance is to Allah, His Messénger and the faithful believers.*[286]

The *Tafsir Ahsanul-Bayan* explained this verse:

> *Believers have been told not to forge intimate relations with the Jews and Christians. Whom to befriend, then, one may well ask? Allah replies that the best friends of believers are Allah, His Messenger, and the believers.*[287]

Chapter 5, Verse 57

> *O you who believe! Take not as Auliya (protectors and helpers) those who take your religion as a mockery and fun from among those who received the Scripture (Jews and Christians) before you, and nor from among the disbelievers; and fear Allah if you indeed are true believers.*

In a section titled *The Prohibition of Being Loyal Friends with Disbelievers*, Ibn Kathir explained:

---

286 *Tafsir Ibn Kathir*, Vol. 3, p. 209.

287 *Tafsir Ahsanul-Bayan*, Vol. 1, p. 620.

This Ayah discourages and forbids taking the enemies of Islam and its people, such as the People of the Book [Jews and Christians] *and the polytheists, as friends.*[288]

The *Tafsir Ibn 'Abbas* explained that this verse meant the Muslims were not to choose as friends Jews, Christians, or "the rest of the disbelievers."[289]

The *Tafsir Ahsanul-Bayan* provided a similar interpretation:

Those who received the Scripture refer to the Jews and Christians, while "disbelievers" refers to the pagans. Here again Allah tells the believers not to take as friends those who make fun of your religion because they are enemies of Allah and His Messenger.[290]

The Tafsir Al-Jalalayn noted:

Show fear of Allah - by not taking them as friends - if you are believers - and are true in your belief.[291]

Chapter 5, Verse 65

And if only the People of the Scripture (Jews and Christians) had believed (in Muhammad) and warded off evil (sin, ascribing partners to Allah) and had become Al-Muttaqun (the pious), We would indeed have expiated

---

288 *Tafsir Ibn Kathir*, Vol. 3, p. 211.

289 *Tafsir Ibn 'Abbas*, p. 144.

290 *Tafsir Ahsanul-Bayan*, Vol. 1, p. 622.

291 *Tafsir Al-Jalalayn*, p. 257.

from them their sins and admitted them to Gardens of pleasure (in Paradise).

Ibn Kathir explained this verse meant:

> *...had the People of the Book believed in Allah and His Messenger and avoided the sins and prohibitions that they committed...We would have removed the dangers from them and granted them their objectives.*[292]

The *Tafsir Ahsanul-Bayan* explained:

> *"And if the People of the Scripture had believed:" That is, if they had the correct belief or, in other words, if they had believed in Muhammad, as their Scriptures told them to. "Warded off evil:" kept away from sins, especially the sin of shirk (ascribing partners to Allah), hostility to Islam and refusing to believe in the mission of Muhammad.*[293]

The *Tafsir Al-Jalalayn* explained that if "the People of the Book had believed in Muhammad...fearing unbelief," they would have been admitted into "Gardens of Delight."[294]

The *Tafsir Ibn 'Abbas* took a similar approach, noting that if the People of the Scripture would believe "in Muhammad and the Qur'an" and "repent of Judaism and Christianity," they would be brought into "Gardens of Delight."[295]

---

292 *Tafsir Ibn Kathir*, Vol. 3, p. 225.

293 *Tafsir Ahsanul-Bayan*, Vol. 1, p. 628.

294 *Tafsir Al-Jalalayn*, p. 260.

295 *Tafsir Ibn 'Abbas*, p. 145.

According to this verse, Jews and Christians, by virtue of their religions, are committing sins that will keep them out of Paradise. Only by believing in Allah and Muhammad could they go to Paradise.

Chapter 5, Verse 66

> *And if only they had acted according to the Taurat (Torah), the Injil (Gospel), and what has (now) been sent down to them from their Lord (the Qur'an), they would surely, have gotten provision from above them and from underneath their feet...*

As Ibn Kathir explained:

> *Had they adhered to the Books that they have with them which they inherited from the Prophets, without altering or changing these Books, these would have directed them to follow the truth and implement the revelation that Allah sent Muhammad with. These Books testify to the Prophet's truth and command that he must be followed.*[296]

The *Tafsir Ahsanul-Bayan* explained this verse:

> *Act according to the Taurat and the Injil means: if they had followed their commandments, including the mention of the advent of Muhammad. (wa ma unzila and what has been sent down): means all the revealed books including the Qur'an. That is, if they had accepted Islam.*[297]

The *Tafsir Ibn 'Abbas* stated this meant:

---

296 *Tafsir Ibn Kathir*, Vol. 3, pp. 225-226.

297 *Tafsir Ahsanul-Bayan*, Vol. 1, p. 629.

...if they had accepted what is in the Torah and the Gospel and demonstrated the traits and description of Muhammad contained therein...[298]

The *Tafsir Al-Jalalayn* explained:

If only they had implemented the Torah and the Gospel by acting on what their Books contain, which includes belief in the Prophet...[299]

This verse claims that the Torah and the "Gospel" had predicted the coming of Muhammad, and the Jews and Christians should have followed those teachings. Had they done so, they would have become Muslims and been provided for.

Chapter 5, Verse 69

Surely, those who believe (in the Oneness of Allah, in His Messenger Muhammad and all that was revealed to him from Allah), and those who are the Jews and the Sabians and the Christians - whosoever believed in Allah and the Last Day, and worked righteousness, on them shall be no fear, nor shall they grieve.

This verse might appear to give credence to the beliefs of the Jews, Sabians, and Christians. However, Ibn Kathir explained:

The meaning here is that if each of these groups believed in Allah and the Hereafter, which is the Day of Judgement and Reckoning, and performed good actions, which to be so, must conform to Muhammad's Law, after Muhammad

---

298 *Tafsir Ibn 'Abbas*, p. 145.

299 *Tafsir Al-Jalalayn*, p. 260.

was sent to all mankind and the Jinns. If any of these groups held these beliefs, then they shall have no fear of what will come or sadness regarding what they lost, nor will grief ever affect them.[300]

The Tafsir Ibn 'Abbas stated that no fear would come upon them

if the Jews repent of Judaism, the Sabaeans of their religion and the Christians of Christianity...[301]

And Ibn 'Abbas said that this verse had actually been abrogated by 3:85.[302] So instead of giving credence to other religions, this verse actually states that everyone must believe in Islam to be saved.

Chapter 5, Verse 82

Verily, you will find the strongest among men in enmity to the believers (Muslims) the Jews and those who are Al-Mushrikun, and you will find the nearest in love to the believers (Muslims) those who say: "We are Christians." That is because amongst them are priests and monks, and they are not proud.

With regard to the Jews, Ibn Kathir wrote:

---

300 *Tafsir Ibn Kathir*, Vol. 3, p. 232. On that same page, Ibn Kathir likened this verse to 2:62. The *Tafsir Ahsanul-Bayan* said that 5:69 and 2:62 had "the same meaning" - see *Tafsir Ahsanul-Bayan*, Vol. 1, p. 633. See the discussion of 2:62 in Chapter 8, *Three Religions with the Same God?*.

301 *Tafsir Ibn 'Abbas*, p. 145.

302 *The Noble Qur'an*, p. 169, n. 1. See the discussion of 3:85 in Chapter 8, *Three Religions with the Same God?*.

> *This describes the Jews, since their disbelief is that of rebellion, defiance, opposing the truth, belittling other people and degrading the scholars. This is why the Jews - may Allah's continued curses descend on them until the Day of Resurrection - killed many of their Prophets and tried to kill the Messenger of Allah several times, as well as, performing magic spells against him and poisoning him.*[303]

The modern *Tafsir Ahsanul-Bayan* explained:

> *That is because the Jews are a stubborn and ungrateful people, self-opinionated, willful, arrogant and unduly critical of religious scholars.*[304]

But why are the Christians considered *the nearest in love to the believers*? Ibn Kathir noted this about the Christians:

> *These people are generally more tolerant of Islam and its people, because of the mercy and kindness that their hearts acquired through part of the Messiah's religion...In their book is the saying: "He who strikes you on the right cheek, then turn the left cheek for him." And fighting was prohibited in their creed...*[305]

The *Tafsir Al-Jalalayn* noted that the Christians were "nearest in love to the believers" because the Christians were

> *not too proud to follow the truth in the way that the Jews and the people of Makka were.*[306]

---

303 *Tafsir Ibn Kathir*, Vol. 3, p. 246.

304 *Tafsir Ahsanul-Bayan*, Vol. 1, p. 644.

305 *Tafsir Ibn Kathir*, Vol. 3, p. 246.

306 *Tafsir Al-Jalalayn*, p. 265.

The *Tafsir Ahsanul-Bayan* provided this explanation about the Christians:

> *They are not stubborn and arrogant like Jews. 'Isa preached tolerance, love and forgiving, preaching not to quarrel. These are high morals. In this respect, they are closer to Muslims. These qualities of Christians make them quite a distinct people, and set them apart from Jews. Even today we see them less hostile to Muslims than the Jews and pagans. Yet, when it comes to the faith of Islam, they are hostile, the proof being a long series of battles between them and the Muslims stretching over centuries. This is one reason why Allah forbids Muslims forging close relations with them both.*[307]

This verse tells Muslims that Jews are their worst enemies. But the Christians were looked upon more favorably because their religion was tolerant, peaceful, and forgiving. Nevertheless, according to our modern *tafsir*, the Christians were hostile *to the faith of Islam*, and Muslims were still forbidden from *forging close relations* with Jews and Christians.

Summary

In Chapter Five the religion of Islam had been completed and finalized, and Muslims did not need any other religion. What Muhammad had allowed became permissible, and what he had prohibited became impermissible. Christians were specifically identified as "disbelievers," which means they are automatically included when verses of the Koran demand intolerance and hostility toward disbelievers. Opposing or criticizing Islam was considered *waging war* against Islam and was punishable by death, crucifixion, or amputation of a hand or a foot. These were the same penalties for making *mischief in the land.* And *mischief* included disobeying, or not believing in Allah, or commanding that others disobey Allah, or even a Muslim taking a disbeliever as a friend. In fact,

---

307 *Tafsir Ahsanul-Bayan*, Vol. 1, p. 644.

this chapter specifically prohibited Muslims from taking Christians and Jews as friends. However, between Christians and Jews, the former were considered the friendliest toward Islam because they were more tolerant, peaceful, and forgiving than were the Jews. The Jews were the worst enemies of Islam. And Jews and Christians were precluded from Paradise because they were not Muslims.

From the practical standpoint of a non-Muslim, whether Chapter Five or Chapter Nine of the Koran is the final chapter is not that important. In both, Islam is the superior religion, and criticism of, or opposition to Islam is to be responded to with violence. In both, friendship between Muslims and non-Muslims is prohibited, and it is replaced with intolerance, hostility, and violence toward non-Muslims. These are the teachings of the last two chapters of the Koran.

And Muhammad, who spoke for Allah and is still considered the timeless standard for good conduct for Muslims, emphasized the excellence of acting on the teachings of the Koran:

> *Narrated 'Abdullah: Allah's Messenger said, "Do not wish to be like anyone, except in two cases: (1) A man whom Allah has given wealth and he spends it righteously (in a just and right way according to what Allah has ordered). (2) A man whom Allah has given Al-Hikmah (wisdom, knowledge of the Qur'an and the Sunna - legal ways of the Prophet) and he acts according to it and teaches it to others."*[308]

And on another occasion, Muhammad talked about the penalty for knowing the Koran and not acting on it. He said that the angels Gabriel and Michael had taken him to the *Sacred Land*:

---

[308] *Sahih Al-Bukhari*, Vol. 9, Book 93, No. 7141, p. 162. Similar *hadiths* about the importance of acting on the teachings of the Koran can be found in: *Sahih Al-Bukhari*, Vol. 7, Book 70, No. 5427, p. 211; *Sahih Muslim*, Vol. 2, No. 815, p. 453; *Sunan Ibn Majah*, Vol. 1, No. 217, pp. 217-218; and *Tafsir Ibn Kathir*, Vol. 2, p. 526.

...we went on till we came to a man lying in a prone position, and another man standing at his head carrying a stone or a piece of rock, and crushing the head of the lying man with that stone. Whenever he struck him, the stone rolled away. The man went to pick it up and by the time he returned to him, the crushed head returned to its normal state and the man came back and struck him again (and so on).[309]

When Muhammad asked about this man, the angels replied:

The one whose head you saw being crushed is the one whom Allah had given the knowledge of the Qur'an (i.e. knowing it by heart), but he used to sleep at night (i.e., he did not recite it then) and did not use to act upon it (i.e., upon its orders etc.) by day; and so this punishment will go on till the Day of Resurrection.[310]

---

309 *Sahih Al-Bukhari*, Vol. 2, Book 23, No. 1386, p. 268.

310 Ibid., p. 269.

7

No Compulsion in Islam?

One of the fundamental truths established by the sacred texts is that no one can be compelled to accept Islam. It is the duty of Muslims to establish the proof of Islam to the people so that truth can be made clear from falsehood. After that, whoever wishes to accept Islam may do so and whoever wishes to continue upon unbelief may do so. No one should be threatened or harmed in any way if he does not wish to accept Islam.[311]

No Compulsion and the Islamic Scholars

It is quite common to hear Muslims say that there is "no compulsion" in Islam. For example, we have the quote at the beginning of this chapter that was used on a number of Muslim websites. And we had another example in the "No Compulsion in Islam" section of Chapter 1, *The Importance of the Tafsirs*. There we had a new, and inaccurate interpretation of 18:29 of the Koran used to maintain that there was no compulsion in Islam.

---

311 This statement, and variations of it with the same message of "no compulsion," were found at the following Muslim websites, accessed July 3, 2012:

1. http://www.islamreligion.com/articles/661/
2. http://en.islamtoday.net/artshow-262-3441.htm
3. http://islamicchamper.wordpress.com/2012/06/26/does-the-noble-quran-let-muslims-convert-people-by-force/
4. http://www.onislam.net/english/ask-the-scholar/quran-and-hadith/456160-verses-on-freedom-of-faith-abrogated.html?Hadith=

But there is an actual verse of the Koran that is used as a basis for the claim of "no compulsion":

Chapter 2, Verse 256

> *There is no compulsion in religion. Verily, the Right Path has become distinct from the wrong path. Whoever disbelieves in Taghut* [[312]] *and believes in Allah, then he has grasped the most trustworthy handhold that will never break. And Allah is All-Hearer, All-Knower.*

From this we are encouraged to believe that one is free to accept or reject Islam. However, once again we come to realize the importance of the *tafsirs* and the authoritative Islamic scholars. When we examine what authoritative scholars of Islam say about the *no compulsion* part of this verse, we find some very different understandings.

According to Ibn Kathir, *no compulsion* meant:

> *Do not force anyone to become Muslim, for Islam is plain and clear, and its proofs and evidence are plain and clear. Therefore, there is no need to force anyone to embrace Islam. Rather, whoever Allah directs to Islam, opens his heart for it and enlightens his mind, will embrace Islam with certainty. Whoever Allah blinds his heart and seals his hearing and sight, then he will not benefit from being forced to embrace Islam.*[313]

So for Ibn Kathir, Islam was the obvious, correct religion. And whomever Allah had given an open heart and enlightened mind would naturally embrace Islam, without compulsion. If someone did not become a Muslim, it was also because Allah willed it, and consequently it was not worth forcing them *to embrace Islam*. So it was up to Allah.

---

312 *Taghut* means false gods and anything worshipped other than Allah.

313 *Tafsir Ibn Kathir*, Vol. 2, p. 30.

A similar approach, with some interesting additional commentary, was presented in the modern *Tafsir Ahsanul-Bayan* when explaining this verse:

> *Nobody will be forced to convert to Islam because Allah has made quite distinct the Right path from the wrong one. Yes, of course, in order to eradicate disbelief and paganism and weaken their force, jihad has been prescribed for the believers. But this is not the same as forced conversion. The purpose of jihad is to make the Word of Allah uppermost, to suppress those hostile forces which impede the progress of the faith, obstruct those who want to practice their faith, and block the missionary work. There will always be people who will try to crush Islam or impede its progress. That is why jihad has been prescribed. The need for jihad will remain till the Day of Judgment.*[314]

So according to this modern *tafsir* there is no such thing as "forced conversion" because Allah has made the right path distinctly different from the wrong path. And the purpose of *jihad* is not "forced conversion," but to "suppress those hostile forces" who attempt to impede the natural progress of Islam along that right path.

The *Tafsir Al-Jalalayn* explained that this verse meant you were in error if you did not believe in Islam:

> *Guidance is clear by the evident signs that belief is right guidance and unbelief is error.*[315]

And there were additional points of view among Islamic scholars. Al-Qurtubi wrote that scholars disagreed about the legal status and meaning

---

[314] *Tafsir Ahsanul-Bayan*, Vol. 1, p. 237.

[315] *Tafsir Al-Jalalayn*, p. 97.

of 2:256. He noted the following variety of opinions about the *no compulsion* section:[316]

1. **Abrogated by 9:73[317]**

> *It is said that it is abrogated because the Prophet, may Allah bless him and grant him peace, forced the Arabs to adopt the din* [religion] *of Islam and fought them and was only pleased with Islam for them. Sulayman ibn Musa took that view, saying "It is abrogated by 'O Prophet! Do jihad against the unbelievers and the hypocrites.' (9:73)" That is related from Ibn Mas'ud and many commentators.*

2. **Applied only to the People of the Book (Jews and Christians)**

This is a variation of the first opinion. The *no compulsion* section applied only to the People of the Book as long as they paid the *Jizya*h. It did not apply to the idolaters:

> *It is not abrogated and was sent down about the people of the Book in particular and means that they are not forced to adopt Islam when they pay jizya. Those who are forced are the idolaters. Only Islam is accepted from them, and they are the ones about whom 'O Prophet! Do jihad against the unbelievers and the hypocrites' (9:73) was revealed.*

3. **Applied only to a Specific Incident**

> *Abu Dawud reported from Ibn 'Abbas that this was revealed about the Ansar. There was a woman, all of whose children had died. She made a vow that if she had a child who lived she would become a Jew. When the*

---

[316] *Tafsir Al-Qurtubi*, Vol. 1, pp. 659-661.

[317] The meaning of 9:73 is discussed in Chapter 5, *The Religion of Peace*.

Banu'n-Nadir were exiled,[318] *among them were many of the children of the Ansar. They said, "We will not leave our sons!" Then Allah revealed this...Whoever wished remained with them and whoever wished, entered Islam.*

4. **Applied only to a Specific Incident and then was Abrogated**

One scholar said the *no compulsion* section applied only to another specific incident involving an *Ansar* in Medina. He said, however, that it was later abrogated by Chapter Nine of the Koran:

> *As-Suddi said that the ayat was revealed about a man of the Ansar called Abu Husayn who had two sons. Some merchants came from Syria to Madina with oil and when they wanted to leave, his sons went to them. They invited the two sons to become Christians and they did so and went back with them to Syria. Their father went to the Messenger of Allah, may Allah bless him and grant him peace, to complain about this and asked the Messenger of Allah to send someone to bring them back. Then "There is no compulsion where the din is concerned" was revealed. He had not then been commanded to fight the People of the Book. He said, "Allah has put them far. They are the first to disbelieve." Abu'l-Husayn felt annoyed that the Prophet did not send someone after them. Then Allah revealed, "No, by your Lord, they are not believers until they make you their judge in the disputes that break out between them" (4:65). Then "No compulsion" was abrogated and he was commanded to fight the People of*

---

318 The Bani al-Nadir were one of the Jewish tribes of Medina. In August 625 Muhammad besieged the Bani al-Nadir because they were supposedly plotting to kill him. After 15 days the Bani al-Nadir surrendered. They were forced to leave Medina taking with them only what their camels could carry. For further details see the entry for August 625 in the *Chronology*.

the Book in Surat at-Tawba [Chapter Nine of the Koran].[319]

5. **An Unusual Interpretation!**

It is said that it means "do not call those who have submitted through the sword compelled and forced."

6. **Applied only to a Certain Category of Captives**

And other scholars said the *no compulsion* section applied only to a certain category of captives, and never applied to captured non-Muslim children, Magians, or idolaters, all of whom must become Muslim:

> *It is said that it was related about captives who were People of the Book. They are not compelled when they are adults. If they are Magians, young or old, or idolaters, they are compelled to adopt Islam because their captivity does not help them when they are idolaters. Do you not see that their sacrifices are not eaten nor their women married. That is what Ibn al-Qasim reported from Malik. Ashhab said that children are considered to have the din* [religion] *of those who captured them. If they refuse that, they are compelled to become Muslim. Children have no din and that is why they are compelled to enter Islam so that they do not go to a false din. When other types of unbelievers pay the jizya, they are forced to become Muslim, whether they are Arabs or non-Arabs, Quraysh or otherwise.*

Among these authoritative Islamic scholars there was no concept of "freedom of religion" as we understand it. And we can see that the

---

319 This was also one of the *hadiths* Al-Wahidi used to explain 2:256. See *Al-Wahidi's Asbab al-Nuzul*, p. 37.

writings of these scholars of Islam actually provide little support for, and many actually counter, the claim that there is *no compulsion* in Islam. To summarize, their approaches consisted of the following:

1. Whomever Allah had given an open heart and enlightened mind would naturally embrace Islam, without compulsion. If someone did not become a Muslim, it was because Allah willed it, and consequently it was not worth forcing them *to embrace Islam*. And *Jihad* had been prescribed to deal with those hostile forces who were so unenlightened that they attempted to impede the natural progress of Islam.

2. The idea of *no compulsion* had been abrogated and Muslims have been ordered by Allah to fight against all non-Muslim.

3. The idea of *no compulsion* applied only to a specific incident, or applied only to a specific incident and then it was specifically abrogated by Chapter Nine of the Koran.

4. The idea of *no compulsion* applied only to the Jews and Christians, as long as they paid the *Jizyah*. It did not apply to the Magians and idolaters.

5. The idea of *no compulsion* did not apply to child captives, even if they were Jews or Christians.

6. Submission *through the sword* was not considered compulsion.

Non-Muslims and Compulsion

What does the Koran have to say about whether or not non-Muslims should be compelled to become Muslims? Here is the first chapter for consideration:

Chapter 2, Verse 193

> *And fight them until there is no more Fitnah (disbelief and worshipping of others along with Allah) and (all and every kind of) worship is for Allah (Alone). But if they cease, let there be no transgression except against Az-Zalimun (the polytheists and wrongdoers).*

Ibn Kathir explained this verse under a section titled *The Order to fight until there is no more Fitnah*:

> *Allah then commanded fighting the disbelievers when he said:...until there is no more Fitnah meaning, Shirk...and the religion (all and every kind of worship) is for Allah (Alone) means, 'So that the religion of Allah becomes dominant above all other religions.'*[320]

Ibn Kathir went on to explain *But if they cease* indicated:

> *If they stop their Shirk and fighting the believers, then cease warfare against them.*[321]

The *Tafsir Al-Jalalayn* explained that this verse meant to fight "until there is no more fitna (*shirk*) in existence" and none but Allah is worshipped.[322]

The *Tafsir Al-Qurtubi* explained this verse:

> *It is an unqualified command to fight without any preconditions of hostilities being initiated by the unbelievers...the reason for fighting is disbelief because Allah says, "until there is no more fitna," meaning*

---

320 *Tafsir Ibn Kathir*, Vol. 1, p. 531.

321 Ibid., p. 532.

322 *Tafsir Al-Jalalayn*, p. 69.

> *disbelief in this case. So the goal is to abolish disbelief and that is clear...fitna here means shirk....*[323]

Al-Qurtubi wrote that *if they cease* meant:

> *If they stop and become Muslim or submit by paying jizya in the case of the people of the Book. Otherwise they should be fought and they are wrongdoers...The wrongdoers are either those who initiate fighting or those who remain entrenched in disbelief and fitna.*[324]

So 2:193 orders Muslims to be at war with non-Muslims, simply because they are not Muslims, until Islam reigns supreme in the world.

And the command to fight until there is no more *Fitnah* is also found in another verse of the Koran:

Chapter 8, Verse 39

> *And fight them until there is no more Fitnah (disbelief and polytheism, i.e., worshipping others besides Allah), and the religion (worship) will all be for Allah Alone (in the whole of the world). But if they cease (worshipping others besides Allah), then certainly, Allah is All-Seer of what they do.*

The *Tafsir Al-Jalalayn* again defined *Fitnah* as *shirk.*[325]

And, in a section titled *The Order to fight to eradicate Shirk and Kufr* (disbelief), Ibn Kathir pointed out that Ibn 'Abbas and other scholars also defined *Fitnah* as *Shirk.*[326]

---

323 *Tafsir Al-Qurtubi*, p. 496.

324 Ibid.

325 *Tafsir Al-Jalalayn*, p. 385.

The modern *Tafsir Ahsanul-Bayan* explained this verse:

> *Here fitnah (affliction) means disbelief or paganism, or the power of disbelievers and pagans. That is, continue fighting until you put an end to the power of disbelievers. Until Allah alone is worshipped in the entire world.*[327]

The Koran also threatens Jews and Christians with punishment if they do not believe in Islam:

Chapter 4, Verse 47

> *O you who have been given the Scripture (Jews and Christians)! Believe in what We have revealed (to Muhammad) confirming what is (already) with you, before we efface faces (by making them look like the back of necks; without nose, mouth and eyes) and turn them hindwards, or curse them as We cursed the Sabbath-breakers. And the Commandment of Allah is always executed.*

In a section titled *Calling the People of the Book to Embrace the Faith, Warning them Against Doing Otherwise*, Ibn Kathir explained that Allah was ordering the Jews and Christians to believe in Islam. If they failed to do so, they would be punished for ignoring the truth of Islam.[328]

The *Tafsir Al-Jalalayn* stated that this verse was

> *a conditional threat and that when some of them became Muslim that threat was removed.*[329]

---

326 *Tafsir Ibn Kathir*, Vol. 4, p. 314.

327 *Tafsir Ahsanul-Bayan*, Vol. 2, p. 293.

328 *Tafsir Ibn Kathir*, Vol. 2, pp. 479-480.

329 *Tafsir Al-Jalalayn*, p. 193.

And the footnote for this verse in *The Noble Qur'an* stated

> *This Verse is a severe warning to the Jews and Christians, and an absolute obligation that they must believe in Allah's Messenger Muhammad and in his Message of Islamic Monotheism and in this Qur'an.*[330]

And as we saw in Chapter 5, *The Religion of Peace*, 9:5 of the Koran orders the Muslims to actively seek out and kill the *Mushrikun*, who in essence are any non-Muslims. This verse stated that only by converting to Islam would the *Mushrikun* be saved. As Ibn Kathir put it,

> *This way, they will have no choice, but to die or embrace Islam.*[331]

We also found that 9:29 of the Koran states that if you are a *Mushrikun* who is a Christian or a Jew, the only way to coexist with the Muslims without fighting them to the death or converting is to pay the *Jizyah*, "with willing submission" and feeling "subdued." According to 9:33 Allah sent Muhammad to make Islam "superior over all religions," and 9:73 and 9:123 command *jihad* against "the disbelievers," with 9:111 promising Paradise for those Muslims who die while engaging in *jihad*. And remember, these are commands from the final chapter of the Koran.

What did Muhammad have to say about compelling non-Muslims to become Muslims? He said Allah had commanded him fight until everyone became a Muslim:

> *It has been narrated on the authority of 'Abdullah b. Umar that the Messenger of Allah said: I have been commanded to fight against people till they testify that there is no god but Allah, and Muhammad is the Messenger of Allah, they establish the prayer, and pay the Zakat. If they do it, their*

---

[330] *The Noble Qur'an*, p. 129, n. 1.

[331] *Tafsir Ibn Kathir*, Vol. 4, p. 376.

blood and property are guaranteed protection on my behalf except when justified by law, and their affairs rest with Allah.[332]

Before Muhammad sent Muslim forces against non-Muslims, he would issue an order that combined the commands of 9:5 and 9:29 of the Koran:

> *It has been reported from Sulaiman b. Buraid through his father that when the Messenger of Allah (may peace be upon him) appointed anyone as leader of an army or detachment he would especially exhort him to fear Allah and to be good to the Muslims who were with him. He would say: Fight in the name of Allah and in the way of Allah. Fight against those who disbelieve in Allah. Make a holy war...When you meet your enemies who are polytheists, invite them to three courses of action. If they respond to any one of these, you also accept it and keep from doing them any harm. Invite them to (accept) Islam; if they respond to you, accept it from them and desist from fighting against them...If they refuse to accept Islam, demand from them the Jizya. If they agree to pay, accept it from them and hold off your hands. If they refuse to pay the tax, seek Allah's help and fight them...*[333]

---

332 *Sahih Muslim*, Vol. 1, No. 22, pp. 21-22. There are similar *hadiths* reporting that Muhammad said he had been commanded to fight until Islam was made supreme, e.g.: *Sahih Al-Bukhari*, Vol. 1, Book 2, No. 25, p. 66; Vol. 4, Book 56, No. 2946, p. 126; *Jami' At-Tirmidhi*, Vol. 5, No. 2606, p. 15, and No. 2608, pp. 17-18; Vol. 6, No. 3341, p. 76; *Sunan Ibn Majah*, Vol. 1, Nos. 71-72, pp. 123-124; *Sunan An-Nasa'i*, Vol. 4, No. 3092, p. 18, and No. 3097, pp. 21-22; and *Sunan Abu Dawud*, Vol. 3, No. 2641, p. 277.

333 *Sahih Muslim*, Vol. 5, No. 1731R1, pp. 162-163. This *hadith* about Muhammad ordering these three courses of action was also reported in *Sunan Abu Dawud*, Vol. 3, No. 2612, pp. 262-264; *Sunan Ibn Majah*, Vol. 4, No. 2858, pp. 98-100; and *Jami' At-Tirmidhi*, Vol. 3, No. 1617, pp. 376-378.

And Muhammad had an interesting approach to *inviting* people to Islam:

> *Al-Kalbi reported from Abu Salih who related that Ibn 'Abbas said: "The Messenger of Allah sent a letter to the people of Hajar, whose chief was Mundhir ibn Sawa, inviting them to Islam, or to pay the Jizyah if they chose not to embrace Islam. When Mundhir ibn Sawa received the letter, he showed it to the Arabs, Jews, Christians, Sabeans and Magians who were around him. They all agreed to pay the Jizyah and disliked embracing Islam. The Messenger of Allah, Allah bless him and give him peace, wrote back to him, saying: As for the Arabs, do not accept from them except Islam* [sic] *otherwise they will have nothing but the sword. As for the people of the Book and the Magians, accept the Jizyah from them. When this letter was read to them, the Arabs embraced Islam while the people of the Book and the Magians agreed to pay the Jizyah..."*[334]

So according to the Koran and Muhammad, non-Muslims should be forced to either become Muslims, die resisting, or become *Dhimmis* and pay the *Jizyah* (if eligible).

Muslims and Apostasy

Is there any compulsion on someone who is already a Muslim? Yes, if they consider leaving Islam for another religion. Let's see what the Koran has to say about a Muslim who leaves Islam for another religion:

1. Chapter 2, Verse 217

> *...And whosoever of you turns back from his religion and dies as a disbeliever, then his deeds will be lost in this life and in the Hereafter, and they will be the dwellers of the Fire. They will abide therein forever.*

---

[334] *Al-Wahidi's Asbab al-Nuzul*, p. 102.

The modern *Tafsir Ahsanul-Bayan* aptly explained the meaning of this section of 2:217:

> *An apostate, that is, a person who renounces the Islamic faith after accepting it, will have a double punishment, in this world as well as in the next. This verse mentions only his punishment in the Hereafter, not his punishment in this world. An apostate, in case he does not repent, shall be slain. A hadeeth says: "Whoever changes his religion, slay him." - (Saheeh-ul-Bukhari, hadeeth 3017). This is his punishment in this world.*[335]

2. Chapter 3, Verse 85

And whoever seeks a religion other than Islam, it will never be accepted of him, and in the Hereafter he will be one of the losers.

Under the heading *The Only Valid Religion To Allah is Islam*, Ibn Kathir explained this verse meant that

> *Allah rebukes those who prefer a religion other than the religion that He sent His Books and*

---

[335] *Tafsir Ahsanul-Bayan*, Vol. 1, p. 193. The *hadith* referred to is found in *Sahih Al-Bukhari*, Vol. 4, Book 56, No. 3017, p. 159:

> *Narrated 'Ikrima: 'Ali burnt some people and this news reached Ibn 'Abbas, who said, "Had I been in his place I would not have burnt them, as the Prophet said, 'Don't punish (anybody) with Allah's punishment.' No doubt, I would have killed them, for the Prophet said, 'If somebody (a Muslim) discards his religion, kill him.'"*

Messengers with, which is the worship of Allah Alone without partners...[336]

And Ibn Kathir added:

> *...whoever seeks other than what Allah has legislated, it will not be accepted from him.*[337]

The *Tafsir Al-Jalalayn* noted that this verse was "revealed" about some Muslims who had "apostatised and joined the unbelievers," and who had become losers because they would, as a result, "go to the Fire and remain in it forever."[338]

The *Tafsir Ibn 'Abbas* also stated that those who sought another religion would "dwell in Hell."[339]

3. Chapter 3, Verses 86-88

How shall Allah guide a people who disbelieved after their Belief and after they bore witness that the Messenger (Muhammad) is true and after clear proofs had come to them? And Allah guides not the people who are Zalimun (polytheists and wrongdoers). They are those whose recompense is that on them (rests) the curse of Allah, of

---

336 *Tafsir Ibn Kathir*, Vol. 2, p. 202.

337 Ibid., p. 204.

338 *Tafsir Al-Jalalayn*, p. 140. Muhammad said the destination for those who left Islam after his death, and consequently died as apostates, was the Fires of Hell - see *Sahih Al-Bukhari*, Vol. 4, Book 60, No. 3349, pp. 343-344. Similar *hadiths* were reported by other narrators - see *Sahih Al-Bukhari*, Vol. 8, Book 81, Nos. 6585-6587, pp. 312-313; and Vol. 9, Book 92, No. 7048, p. 123.

339 *Tafsir Ibn 'Abbas*, p. 78.

the angels and of all mankind. They will abide therein (Hell). Neither will their torment be lightened, nor will it be delayed or postponed (for a while).

Ibn Kathir plainly stated what these verses said about the consequences for those leaving Islam: "Allah curses them and His creation also curses them," and their "torment will not be lessened, not even for an hour."[340]

The *Tafsir Ibn 'Abbas* explained that the apostates would receive the punishment of Allah, and the curses of the angels and of the believers.[341]

The *Tafsir Ahsanul-Bayan* pointed out that apostasy from Islam was "a horrible crime, since the apostate knew the truth and yet turned away from it..."[342]

4. Chapter 3, Verse 102

O you who believe! Fear Allah (by doing all that He has ordered and by abstaining from all that He has forbidden) as He should be feared. (Obey Him, be thankful to Him, and remember Him always,) and die not except in a state of Islam [as Muslims (with complete submission to Allah)].

Ibn Kathir explained the last part of this verse:

> *Allah's statement, and die not except as (true) Muslims, means preserve your Islam while you*

---

340 *Tafsir Ibn Kathir*, Vol. 2, p. 206.

341 *Tafsir Ibn 'Abbas*, p. 78.

342 *Tafsir Ahsanul-Bayan*, Vol. 1, p. 331.

> *are well and safe, so that you die as a Muslim...We seek refuge from dying on other than Islam.*[343]

So Allah has plainly commanded Muslims to die as Muslims. It is then defiance of Allah to leave Islam and die as a non-Muslim. And Muhammad added to the reasons for why a Muslim would not want to defy Allah:

> *Narrated Abu Hurairah: The Prophet said, "Allah has a sense of Ghaira, and Allah's Sense of Ghaira is provoked when a believer does something which Allah has prohibited.*[344]

Ghaira is "a feeling of great fury and anger when one's honour and prestige is injured or challenged."[345]

5. Chapter 4, Verse 137

> *Verily, those who believe, then disbelieve, then believe (again), and (again) disbelieve, and go on increasing in disbelief; Allah will not forgive them, nor guide them on the (right) path.*

Ibn Kathir explained this verse:

---

343 *Tafsir Ibn Kathir*, Vol. 2, p. 228.

344 *Sahih Al-Bukhari*, Vol. 7, Book 67, No. 5223, p. 103. For other narrations about Allah having a sense of *Ghaira*, see *Sahih Al-Bukhari*, Vol. 7, Book 67, Nos. 5220-5222, pp. 102-103; and Vol. 9, Book 97, No. 7403, p. 301.

345 *Sahih Al-Bukhari*, Vol. 9, Glossary, p. 406. This is the same definition used in *The Noble Qur'an* - see the Glossary, p. 857.

> *Allah states that whoever embraces the faith, reverts from it, embraces it again, reverts from it and remains on disbelief and increases in it until death, then he will never have a chance to gain accepted repentance after death. Nor will Allah forgive him, or deliver him from his plight to the path of correct guidance.*[346]

Both the *Tafsir Al-Jalalayn* and the *Tafsir Ibn 'Abbas* stated that Allah would not forgive those who increased their depth of unbelief by disbelieving in Muhammad.[347]

6. Chapter 16, Verse 106

Whosever disbelieved in Allah after his belief, except him who is forced thereto and whose heart is at rest with Faith; but such as open their breasts to disbelief, on them is wrath from Allah, and theirs will be a great torment.

Ibn Kathir explained the meaning of this verse in a section titled *Allah's Wrath against the Apostate, except for the One Who is forced into Disbelief*:

> *Allah tells us that He is angry with them who willingly disbelieve in Him after clearly believing in Him, who open their hearts to disbelief finding peace in that, because they understood the faith yet they still turned away from it. They will suffer severe punishment in the Hereafter, because they preferred this life to the Hereafter, and they left the faith for the sake of this world and Allah did*

---

346 *Tafsir Ibn Kathir*, Vol. 2, p. 611.

347 *Tafsir Al-Jalalayn*, p. 222; and *Tafsir Ibn 'Abbas*, p. 125.

not guide their hearts and help them to stand firm in the true religion...[348]

Ibn Kathir explained the exception mentioned in this verse, *except him who is forced thereto*:

> *This is an exception in the case of one who utters statements of disbelief and verbally agrees with the Mushrikin because he is forced to do so by the beatings and abuse to which he is subjected, but his heart refuses to accept what he is saying, and he is, in reality, at peace with his faith in Allah and His Messenger.*[349]

The *Tafsir Al-Jalalayn* also acknowledged the exception mentioned in this verse, and then pointed out that this verse was "a severe threat" to those who apostatize.[350]

The *Tafsir Ahsanul-Bayan* provided a similar explanation:

> *As Al-Qurtubi said, scholars are unanimous that whoever renounces the faith under duress to save his life, his heart content with the faith, he is not*

---

348 *Tafsir Ibn Kathir*, Vol. 5, p. 529.

349 Ibid., p. 530. For the incident that led to the "revelation" of this verse, see *Al-Wahidi's Asbab al-Nuzul*, p. 142. Here we find that Yasir and his wife Sumayyah (Muslims) "were the first two persons who were killed in Islam." Their son 'Ammar ibn Yasir, after witnessing his parents murder by the Quraysh, renounced Islam ("...he was coerced to let them hear what they wanted to hear."). He went to Muhammad crying, and Muhammad forgave him. It is interesting to note that Muhammad encouraged the deception to continue by telling 'Ammar, "if they return to you, let them hear again what you told them."

350 *Tafsir Al-Jalalayn*, p. 583.

> *to be considered a disbeliever. The punitive laws relating to heresy...do not apply to him.*[351]

This *tafsir* then explained the phrase *on them is wrath from Allah*:

> *That is the punishment of heresy: Awful doom and the wrath of Allah. A heretic shall be slain. That is his temporal punishment...*[352]

7. Chapter 47, Verse 25

Verily, those who have turned back (have apostatised) as disbelievers after the guidance has been manifested to them - Shaitan (Satan) has beautified for them (their false hopes), and (Allah) prolonged their term (age).

In a section titled *Condemning Apostasy*, Ibn Kathir explained that this verse meant those who leave Islam are guided by Satan:

> *Allah then says, (Verily, those who have turned back) meaning, they departed from the faith and returned to disbelief...after guidance had become clear to them - Shaytan has enticed them meaning he adorned and beautified that (apostasy) for them...he tempted them and deceived them.*[353]

So we see the Koran states that an apostate from Islam has been guided by Satan and faces severe punishment in the after-life. But what is the punishment in this life? For that we look to Muhammad.

---

351 *Tafsir Ahsanul-Bayan*, Vol. 3, p. 247.

352 Ibid., p. 247.

353 *Tafsir Ibn Kathir*, Vol. 9, p. 112.

Simply put, Muhammad said it was legal to kill a Muslim who left Islam:

> *Narrated 'Abdullah: Allah's Messenger said, "The blood of a Muslim who confesses that La ilaha illallah (none has the right to be worshipped but Allah) and that I am the Messenger of Allah, cannot be shed except in three cases:...(3) the one who turns renegade from Islam (apostate) and leaves the group of Muslims (by innovating heresy, new ideas and new things, etc. in the Islamic religion)."*[354]

Muhammad's command is generally reflected in the rulings about apostasy by the five major schools of Sharia Law. These schools say that a male who leaves Islam should be killed. However, there can be an exception for a female. Instead of facing a death sentence for apostasy, as she would with the Shafi'i, Hanbali, and Maliki schools,[355] the Hanafi school believes

---

[354] *Sahih Al-Bukhari*, Vol. 9, Book 87, No. 6878, p. 20. For other reports that Muhammad commanded the death penalty for apostasy from Islam, see *Sahih Al-Bukhari*, Vol. 4, Book 56, No. 3017, p. 159; Vol. 9, Book 87, No. 6899, pp. 31-32; Vol. 9, Book 88, No. 6923, pp. 46-47; and Vol. 9, Book 93, No. 7157, pp. 168-169; *Sahih Muslim*, Vol. 5, No. 1676, pp. 118-119; and Vol. 6, No. 1733R3, pp. 240-241; *Sunan Ibn Majah*, Vol. 3, Nos. 2533-2535, pp. 451-453; *Jami' At-Tirmidhi*, Vol. 3, No. 1402, pp. 188-189, and No. 1458, pp. 243-244; and Vol. 4, No. 2158, pp. 219-220; *Sunan An-Nasa'i*, Vol. 5, Nos. 4025-4028, pp. 42-44; No. 4053, pp. 56-57; and Nos. 4062-4071, pp. 59-63; and *Sunan Abu Dawud*, Vol. 5, Nos. 4351-4359, pp. 15-20.

It was also reported that Muhammad specifically said,

> *If someone changes his religion - then strike off his head!*

Al-Muwatta of Imam Malik ibn Anas, 36.18.15.

See Footnote 841 for examples of apostates Muhammad ordered to be killed after the conquest of Mecca in January 630.

[355] Ahmad ibn Naqib al-Misri, *Reliance of the Traveller (Umdat al-Salik), A Classic Manual of Islamic Sacred Law*, edited and translated by Nuh Ha Mim

"that women should be forced to return to Islam by such punishment as beating or imprisonment."[356] Her imprisonment would last until she returned to Islam or died.[357] But under the Jafari school "she will be imprisoned and beaten at the times of the prescribed prayer until she repents or dies,"[358] or she will be "condemned to perpetual imprisonment, and is to be beaten with rods at the hours of prayer."[359]

So a Muslim considering leaving Islam knows that once they do so, they can be legally killed by another Muslim, or imprisoned and beaten until they return to Islam. And if they die as an apostate, they will be cursed and live eternally in the Fires of Hell.

In spite of this, after Muhammad's death there were numerous Arab tribes who tried to leave Islam, along with many Meccans. Ibn Hisham wrote:

> *Abu 'Ubayda and other traditionists* [sic] *told me that when the apostle was dead most of the Meccans meditated*

Keller (Revised Edition 1994; rpt. Beltsville, Maryland: Amana Publications, 2008), o8.1; Imam Muwaffaq ad-Din Abdu'llah ibn Ahmad ibn Qudama al-Maqdisi, *The Mainstay Concerning Jurisprudence (Al-Umda fi 'l-Fiqh)*, trans. Muhtar Holland (Ft. Lauderdale, FL: Al-Baz Publishing, Inc., 2009), p. 309; and *Al-Muwatta of Imam Malik ibn Anas*, 36.18.

356 Majid Khadduri, *War and Peace in the Law of Islam* (Clark, NJ: The Lawbook Exchange Ltd., 2006), p. 151.

357 Abu Hanifah Nu'man ibn Thabit ibn Nu'man ibn al-Marzuban ibn Zuta ibn Mah, *The Kitab al-Athar of Imam Abu Hanifah: The Narration of Imam Muhammad Ibn Al-Hasan Ash-Shaybani*, trans. 'Abdassamad Clarke (London: Turath Publishing, 2007), 186.591, and p. 347, n. 1650.

358 *Encyclopedia of Islamic Law: A Compendium of the Views of the Major Schools*, adapted by Laleh Bakhtiar (Chicago: Kazi Publications, Inc., 1996), p. 291.

359 Samuel M. Zwemer, *The Law of Apostasy in Islam* (1924; rpt. Cornwall, United Kingdom: Diggory Press Ltd., 2006), p. 45.

> *withdrawing from Islam and made up their minds to do so. 'Attab b. Asid* [the governor of Mecca] *went in such fear of them that he hid himself. Then Suhayl b. 'Amr arose and after giving thanks to God mentioned the death of the apostle and said, 'That will increase Islam in force. If anyone troubles us we will cut off his head.' Thereupon the people abandoned their intention and 'Attab reappeared once more.*[360]

The threat of force then served to keep the Meccans as part of the Muslim community. However, there began a period known as the Wars of Apostasy (*Riddah* Wars). Abu Bakr, who was chosen to lead the Muslims after Muhammad's death, sent eleven Muslim armies out to deal with the various uprisings. Majid Khadduri described this period:

> *The outstanding case of apostasy was the secession of the tribes of Arabia after the death of Muhammad. Abu Bakr, the first caliph, warned them first to return to Islam, and those who did not return were severely fought, especially by Khalid ibn al-Walid,*[[361]] *who burned a great number of them in spite of objections raised regarding the penalty of burning. The leaders of the apostate tribes were severely punished and most of them were slain. An eminent chronicler, al-Baladhuri, reports that nobody escaped death save those who returned to Islam.*[362]

The Muslim armies marched not only against apostate tribes, but also against Arab tribes that had not been previously conquered during the time of Muhammad. The commander of each army had a letter from Abu Bakr to be read to the people before any non-Muslim tribe was attacked. The letter explained:

---

[360] *The Life of Muhammad*, pp. 794-795, n. 920.

[361] Khalid ibn al-Walid was known as *The Sword of Allah.*

[362] *War and Peace in the Law of Islam*, p. 77.

> *I have sent to you someone at the head of an army of the Muhajirun and the Ansar and those who follow [them] in good works. I ordered him not to fight anyone or to kill anyone until he has called him to the cause of God; so that those who respond to him and acknowledge [Him] and renounce [unbelief] and do good works, [my envoy] shall accept him and help him to [do right], but I have ordered him to fight those who deny [Him] for that reason. So he will not spare any one of them he can gain mastery over, [but may] burn them with fire, slaughter them by any means, and take women and children captive; nor shall he accept from anyone anything except Islam.*[363]

The fighting lasted for almost two years, including two thwarted attacks on Medina, before Islam was victorious on the Arabian Peninsula.

And in terms of compulsion for the average Muslim, Muhammad even considered using deadly force to compel attendance at congregational prayers:

> *It was narrated that Abu Hurairah said: "The Messenger of Allah said: 'I was thinking of commanding that the call to prayer be given, then I would tell a man to lead the people in prayer, then I would go out with some other men carrying bundles of wood, and go to people who do not*

---

[363] *The History of al-Tabari: The Conquest of Arabia*, p. 57. Abu Bakr set the example when a captive who had fought against the Muslims was brought to him. Abu Bakr

> *ordered a fire to be kindled with much firewood in the prayer yard (musalla) of Medina and threw him, with arms and legs bound, into it.*

Ibid., pp. 79-80. For additional statements from Abu Bakr about fighting the apostates, see, for example, *Sahih Al-Bukhari*, Vol. 2, Book 24, Nos. 1399-1400, p. 279.

attend the prayer, and burn their houses down around them."[364]

Conclusion

We started out this chapter with a quote from some Muslim websites about there being no compulsion in Islam. However, we found that in spite of the claims that there is no threat or harm if one does not wish to accept Islam, there is actually a doctrinal and historical basis showing *compulsion* has played a prominent role in conversions to Islam and the retention of its adherents. It is therefore more appropriate, and more accurate, to end this chapter with the following warnings from Muhammad:

To non-Muslims:

> *Narrated Ibn 'Umar: Allah's Messenger said: "I have been ordered (by Allah) to fight against the people till they testify that La ilaha illallah, wa anna Muhammad-ar-Rasul-Allah (none has the right to be worshipped but Allah and that Muhammad is the Messenger of Allah)...then they save their lives and properties from me...*"[365]

---

[364] *Sunan Ibn Majah*, Vol. 1, No. 791, pp. 513-514. Similar *hadiths* were reported in *Sunan Ibn Majah*, Vol. 1, No. 795, pp. 515-516; *Sahih Al-Bukhari*, Vol. 1, Book No. 10, No. 644, pp. 371-372; and *Sunan An-Nasa'i*, Vol. 1, No. 849, p. 502.

According to the Hanbali School of Sharia Law, denial of the obligatory aspect of the five daily prayers is unbelief/apostasy, and death should be the penalty if there is no repentance; see *The Mainstay Concerning Jurisprudence*, p. 37.

[365] *Sahih Al-Bukhari*, Vol. 1, Book 2, No. 25, p. 66.

To Muslims:

> *Ibn 'Abbas said: "The Messenger of Allah said: 'Whoever changes his religion, kill him.'"*[366]

[366] *Sunan An-Nasa'i*, Vol. 5, No. 4064, p. 60.

8

Three Religions with the Same God?

The opening prayer of the Koran being seen as really the Lord's Prayer of Islam is something that if you shared that with a group of Christians in Middle America they would probably fall over and need resuscitation. You know, I marvel when, when people ask me the question about or they say did you know that the opening prayer in the Koran is, is, is sometimes referred to as the Lord's Prayer of Islam? And my response is, so what? It is true. How did it get there? Common, common heritage, common linkages. Common pieces of respectful dialogue and information sharing. Recognizing that we are connected. We do have a common source. There is one God.

The Rt. Rev. John B. Chane, Episcopal Bishop of Washington, DC, *Three Faiths, One God: Judaism, Christianity, Islam* (Documentary Preview, 2011)

Introduction

There are numerous efforts in the Western world to portray Islam as quite similar in beliefs, and closely related to Christianity and Judaism. One hears comments about these three religions all believing in one God, or even having the same God, and about tri-faith initiatives in which people seek to work together toward common goals. There are even some efforts to meld Islam and Christianity into a new inclusive belief system named *Chrislam*, in which the Bible and the Koran are placed side-by-side and given equal authority.

But what does Islam really teach about Christianity and Judaism? We have seen examples of those teaching in previous chapters. In this chapter we will take a closer look.

The Episcopal Church in the United States teaches that Jesus gave the *Lord's Prayer* to his disciples as an example of how they should pray. And the Rt. Rev. Chane pointed out that the first chapter of the Koran, *Al-Fatihah* (The Opening), is the *Lord's Prayer of Islam*. So, considering *lex orandi, lex credendi*[367], let's take a look at *Al-Fatihah.*

Al-Fatihah

Al-Fatihah consists of only seven verses:

1. *In the name of Allah, the Most Gracious, the Most Merciful.*
2. *All praise and thanks are Allah's, the Lord of the 'Alamin (mankind, jinn, and all that exists).*
3. *The Most Gracious, the Most Merciful.*
4. *The Only Owner (and the Only Ruling Judge) of the Day of Recompense (i.e. the Day of Resurrection).*
5. *You (Alone) we worship, and You (Alone) we ask for help (for each and everything).*
6. *Guide us to the Straight Way.*
7. *The way of those on whom You have bestowed Your Grace, not (the way) of those who earned Your Anger, nor of those who went astray.*

Muhammad said this was the "greatest" chapter in the Koran,[368] and he referred to it as the "Mother" of the Koran.[369] Muhammad said that any

---

367 The way we pray is the way we believe.

368 *Tafsir Al-Qurtubi*, p. 94; *Tafisr Ibn Kathir*, Vol. 1, p. 44; *Sahih Al-Bukhari*, Vol. 6, Book 65, No. 4474, pp. 21-22; and *Sunan Abu Dawud*, Vol. 2, No. 1458, pp. 186-187.

369 Muhammad referred to *Al- Fatihah* as *Umm Al-Kitab*, the Mother of the Book (the Koran) - for example, see *Tafsir Ibn Kathir*, Vol. 1, p. 41; *Tafsir Al-Qurtubi*, p. 97; and *Sunan Abu Dawud*, Vol. 1, No. 821, p. 483.

prayer that did not include *Al-Fatihah* was "invalid,"[370] a position naturally still held today among Muslims with regard to each cycle of the five daily, obligatory prayers.[371] Muslims also include *Al-Fatihah* in a number of their other prayers, such as the Friday Prayer, the Eid Prayer, and the Funeral Prayer.[372]

Since this first chapter of the Koran is so important, let's take a look at it, focusing on the last two verses. In Verse 6 Muslims ask to be guided to the *Straight Way*. Muhammad said the *Straight Way* (or Path) was Islam.[373] The modern *Tafsir Ahsanul-Bayan* explained the meaning of the *Straight Path*:

> *The Straight Path here means the religion of Islam as enshrined, enunciated and explained in the final Revelation, the Qur'an, and the authentic sayings and acts of Allah's Messenger, called hadeeth.*[374]

---

370 *Tafsir Ibn Kathir*, Vol. 1, pp. 47, 50, and 79; *Tafsir Al-Qurtubi*, p. 104; *Tafsir Ahsanul-Bayan*, Vol. 1, pp. 12-13; *Sahih Al-Bukhari*, Vol. 1, Book 10, No. 756, p. 424; *Sahih Muslim*, Vol. 1, Nos. 394-396, pp. 240-243; *Sunan Abu Dawud*, Vol. 1, No. 821, p. 483; *Jami' At-Tirmidhi*, Vol. 1, No. 247, pp. 271-272, and Vol. 5, No. 2953, pp. 276-278; *Sunan Ibn Majah*, Vol. 2, Nos. 838-841, pp. 34-36; and *Sunan An-Nasa'i*, Vol. 2, Nos. 910-912, pp. 38-40.

371 *Salaat: The Islamic Prayer from A to Z*, pp. 53-54, 61, 75-76, 95-96, and 137.

372 Ibid., p. 105.

373 *Tafsir Ibn Kathir*, Vol. 1, p. 84. Also see *Tafsir Al-Qurtubi*, p. 125, where an interpretation is that the *Straight Way* (Path) was Muhammad himself.

374 *Tafsir Ahsanul-Bayan*, Vol. 1, p. 23.

In Verse 7 Muslims state that the Straight Way is the *way of those on whom You* [Allah] *have bestowed Your Grace*. So on whom has Allah bestowed his grace? The answer is found in this verse of the Koran:[375]

Chapter 4, Verse 69

> *And whoso obeys Allah and the Messenger (Muhammad), then they will be in the company of those on whom Allah has bestowed His Grace, of the Prophets, the Siddiqun (those followers of the Prophets who were first and foremost to believe in them, like Abu Bakr As-Siddiq), the martyrs, and the righteous. And how excellent these companions are!*

So it is the believing Muslim upon whom Allah has bestowed his grace.

Muslims then ask not to be guided to the way of those who have earned Allah's anger or to the way of those who have gone astray. So who are

---

375 This was explicitly pointed out in the *Tafsir Ibn Kathir*, Vol. 1, p. 86. Ibn Kathir explained the meaning of 4:69:

> *Consequently, whosoever implements what Allah and His Messenger have commanded him and avoids what Allah and His Messenger have prohibited, then Allah will grant him a dwelling in the Residence of Honor. There, Allah will place him in the company of the Prophets, and those who are lesser in grade, the true believers, then the martyrs and then the righteous, who are righteous inwardly and outwardly. Allah then praised this company.*

See *Tafsir Ibn Kathir*, Vol. 2, p. 508. Al-Qurtubi, in explaining *Al-Fatihah*, also pointed to 4:69 to explain who had received Allah's grace; Al-Qurtubi wrote that those listed in 4:69 had followed the "Straight Path." See *Tafsir Al-Qurtubi*, p. 126. The *Tafsir Ahsanul-Bayan* also referred to 4:69 to explain who had received Allah's grace. See *Tafsir Ahsanul-Bayan*, Vol. 1, pp. 23-24.

those who have earned the anger of Allah? Muhammad said they were the Jews.[376] And Al-Qurtubi pointed out that this anger was not passive:

> *The meaning of anger when it is attributed to Allah is the desire to punish...*[377]

So Allah wants to *punish* the Jews.

And who has gone astray? Muhammad said that those who had gone astray, or were misguided, were the Christians.[378] Al-Qurtubi used the word "misguided" for the Christians, and he explained

> *The word "misguidance" (dalal) in Arabic means "missing the target and straying from the path of Truth."*[379]

Ibn Kathir explained these two deviations from the Straight Way:

> *These two paths are the paths of the Christians and Jews, a fact that the believer should beware of so that he avoids them. The path of the believers is knowledge of the truth*

---

376 *Tafsir Al-Qurtubi*, p. 127; *Tafsir Ibn Kathir*, Vol. 4, p. 410; *Sahih Al-Bukhari*, Vol. 6, Book 65, No. 4475, p. 22; *Jami' At-Tirmidhi*, Vol. 5, No. 2954, p. 281; *The Noble Qur'an*, p. 12, n. 1; and *The Sealed Nectar*, p. 493. Commentary about the Jews being those with whom Allah is angry is found in: *Tafsir Ibn Kathir*, Vol. 1, p. 87; *Tafsir Ahsanul-Bayan*, Vol. 1, p. 24; and *Tafsir Al-Jalalayn*, p. 2.

377 *Tafsir Al-Qurtubi*, p. 128.

378 *Tafsir Al-Qurtubi*, p. 127; *Tafsir Ibn Kathir*, Vol.4, p. 410; *Sahih Al-Bukhari*, Vol. 6, Book 65, No. 4475, p. 22; *Jami' At-Tirmidhi*, Vol. 5, No. 2954, p. 281; *The Noble Qur'an*, p. 12, n. 1; and *The Sealed Nectar*, p. 493. Commentary about the Christians being those who had gone astray is found in: *Tafsir Ibn Kathir*, Vol. 1, p. 87; *Tafsir Ahsanul-Bayan*, Vol. 1, p. 24; and *Tafsir Al-Jalalayn*, p. 2.

379 *Tafsir Al-Qurtubi*, p. 128.

and abiding by it. In comparison, the Jews abandoned practicing the religion, while the Christians lost the true knowledge. This is why 'anger' descended upon the Jews, while being described as 'led astray' is more appropriate of the Christians. Those who know, but avoid implementing the truth, deserve the anger, unlike those who are ignorant. The Christians want to seek the true knowledge, but are unable to find it because they did not seek it from its proper resources. This why they were led astray. We should also mention that both the Christians and the Jews have earned the anger and are led astray, but the anger is one of the attributes more particular of the Jews.[380]

So according to Ibn Kathir, the Jews and Christians have been led astray, and Allah is angry with both of them.

Some would regard *Al-Fatihah* as reflecting a common heritage, common linkages and pieces of respectful dialogue, and the recognition that we are connected. On the other hand, Ibn Kathir sees *Al-Fatihah* as telling Muslims that Islam is the true religion and warning them against following the two misguided paths, because the Jews and Christians will be gathered up with the sinners on the Day of Resurrection:

Al-Fatihah directs the believers to invoke Allah to guide them to the straight path, which is the true religion, and to help them remain on that path in this life, and to pass over the actual Sirat (bridge over hell that everyone must pass over) on the Day of Judgment. On that Day, the believers will be directed to the gardens of comfort in the company of the Prophets, the truthful ones, the martyrs and the righteous. Al-Fatihah also encourages performing good deeds, so that the believers will be in the company of the good-doers on the Day of Resurrection. The Surah

---

380 *Tafsir Ibn Kathir*, Vol. 1, p. 87.

> [chapter] *also warns against following the paths of misguidance, so that one does not end up being gathered with those who indulge in sin, on the Day of Resurrection, including those who have earned the anger and those who were led astray.*[381]

A similar admonition can be found in the modern *Tafsir Ahsanul-Bayan*:

> *Hence, those who want to follow the Straight Way should avoid the errors of both Jews and Christians, the Jews because they deliberately followed the wrong way, tampered with the verses of their Book, played tricks, called prophet 'Uzair a son of God, and gave their rabbis the authority to prohibit or permit. And the Christians, because they elevated 'Isa to the level of "son of God" and "the third of three."*[382]

So the Muslim recitation of *Al-Fatihah* not only reinforces differences instead of commonalities, but also maligns Judaism and Christianity, multiple times a day.

What Does the Koran Say about Jews and Christians?

In search of "common linkages" and "pieces of respectful dialogue," let's take a stroll through some verses of the Koran:

1. Chapter 2, Verse 62

> *Verily, those who believe and those who are Jews and Christians, and Sabians, whoever believes in Allah and the Last Day and does righteous good deeds shall have*

---

381 Ibid., p. 89.

382 *Tafsir Ahsanul-Bayan*, Vol. 1, p. 24.

their reward with their Lord, on them shall be no fear, nor shall they grieve.

It would appear that this verse provides support for the idea of "common linkages." However, the *Tafsir Ahsanul-Bayan* provides a pertinent commentary:

> *Some modernists advance this verse as proof that all the religions, despite their apparent diversity in beliefs and rites of worship, are in essence one, and that it is not essential to believe in the prophetic mission of Muhammad and that deliverance depends on faithfully following one's own religion and doing good works. This is an absolutely erroneous idea.*[383]

This *tafsir* went on to explain that this verse only pertained to good deeds done before the advent of Islam; after that point people needed to believe in Islam to receive their reward. This *tafsir* used the following *hadith* to explain this:

> *"By the One in Whose hand is the soul of Muhammad, anyone, be he a Jew or Christian, who hears about me, and does not believe in my mission will, upon his death, be among the dwellers of the Fire."*[384]

Ibn Kathir provided a similar explanation:

> *...Allah does not accept any deed or work from anyone, unless it conforms to the Law of Muhammad that is, after Allah sent Muhammad.*

---

383 Ibid., p. 71.

384 Ibid., p. 72-73. For this particular *hadith*, see *Sahih Muslim*, Vol. 1, No. 153, p. 103.

> *Before that, every person who followed the guidance of his own Prophet was on the correct path, following the correct guidance and was saved.*[385]

And Ibn Kathir was very specific about the change that had arrived with Muhammad:

> *When Allah sent Muhammad as the Last and Final Prophet and Messenger to all the Children of Adam, mankind was required to believe in him, obey him and refrain from what he prohibited them; those who do this are true believers.*[386]

So this verse actually means that, after the advent of Islam, *righteous good deeds* will be accepted only if they are done by Muslims. And it is interesting to note that this verse was abrogated by the following verse:[387]

2. Chapter 3, Verse 85

> *And whosoever seeks a religion other than Islam, it will never be accepted of him, and in the Hereafter he will be one of the losers.*

---

[385] *Tafsir Ibn Kathir*, Vol. 1, p. 249.

[386] Ibid., p. 250.

[387] *The Noble Qur'an*, p. 24, n. 2 (which also stated that a similar verse, 5:69, had been abrogated by 3:85). That 2:62 was abrogated by 3:85 was also noted in the *Tafsir Ahsanul-Bayan*, Vol. 1, p. 72; *Tafsir Ibn Kathir*, Vol. 1, pp. 248-249; and *Tafsir Al-Qurtubi*, p. 267. Although Al-Qurtubi also pointed out that some scholars said 2:62 was not abrogated because the verse was only

> *about those who believe in the Prophet, peace be upon him, and who are firm in their belief.* [i.e. those who are Muslim]

Tafsir Al-Qurtubi, p. 267.

Under the heading *The Only Valid Religion To Allah is Islam*, Ibn Kathir explained this verse meant that

> *Allah rebukes those who prefer a religion other than the religion that He sent His Books and Messengers with, which is the worship of Allah Alone without partners...*[388]

The *Tafsir Al-Jalalayn* and *Tafsir Ibn* 'Abbas explained that the "losers" are in Hell.[389]

This verse states that after the coming of Muhammad, no other religion than Islam will be accepted. And we have the Koran stating that Jews and Christians are "losers" destined for Hell.

3. Chapter 2, Verse 105

Neither those who disbelieve among the people of the Scripture (Jews and Christians) nor Al-Mushrikun (the idolaters, polytheists, disbelievers in the Oneness of Allah, pagans) like that there should be sent down to you any good from your Lord. But Allah chooses for His Mercy whom He wills. And Allah is the Owner of Great Bounty.

In a section titled *The extreme Enmity that the Disbelievers and the People of the Book have against Muslims*, Ibn Kathir explained this verse:

> *Allah described the deep enmity that the disbelieving polytheists and People of the Scripture, whom Allah warned against imitating,*

---

388 *Tafsir Ibn Kathir*, Vol. 2, p. 202.

389 *Tafsir Al-Jalalayn*, p. 140; and *Tafsir Ibn 'Abbas*, p. 78.

have against the believers, so that Muslims should sever all friendship with them.[390]

4. Chapter 3, Verse 110

You (true believers in Islamic Monotheism, and real followers of Prophet Muhammad and his Sunnah) are the best of peoples ever raised up for mankind; you enjoin Al-Ma'ruf (i.e. Islamic Monotheism and all that Islam has ordained) and forbid Al-Munkar (polytheism, disbelief and all that Islam has forbidden), and you believe in Allah. And had the people of the Scripture (Jews and Christians) believed, it would have been better for them; among them are some who have Faith, but most of them are Al-Fasiqun (disobedient to Allah and rebellious against Allah's Command).

Ibn Kathir explained that this verse meant "the *Ummah* [Muslim community] of Muhammad is the most righteous and beneficial nation for mankind."[391] He further explained that although some of the Jews and Christians believed in Allah and Muhammad, the "majority of them follow deviation, disbelief, sin and rebellion."[392]

The modern *Tafsir Ahsanul-Bayan* stated:

The Muslims have been called the best ummah (the best community) by virtue of the fact that they enjoin right conduct and forbid indecency and believe in Allah. The point to note here is that this quality is conditional...those who do not enjoin

---

390 *Tafsir Ibn Kathir*, Vol. 1, p. 323.

391 Ibid., Vol. 2, p. 238.

392 Ibid., p. 242.

right conduct and do not forbid indecency are no better than the People of the Book [Jews and Christians]...[393]

The *Tafsir Al-Jalalayn* stated that this verse meant that most of the Jews and Christians were "degenerate and unbelievers."[394]

So in this verse the Jews and Christians are presented as the epitome of sinful conduct and disbelief.

5. Chapter 4, Verse 47

O you who have been given the Scripture (Jews and Christians)! Believe in what We have revealed (to Muhammad) confirming what is (already) with you, before we efface faces (by making them look like the back of necks; without nose, mouth and eyes) and turn them hindwards, or curse them as We cursed the Sabbath-breakers. And the Commandment of Allah is always executed.

In a section titled *Calling the People of the Book to Embrace the Faith, Warning them Against Doing Otherwise*, Ibn Kathir explained that Allah was ordering the Jews and Christians to believe in Islam. If they failed to do so, they would be punished for ignoring the truth of Islam.[395]

The *Tafsir Al-Jalalayn* stated that this verse was

---

393 *Tafsir Ahsanul-Bayan*, Vol. 1, p. 347.

394 *Tafsir Al-Jalalayn*, p. 147.

395 *Tafsir Ibn Kathir*, Vol. 2, pp. 479-480.

a conditional threat and that when some of them became Muslim that threat was removed.[396]

And the footnote for this verse in *The Noble Qur'an* stated

This Verse is a severe warning to the Jews and Christians, and an absolute obligation that they must believe in Allah's Messenger Muhammad and in his Message of Islamic Monotheism and in this Qur'an.[397]

So instead of accepting them as adherents of credible faiths, the Koran threatens Jews and Christians with punishment if they do not believe in Islam.

6. Chapter 5, Verse 51

O you who believe! Take not the Jews and the Christians as Auliya' (friends, protectors, helpers), they are but Auliya' of each other. And if any amongst you takes them as Auliya', then surely, he is one of them. Verily, Allah guides not those people who are the Zalimun (polytheists and wrongdoers and unjust).

In a section titled *The Prohibition of Taking the Jews, Christians and Enemies of Islam as Friends*, Ibn Kathir explained this verse by pointing out that

Allah forbids His believing servants from having Jews and Christians as friends, because they are the enemies of Islam and its people, may Allah curse them. Allah then states that they are friends

---

396 *Tafsir Al-Jalalayn*, p. 193.

397 *The Noble Qur'an*, p. 129, n. 1.

> *of each other and He gives a warning threat to those who do this, And if any among you befriends them, then surely he is one of them.*[398]

The *Tafsir Al-Jalalayn* explained that this verse meant Muslims were not to join Jews and Christians "in mutual friendship and love," or "in their unbelief."[399]

The *Tafsir Ibn 'Abbas* stated that Muslims who take Jews and Christians as friends are "not included in Allah's protection and safety."[400]

Our modern *Tafsir Ahsanul-Bayan* agreed with these interpretations:

> *The verse forbids Muslims to keep intimate relations with them and take them as protectors and helpers, because they are the enemies of Allah, the Muslims, and Islam. It should be noted that those who take them as protectors and helpers will be considered among them .*[401]

7. Chapter 5, Verse 55

Verily, your Wali (Protector or Helper) is none other than Allah, His Messenger, and the believers - those who perform As-Salat (the prayers), and give Zakat (obligatory

---

398 *Tafsir Ibn Kathir*, Vol. 3, p. 204.

399 *Tafsir Al-Jalalayn*, p. 256.

400 *Tafsir Ibn 'Abbas*, p. 143.

401 *Tafsir Ahsanul-Bayan*, Vol. 1, p. 616.

charity), and they are Raki'un (those who bow down or submit themselves with obedience to Allah in prayer).

Ibn Kathir explained that this verse meant:

> *the Jews are not your friends. Rather, your allegiance is to Allah, His Messenger and the faithful believers.*[402]

The *Tafsir Ahsanul-Bayan* explained this verse:

> *Believers have been told not to forge intimate relations with the Jews and Christians. Whom to befriend, then, one may well ask? Allah replies that the best friends of believers are Allah, His Messenger, and the believers.*[403]

8. Chapter 5, Verse 57

O you who believe! Take not as Auliya (protectors and helpers) those who take your religion as a mockery and fun from among those who received the Scripture (Jews and Christians) before you, and nor from among the disbelievers; and fear Allah if you indeed are true believers.

In a section titled *The Prohibition of Being Loyal Friends with Disbelievers*, Ibn Kathir explained:

> *This Ayah discourages and forbids taking the enemies of Islam and its people, such as the*

---

402 *Tafsir Ibn Kathir*, Vol. 3, p. 209.

403 *Tafsir Ahsanul-Bayan*, Vol. 1, p. 620.

> *People of the Book* [Jews and Christians] *and the polytheists, as friends.*[404]

The *Tafsir Ibn 'Abbas* explained that this verse meant the Muslims were not to choose as friends Jews, Christians, or "the rest of the disbelievers."[405]

The *Tafsir Ahsanul-Bayan* provided a similar interpretation:

> *Those who received the Scripture refer to the Jews and Christians, while "disbelievers" refers to the pagans. Here again Allah tells the believers not to take as friends those who make fun of your religion because they are enemies of Allah and His Messenger.*[406]

The Tafsir Al-Jalalayn noted:

> *Show fear of Allah - by not taking them as friends - if you are believers - and are true in your belief.*[407]

9. Chapter 5, Verse 82

Verily, you will find the strongest among men in enmity to the believers (Muslims) the Jews...

Ibn Kathir explained what this verse said about the Jews:

---

404 *Tafsir Ibn Kathir*, Vol. 3, p. 211.

405 *Tafsir Ibn 'Abbas*, p. 144.

406 *Tafsir Ahsanul-Bayan*, Vol. 1, p. 622.

407 *Tafsir Al-Jalalayn*, p. 257.

This describes the Jews, since their disbelief is that of rebellion, defiance, opposing the truth, belittling other people and degrading the scholars. This is why the Jews - may Allah's continued curses descend on them until the Day of Resurrection - killed many of their Prophets and tried to kill the Messenger of Allah several times, as well as, performing magic spells against him and poisoning him.[408]

The modern *Tafsir Ahsanul-Bayan* added to this:

That is because the Jews are a stubborn and ungrateful people, self-opinionated, willful, arrogant and unduly critical of religious scholars.[409]

10. Chapter 60, Verse 13

O you who believe! Take not as friends the people who incurred the Wrath of Allah (i.e. the Jews). Surely, they have despaired of (receiving any good in) the Hereafter, just as the disbelievers have despaired of those (buried) in graves (that they will not be resurrected on the Day of Resurrection).

Ibn Kathir explained that this verse "forbids taking disbelievers as protecting friends," and the verse specifically referred

---

408 *Tafsir Ibn Kathir*, Vol. 3, p. 246.

409 *Tafsir Ahsanul-Bayan*, Vol. 1, p. 644.

to the Jews, Christians and the rest of the disbelievers whom Allah became angry with and cursed.[410]

Al-Wahidi, the *Tafsir Al-Jalalayn*, and the *Tafsir Ibn 'Abbas* all pointed out that the people who had *incurred the Wrath of Allah* were the Jews.[411]

The preceding five verses forbade Muslims from taking the Jews and Christians as friends. However, there is an interesting exception to this prohibition of Muslims taking Jews and Christians as friends. It is found in this verse of the Koran:

Chapter 3, Verse 28

Let not the believers take the disbelievers as Auliya (supporters, helpers) instead of the believers, and whoever does that, will never be helped by Allah in any way, except if you indeed fear a danger from them. And Allah warns you against Himself (His punishment), and to Allah is the final return.

Ibn Kathir explained this verse and the exception it mentioned:

Allah prohibited His believing servants from becoming supporters of the disbelievers, or to take them as comrades with whom they develop friendships, rather than the believers...except those believers who in some areas or times fear for their safety from the disbelievers. In this case, such believers are allowed to show friendship to the disbelievers outwardly, but never inwardly. For instance, Al-Bukhari recorded that Abu Ad-Darda' said, "We smile

---

410 *Tafsir Ibn Kathir*, Vol. 9, p. 610.

411 *Al-Wahidi's Asbab al-Nuzul*, p. 228; *Tafsir Al-Jalalayn*, p. 1197, and *Tafsir Ibn 'Abbas*, p. 761.

> *in the face of some people although our hearts curse them." Al-Bukhari said that Al-Hasan said, "The Tuqyah is allowed until the Day of Resurrection."*[412]

The *Tafsir Al-Jalalayn* explained the exception allowed in this verse:

> *...unless it is dissimulation out of fear of them so that the befriending takes place with the tongue alone and not the heart. This was before Islam became mighty, when Islam had no power in the land.*[413]

The *Tafsir Ibn 'Abbas* presented a similar explanation:

> *...saving yourselves from them by speaking in a friendly way towards them with* [sic], *while your hearts dislikes* [sic] *this.*[414]

The modern *Tafsir Ahsanul-Bayan* explained:

> *In this verse, Allah has strictly forbidden the believers to make friends with disbelievers, because the latter are the enemies of Allah as well as enemies of the believers. Hence, there is no reason to make friends with them. There are many verses in the Qur'an warning believers against making friends with disbelievers, except for reasons of expediency or need or trade. Treaties and*

---

412 *Tafsir Ibn Kathir*, Vol. 2, pp. 141-142; n. 2 on p. 142 defines *Tuqyah* (*Taqiyya*) as "To shield what is in one's heart." For an informative article discussing the significance of *Taqiyya* to Islam, see Raymond Ibrahim, "How Taqiyya Alters Islam's Rules of War, Defeating Jihadist Terrorism," *The Middle East Quarterly*, Volume 17, No. 1 (Winter 2010). This article is accessible at http://www.meforum.org/2538/taqiyya-islam-rules-of-war.

413 *Tafsir Al-Jalalayn*, pp. 122-124.

414 *Tafsir Ibn 'Abbas*, p. 68.

pacts of mutual benefit may also be concluded with them...because all these are quite different things and have nothing to do with friendship.[415]

Our modern *tafsir* then explained the exception:

This permission is for those Muslims who live in a non-Muslim state. If they fear repression, they may profess friendship with the non-Muslims verbally.[416]

So Muslims professing friendship with non-Muslims are not contravening 5:51; they can simply be following the exception allowed in 3:28. And the same principle is applied in 16:106 where Muslims are allowed to deny their faith under duress (see the explanations for 16:106 in Chapter 7, *No Compulsion in Islam?*).

Let's continue with our journey through the Koran:

11. Chapter 9, Verse 29

Fight against those who believe not in Allah, nor in the Last Day, nor forbid that which has been forbidden by Allah and His Messenger (Muhammad), and those who acknowledge not the religion of truth (i.e. Islam) among the people of the Scripture (Jews and Christians), until they pay the Jizyah with willing submission, and feel themselves subdued.

In a paragraph titled *The Order to fight People of the Scriptures until They give the Jizyah*, Ibn Kathir explained the meaning of this verse:

---

415 *Tafsir Ahsanul-Bayan*, Vol. 1, p. 290.

416 Ibid.

> *Therefore, when People of the Scriptures disbelieved in Muhammad, they had no beneficial faith in any Messenger or what the Messengers brought. Rather, they followed their religions because this conformed with their ideas, lusts and ways of their forefathers, not because they are Allah's Law and religion. Had they been true believers in their religions, that faith would have directed them to believe in Muhammad...Allah commanded His Messenger to fight the People of the Scriptures, Jews and Christians...*[417]

So had the Jews and Christians been "true believers" in their own religions, they would have become Muslim! As a consequence of the lack of this true belief, the Muslims were therefore commanded by Allah to fight against the Jews and Christians *until they pay the Jizyah with willing submission, and feel themselves subdued.* The *Jizyah* is a

> *Head tax imposed by Islam on all non-Muslims [Dhimmis] living under the protection of an Islamic government.*[418]

But what about it having to be paid *with willing submission* and with a sense of feeling *subdued*?

In a paragraph titled *Paying Jizyah is a Sign of Kufr* [unbelief] *and Disgrace*, Ibn Kathir explained that if the Jews and Christians chose not to embrace Islam, they would have to pay the *Jizyah* "in defeat and subservience," and feel "disgraced, humiliated, and belittled." He continued

---

417 *Tafsir Ibn Kathir*, Vol. 4, pp. 404-405.

418 *The Noble Qur'an*, Glossary, p. 862.

> *Therefore, Muslims are not allowed to honor the people of Dhimmah* [those who are *Dhimmis*] *or elevate them above Muslims, for they are miserable, disgraced and humiliated.*[419]

This was affirmed in the *Tafsir Al-Jalalayn* when the *Jizyah* section of 9:29 was being discussed:

> *...until they pay the jizya with their own hands - meaning the Jews and the Christians who must pay it in submission or directly with their actual hands - in a state of complete abasement - humble and subject to the judgements of Islam.*[420]

The *Tafsir Ibn 'Abbas* reiterated that the people to be fought were the Jews and Christians, until they paid "the tribute" and were "abased."[421]

This was also noted in the modern *Tafsir Ahsanul-Bayan*:

> *The command to fight the pagans was already given. Now Allah commands the believers to fight the Jews and Christians (if they do not accept Islam) until they pay the jizya and live under the rule of the Muslims.*[422]

So the Koran is quite explicit that the Muslims are to fight the Jews and Christians until the latter agree to become *Dhimmis* and submissively pay the *Jizyah*.

---

419 *Tafsir Ibn Kathir*, Vol. 4, pp. 405-406.

420 *Tafsir Al-Jalalayn*, pp. 404-406.

421 *Tafsir Ibn 'Abbas*, p. 231.

422 *Tafsir Ahsanul-Bayan*, Vol. 2, pp. 345-346.

12. Chapter 9, Verse 30

> *And the Jews say: 'Uzair (Ezra) is the son of Allah, and the Christians say: Messiah is the son of Allah. That is their saying with their mouths, resembling the saying of those who disbelieved aforetime. Allah's curse be on them, how they are deluded away from the truth!*

In a paragraph titled *Fighting the Jews and Christians is legislated because They are Idolators and Disbelievers*, Ibn Kathir explained the meaning of this verse:

> *Allah the Exalted encourages the believers to fight the polytheists, disbelieving Jews and Christians, who uttered this terrible statement and utter lies against Allah, the Exalted. As for the Jews, they claimed that 'Uzayr was the son of God, Allah is free of what they attribute to Him. As for the misguidance of Christians over 'Isa [Jesus], it is obvious. This is why Allah declared both groups to be liars.*[423]

The *Tafsir Ibn 'Abbas* stated that Allah cursed the Jews and Christians because of their lies.[424] The *Tafsir Al-Jalalayn* said that Allah cursed the Jews and Christians because they had "turned aside from the truth when the proof has been established!"[425]

So the Jews and Christians are liars who have been cursed by Allah.

---

423 *Tafsir Ibn Kathir*, Vol. 4, p. 408.

424 *Tafsir Ibn 'Abbas*, p. 233.

425 *Tafsir Al-Jalalayn*, p. 406.

13. Chapter 9, Verse 32

They (the disbelievers, the Jews and the Christians) want to extinguish Allah's Light (with which Muhammad has been sent - Islamic Monotheism) with their mouths, but Allah will not allow except that His Light should be perfected even though the Kafirun (disbelievers) hate (it).

In a section titled *People of the Scriptures try to extinguish the Light of Islam*, Ibn Kathir explained this verse:

> *Allah says, the disbelieving idolators and People of the Scriptures want to, extinguish the Light of Allah. They try through argument and lies to extinguish the guidance and religion of truth that the Messenger of Allah was sent with.*[426]

The *Tafsir Ibn 'Abbas* also pointed out that the Jews and Christians used lies to "thwart" Islam.[427]

The *Tafsir Ahsanul-Bayan* explained the verse:

> *The Jews and the Christians would love to blot out the guidance and the right religion that Allah has sent through His Messenger by their subtle arguments. But this they cannot do...The religion of Allah shall triumph and prevail over all other religions...*[428]

---

426 *Tafsir Ibn Kathir*, Vol. 4, p. 411.

427 *Tafsir Ibn 'Abbas*, p. 234.

428 *Tafsir Ahsanul-Bayan*, Vol. 2, p. 348.

So according to this verse, the Jews and Christians are hostile to Islam, which is the religion of truth, and use lies in an attempt to "blot" it out. Nevertheless, Islam will be triumphant.

14. Chapter 9, Verse 33

> *It is He Who has sent His Messenger (Muhammad) with guidance and the religion of truth (Islam), to make it superior over all religions even though the Mushrikun (polytheists, pagans, idolaters, disbelievers in the Oneness of Allah) hate (it).*

Under a section titled *Islam is the Religion That will dominate over all Other Religions*, Ibn Kathir provided a *hadith* to explain this verse: Muhammad said,

> *This matter (Islam) will keep spreading as far as the night and day reach, until Allah will not leave a house made of mud or hair, but will make this religion enter it, while bringing might to a mighty person (a Muslim) and humiliation to a disgraced person (who rejects Islam). Might with which Allah elevates Islam (and its people) and disgrace with which Allah humiliates disbelief (and its people).*[429]

Ibn Kathir then added,

> *Tamim Ad-Dari [who was a Christian before Islam] used to say, "I have come to know the meaning of this Hadith in my own people. Those who became Muslims among them acquired goodness, honor and might. Disgrace,*

---

429 *Tafsir Ibn Kathir*, Vol. 4, p. 413.

humiliation and Jizyah befell those who remained disbelievers."[430]

The *Tafsir Ahsanul-Bayan* provided a more contemporary explanation:

> *When the Muslims practiced Islam faithfully and completely, they were a dominant power in the world, and if they practice it now as their earlier generations did, they would again be entrusted with ruling the world, because Allah has promised the Party of Allah domination and power.*[431]

So Islam is to be superior over all other religions, whether non-Muslims like it or not.

15. Chapter 18, Verse 103

Say (O Muhammad): "Shall We tell you the greatest losers in respect of (their) deeds?

Ibn Kathir reported that this referred to the Jews and Christians, because

> *the Jews, they disbelieved in Muhammad, and as for the Christians, they disbelieved in Paradise and said that there is no food or drink there...*[432]

---

430 Ibid., p. 413.

431 *Tafsir Ahsanul-Bayan*, Vol. 2, p. 349.

432 *Tafsir Ibn Kathir*, Vol. 6, p. 217. This reference is also reported in *Sahih Al-Bukhari*, Vol. 6, Book 65, No. 4728, p. 209.

The *Tafsir Ahsanul-Bayan* stated that some commentators said this referred specifically to Jews and Christians, and "generally to all disbelievers."[433]

So the Jews and Christians are among "the greatest losers."

16. Chapter 48, Verse 28

He it is Who has sent His Messenger (Muhammad) with guidance and the religion of truth (Islam), that He may make it (Islam) superior to all religions. And All-Sufficient is Allah as a Witness.

Ibn Kathir explained this verse in a section titled *The Good News that Muslims will conquer the Known World, and ultimately the Entire World*:

> *Allah the Exalted and Most Honored said, while delivering the glad tidings to the believers that the Messenger will triumph over his enemies and the rest of the people of the earth...that He may make it superior to all religions...all the religions of the people of the earth, Arabs and non-Arabs alike, whether having certain ideologies or being atheists or idolators.*[434]

The *Tafsir Ibn 'Abbas* explained:

> *(that He may cause it to prevail over all religion) such that the Hour will not come until there is*

---

433 *Tafsir Ahsanul-Bayan*, Vol. 3, p. 394.

434 *Tafsir Ibn Kathir*, Vol. 9, pp. 176-177.

none but a Muslim or someone who is in a peace treaty with him.[435]

So here we have another verse stating that Islam is to be superior over all other religions.

17. Chapter 58, Verse 22

You (O Muhammad) will not find any people who believe in Allah and the Last Day, making friendship with those who oppose Allah and His Messenger (Muhammad), even though they were their fathers or their sons or their brothers or their kindred (people). For such He has written Faith in their Hearts, and strengthened them with Ruh (proofs, light and true guidance) from Himself. And He will admit them to Gardens (Paradise) under which rivers flow, to dwell therein (forever). Allah is pleased with them, and they with Him. They are the party of Allah. Verily it is the party of Allah that will be the successful.

The *Tafsir Al-Jalalayn* explained this verse:

If they oppose Allah and His Messenger, the believers should oppose them and fight them.[436]

In a section titled *The Believers do not befriend the Disbelievers*, Ibn Kathir wrote that this verse simply meant, "do not befriend the deniers, even if they are among the closest relatives."[437] Ibn Kathir then mentioned

---

435 *Tafsir Ibn 'Abbas*, p. 689.

436 *Tafsir Al-Jalalayn*, p. 1184.

437 *Tafsir Ibn Kathir*, Vol. 9, p. 537.

numerous instances of Muslims killing, or intending to kill, their non-Muslim relatives.[438] He then went on to explain the meaning of the rest of 58:22:

> *For such He has written faith in their hearts...means, those who have the quality of not befriending those who oppose Allah and His Messenger, even if they are their fathers or brothers, are those whom Allah has decreed faith, meaning, happiness, in their hearts and made faith dear to their hearts and happiness reside therein...When the believers became enraged against their relatives and kindred in Allah's cause, He compensated them by being pleased with them and making them pleased with Him from what He has granted them of eternal delight, ultimate victory and encompassing favor.*[439]

Al-Wahidi also noted instances in which Muslims killed or confronted their non-Muslim relatives as the basis for this verse.[440]

So it pleases Allah when Muslims become enraged and fight against their non-Muslim relatives and acquaintances.

18. Chapter 98, Verse 6

Verily, those who disbelieve (in the religion of Islam, the Qu'ran and the Prophet Muhammad) from among the people of the Scripture (Jews and Christians) and Al-

---

[438] Ibid., pp. 538-539.

[439] Ibid., pp. 539-540.

[440] *Al-Wahidi's Asbab al-Nuzul*, p. 222.

Mushrikun, will abide in the fire of Hell. They are the worst of creatures.

Allah tells us that those (in particular the Jews and Christians) who do not believe in Islam, the Koran, and Muhammad, are the "worst of creatures" and will be sent to the Fires of Hell.

The *Tafsir Ahsanul-Bayan* pointed out that this "is the end result of disbelief."[441] In contrast, 98:7 says that the Muslims "are the best of creatures." And as earlier noted, 3:110 states that "Muslims are the best of peoples ever raised up for mankind."

Since we have not yet found them, let's continue looking for the common heritage, common linkages, and common pieces of respectful dialogue.

What Did Muhammad Say about Jews and Christians?

What did Muhammad himself have to say about Jews and Christians? Consider the following:

1. *It was narrated from 'Amr bin Shu'aib, from his father, from his grandfather, that the Messenger of Allah ruled that the blood money for the People of the Book is half of that of the blood money for the Muslims, and they are the Jews and Christians.*[442]

2. *Abu Huraira reported that Allah's Messenger (may peace*

---

441 *Tafsir Ahsanul-Bayan (Part 30)*, p. 248.

442 *Sunan Ibn Majah*, Vol. 3, No. 2644, p. 521. Similar *hadiths* are reported in *Sunan An-Nasa'i*, Vol. 5, No. 4810-4811, pp. 427-428.

be upon him) had said: Do not greet the Jews and the Christians before they greet you and when you meet any one of them on the roads force him to go to the narrowest part of it.[443]

---

[443] *Sahih Muslim*, Vol. 6, No. 2167, p. 439. Also mentioned in *Sunan Abu Dawud*, Vol. 5, No. 5205, p. 458. See *Jami' At-Tirmidhi*, Vol. 3, No. 1602, p. 365, where At-Tirmidhi wrote the following explanation for this *hadith*:

> *"Do not precede the Jews and the Christians*[in greeting]*": Some of the people of knowledge said that it only means that it is disliked because it would be honoring them, and the Muslims were only ordered to humiliate them. For this reason, when one of them is met on the path, then the path is not yielded for him, because doing so would amount to honoring them.*

And there was an interesting, more contemporary commentary on this *hadith*:

> *In normal conditions when Muslims are in power and they are not living as a minority, and they are not under any compulsion or subjugation, it is an order for Muslims that they should not give such leeway to the non-Muslims and they should not greet them first nor yield the way for them...In a country where Muslims are living as a minority, they are allowed to give such leeway to non-Muslim rulers for the greater interest of the Muslim community.*

Jami' At-Tirmidhi, Vol. 3, Comments, p. 366.

There was a similar contemporary explanation for a similar *hadith* in which Muhammad said that the Muslims must not be the first to greet Jews and Christians:

> *Saying Salam* [greeting] *is a means to express honor and respect to others and paying respect and honor to the non-believers, thus, is not correct; if a disbeliever comes across a path, he should not be given the right of way rather he should be forced to walk on the side of the road so that he does not regard himself honorable and respectable.*

See *Jami' At-Tirmidhi*, Vol. 5, No. 2700, Comments, p. 93.

3. *Narrated Abu Hurairah: Allah's Messenger said, "The Hour will not be established until you fight against the Jews, and the stone behind which a Jew will be hiding will say, 'O Muslim! There is a Jew hiding behind me, so kill him."*[444]

Muhammad said that the Jews were grave robbers. Al-Bukhari reported this *hadith* under the heading of *What has been said about Bani Israel*:

> *'Uqba bin 'Amir said, "I heard him* [Muhammad] *saying that the Israeli used to dig the grave of the dead (to steal their shrouds)."*[445]

Muhammad even said that Jews would be accompanying the anti-Christ:

---

[444] *Sahih Al-Bukhari*, Vol. 4, Book 56, No. 2926, p. 113. For a similarly worded *hadith* (narrated by 'Abdullah bin 'Umar), see *Sahih Al-Bukhari*, Vol. 4, Book 56, No. 2925, p. 113. This was also reported in *Sahih Muslim,* Vol. 8, No. 2921, p. 348; *Jami At-Tirmidhi*, Vol. 4, No. 2236, p. 283; and *Tafsir Ibn Kathir*, Vol. 3, p. 34. A variation of this is also found in *Sunan Ibn Majah*, Vol. 5, No. 4077, p. 268.

In another *hadith* Muhammad said that the Jews would hide behind stones and trees, and these stones and trees would call out,

> *Muslim, or the servant of Allah, there is a Jew behind me; come and kill him; but the tree Gharqad would not say, for it the tree of the Jews.*

Sahih Muslim, Vol. 8, No. 2922, p. 349. A similar *hadith* was reported in the *Tafsir Ibn Kathir*, Vol. 3, p. 34. The *Gharqad* is a thorny tree.

[445] *Sahih Al-Bukhari*, Vol. 4, Book 60, No. 3452, p. 413. *Bani Israel*, or *Banii Israa'iil*, is an expression used in the Koran to refer to the early Jews. See the entry for *Israa'iil* in Mahmoud Ismail Saleh, *Dictionary of Islamic Words & Expressions*, 3rd ed. (Riyadh, Kingdom of Saudi Arabia: Darussalam, 2011), p. 102.

Anas b. Malik reported that Allah's Messenger (may peace be upon him) said: The antichrist would be followed by seventy thousand Jews of Isbahan wearing Persian shawls.[446]

At one point Muhammad had a peace treaty with the Christians of the Bani Taglib tribe, but one of the conditions of the treaty was that the Christians would not baptize their children into Christianity.[447]

Muhammad said that Jews and Christians will go to Hell. He talked about the Day of Resurrection, when people will be gathered in front of Allah by religious groupings:

Then it will be said to the Jews, 'What did you use to worship?' They will reply, 'We used to worship Uzair (Ezra), the son of Allah.' It will be said to them, 'You are liars, for Allah has neither a wife nor a son. What do you want (now)?' They will reply, 'We want You to provide us with water.' Then it will be said to them 'Drink,' and they will fall down in Hell (instead). Then it will be said to the Christians, 'What did you use to worship?' They will reply, 'We used to worship Masih (Messiah), the son of Allah.' It will be said, 'You are liars, for Allah has neither a wife nor a son. What do you want (now)?' They will say, 'We want You to provide us with water.' It will be

---

446 *Sahih Muslim*, Vol. 8, No. 3944, p. 366. Also reported in *Sunan Ibn Majah*, Vol. 5, No. 4077, p. 267, where each Jew is "carrying an adorned sword." An earlier *hadith* commentary stated that the antichrist (the "False Christ") "is a Jew." See *Sunan Ibn Majah*, Vol. 5, p. 255, Comment "a." This was also stated in the Glossary of the *Sunan Abu Dawud* collection under the entry for *Dajjal* (Antichrist). See *Sunan Abu Dawud*, Vol. 5, pp. 507-508.

447 'Imaduddeen Isma'eel Ibn Katheer Al-Qurashi, *Winning the Hearts and Souls: Expeditions and Delegations in the Lifetime of Prophet Muhammad*, trans. Research Department of Darussalam (Riyadh, Kingdom of Saudi Arabia: Darussalam, 2010), p. 227.

said to them, 'Drink,' and they will fall down in Hell (instead)...[448]

And on the Day of Resurrection, Muhammad said that mountains of sins would be removed from the backs of Muslims and put onto the Jews and Christians:

> . *Narrated Abu Musa: Allah's Messenger said: On the Day of Resurrection, my Ummah (nation) will be gathered into three groups. One sort will enter Paradise without rendering an account (of their deeds). Another sort will be reckoned an easy account and admitted into Paradise. Yet another sort will come bearing on their backs heaps of sins like great mountains. Allah will ask the angels though He knows best about them: Who are these people? They will reply: They are humble slaves of yours. He will say: Unload the sins from them and put the same over the Jews and Christians; then let the humble slaves get into Paradise by virtue of My Mercy.*[449]

Muhammad even said that Jews and Christians would take the place of Muslims in Hell:

> *Abu Burda reported on the authority of his father that Allah's Apostle (may peace be upon him) said: No Muslim would die but Allah would admit instead of him a Jew or a Christian in Hell-Fire.*[450]

---

[448] *Sahih Al-Bukhari*, Vol. 9, Book No. 97, No. 7439, p. 323. This story is also reported in *Sahih Muslim*, Vol. 1, No. 183, p. 132.

[449] *110 Ahadith Qudsi: Sayings of the Prophet Having Allahs Statement*, 3rd ed., trans. Syed Masood-ul-Hasan (Riyadh, Kingdom of Saudi Arabia: Darussalam, 2006), No. 8, titled *Superiority of the believers in the Oneness of Allah and the punishment of Jews and Christians*, pp. 19-20.

[450] *Sahih Muslim*, Vol. 8, No. 2767R1, p. 269. Here is the translator's explanation for this statement on p. 269, n. 1:

Muhammad also wanted to expel Jews from the land:

> *Narrated Abu Hurairah: While we were in the mosque, the Prophet came out and said, "Let us go to the Jews." We went out till we reached Bait-ul-Midras. He said to them, "If you embrace Islam, you will be safe. You should know that the earth belongs to Allah and His Messenger, and I want to expel you from this land. So, if anyone amongst you owns some property, he is permitted to sell it, otherwise you should know that the earth belongs to Allah and His Messenger.*[451]

And on his death bed Muhammad had some interesting things to say regarding Jews and Christians:

1. *It was narrated by 'Umar b. Al-Khattab that he heard the Messenger of Allah (may peace be upon him) saying: I will expel the Jews and Christians from the Arabian Peninsula and will not leave any but Muslims.*[452]

> *As a Jew and a Christian would get into Hell-Fire for their wrong beliefs, there would be therefore, ample scope in the Paradise. It is a metaphorical expression for saying that space in Paradise would be provided by Christian* [sic] *and Jews being thrown into Hell-Fire.*

451 *Sahih Al-Bukhari*, Vol. 4, Book 58, No. 3167, p. 248. A longer version of this *hadith* is reported in *Sahih Al-Bukhari*, Vol. 9, Book 96, No. 7348, pp. 268-269. This *hadith* was also reported in *Sahih Muslim*, Vol. 5, No. 1765, p. 186.

452 *Sahih Muslim*, Vol. 5, No. 1767, p. 189. Versions of this *hadith*, also specifically mentioning Jews and Christians, are in *Sunan Abu Dawud*, Vol. 3, No. 3030, p. 517; *Jami' At-Tirmidhi*, Vol. 3, Nos. 1606-1607, p. 368; and *The Sealed Nectar*, p. 554 (where it is stated that Muhammad said this four days before his death). For reports that Muhammad actually mentioned expelling non-Muslims in general, see *Sahih Al-Bukhari*, Vol. 4, Book 56, No. 3053, pp. 179-180; and Vol. 5, Book 64, No. 4431, pp. 438-439; *The Life of Muhammad*, p. 689; and *The History of al-Tabari: The Last Years of the Prophet*, p. 175.

2. *Yahya related to me from Malik from Isma'il ibn Abi Hakim that he heard 'Umar ibn 'Abd al-'Aziz say, "One of the last things that the Messenger of Allah, may Allah bless him and grant him peace, said was, 'May Allah fight the Jews and the Christians! They took the graves of their Prophets as places of prostration. Two deens* [religions] *shall not co-exist in the land of the Arabs.'"*[453]

***Shirk*, the Unforgiveable Sin of Christians**

There is an unforgiveable sin in Islam that pertains in particular to Christians: Major *Shirk*, meaning polytheism, worshipping others along with Allah, and/or ascribing partners to Allah (including ascribing a Son to him). In the Koran and the writings of the Islamic scholars the word *Shirk* is generally used alone, with the adjective "Major" implied, based on the context.

There are three levels of *Shirk*:[454]

1. Major (*Ash-Shirk Al-Akbar*). There are four aspects to this level:

    a) Invoking, supplicating or praying to other deities besides Allah;

    b) Acts of worship or religious deeds not for the sake of Allah but directed towards other deities;

    c) Rendering obedience to any authority against the Order of Allah;

---

453 *Al-Muwatta of Imam Malik ibn Anas*, 45.5.17.

454 *The Noble Qur'an*, Appendix II, *Ash-Shirk: Polytheism and its Various Manifestations*, pp. 884-885. For additional reading about *Shirk*, see Fadlur Rahman Kalim Kashmiri, *The Many Shades of Shirk*, trans. Khola Hasan (Riyadh, Kingdom of Saudi Arabia: Darussalam, 1996).

d) Showing the love that is due to Allah to others than Him.

2. Minor (*Ash-Shirk Al-Asghar*). Any act of worship or any religious deed done to gain praise, fame or for worldly benefit.

3. Inconspicuous (*Ash-Shirk Al-Khafi*). Being inwardly dissatisfied with the inevitable condition that has been ordained for one by Allah.

There is no question that *Shirk* is forbidden. In the following verse of the Koran Allah provides a list of things he has prohibited, beginning with *Shirk*:

Chapter 6, Verse 151

> *Say (O Muhammad): " Come, I will recite what your Lord has prohibited you from: Join not anything in worship with him...This He has commanded you that you may understand."*

Our modern *tafsir* explained this verse:

> *That is, Allah has commanded you not to join others with Him in worship because it is the greatest sin, a sin which is unpardonable. Allah has banned Paradise for those who commit the sin of shirk and Hell is their inevitable lot. This warning is repeated often in the Qur'an, and hadeeths. But, despite all these warnings, people are often lured away by the devil to this very sin.*[455]

So Christians have been *lured* to Christianity by the devil.

The Koran also states that *Shirk* is the one sin that Allah will not forgive:

---

455 *Tafsir Ahsanul-Bayan*, Vol. 2, p. 119.

Chapter 4, Verse 48

> *Verily, Allah forgives not that partners should be set up with him (in worship), but He forgives except that (anything else) to whom He wills; and whoever sets up partners with Allah in worship, he has indeed invented a tremendous sin.*

Ibn Kathir pointed out that this verse simply meant that Allah does not forgive *Shirk*, unless one repents from it.[456] The *Tafsir Al-Jalalayn* agreed that *Shirk* was unforgivable, and called attributing partners to Allah "a terrible crime."[457] The *Tafsir Ibn 'Abbas* also agreed and called such attribution "a tremendous lie."[458]

The *Tafsir Ahsanul-Bayan* stated that:

> *As for shirk (ascribing partners to Allah), Allah will never forgive that, because He has prohibited Paradise for those who commit shirk, the unforgivable sin.*[459]

And this is reiterated in another verse:

Chapter 4, Verse 116

> *Verily, Allah forgives not (the sin of) setting up partners (in worship) with Him, but He forgives whom He wills, sins other than that, and whoever sets up partners in worship with Allah, has indeed strayed far away.*

---

456 *Tafsir Ibn Kathir*, Vol. 2, p. 481.

457 *Tafsir Al-Jalalayn*, pp. 193-194.

458 *Tafsir Ibn 'Abbas*, p. 108.

459 *Tafsir Ahsanul-Bayan*, Vol. 1, p. 463.

Ibn Kathir said this verse meant that anyone who set up partners in worship with Allah

> *will have taken other than the true path, deviated from guidance and righteousness, destroyed himself in this life and the Hereafter, and lost contentment in this life and the Hereafter.*[460]

The *Tafsir Al-Jalalayn* explained that anyone "who attributes partners to Allah has gone far from the Truth into misguidance."[461] The *Tafsir Ibn 'Abbas* again noted that with this verse Allah forgives all, "save the ascription of partners to Him."[462]

And what does the Koran say is to be done to those engaging in *Shirk*?

Chapter 3, Verse 151

> *We shall cast terror into the hearts of those who disbelieve, because they joined others in worship with Allah, for which He had sent no authority; their abode will be the Fire and how evil is the abode of the Zalimun (polytheists and wrongdoers).*

Ibn Kathir explained this verse:

> *Allah next conveys the good news that He will put fear of the Muslims, and feelings of subordination to the Muslims in the hearts of their disbelieving enemies, because of their Kufr* [disbelief] *and Shirk. And Allah has prepared torment and punishment for them in the Hereafter.*[463]

---

460 *Tafsir Ibn Kathir*, Vol. 2, p. 583.

461 *Tafsir Al-Jalalayn*, p. 216.

462 *Tafsir Ibn 'Abbas*, p. 121.

463 *Tafsir Ibn Kathir*, Vol. 2, pp. 287-288.

So those engaging in *Shirk* will have terror cast into their hearts and they are destined for the Fires of Hell.

And there are additional verses in the Koran condemning *Shirk* and those who engage in it, e.g. 2:22, 2:116, 5:72-73, 9:30-31, 16:86, 18:4-5, 18:102, 19:37, 19:88-95, 23:117, 27:59-60, 31:13, and 39:64-65.

Muhammad also reported that *Shirk* was unforgivable:

> *Imam Ahmad recorded that Abu Dharr said that the Messenger of Allah said, Allah said, "O My servant! As long as you worship and beg Me, I will forgive you, no matter your shortcomings. O My servant! If you meet Me with the earth's fill of sin, yet you do not associate any partners with Me, I will meet you with its fill of forgiveness."*[464]

Muhammad said that *Shirk* was the first of the "great destructive sins":

> *Narrated Abu Hurairah: The Prophet said, "Avoid seven great destructive sins." They (the people) asked, "O Allah's Messenger! What are they?" He said, (they are): (1) To join partners in worship with Allah...*[465]

Muhammad also said that *Shirk* was "the greatest sin in consideration with Allah."[466]

And Muhammad said that those engaging in *Shirk* would go to Hell:

---

[464] Ibid., p. 482.

[465] *Sahih Al-Bukhari*, Vol. 8, Book 86, No. 6857, p. 447.

[466] Ibid., Vol. 6, Book 65, No. 4477, p. 25. For a similar statement see *Sahih Al-Bukhari*, Vol. 3, Book 52, No. 2654, p. 474.

Narrated 'Abdullah: The Prophet said one statement and I said another. The Prophet said "Whoever dies while still invoking anything other than Allah as a rival to Allah, will enter Hell (Fire)." And I said, "Whoever dies without invoking anything as a rival to Allah, will enter Paradise."[467]

So Christians, by definition, engage in *Shirk*, the unforgivable sin in Islam that condemns Christians to the Fires of Hell. And it is interesting to note that, as we have already seen, 2:193, 8:39, and 9:5 are verses of the Koran commanding Muslims to fight until there is no more *Shirk*. Consequently, Muslims are commanded to be at war with Christians until there are no more Christians, or, thanks to 9:29, until they become *Dhimmis* and pay the *Jizyah*.

Conclusion

In terms of the Islamic teachings about Jews and Christians, where do we find the common heritage, common linkages, and common pieces of respectful dialogue? The modern *Tafsir Ahsanul-Bayan* summed it up with its concluding comments about 2:62 of the Koran:

This leads to the conclusion that the erroneous creed of the unity of faiths originates from two causes: Interpreting a verse of Qur'an independently, without keeping other relevant verses in view, and disregarding hadeeth as an aid to understanding the Qur'an. Obviously, it is right to say that the Qur'an cannot be understood without the use of the hadeeths.[468]

---

467 Ibid., Vol. 6, Book 65, No. 4497, pp. 37-38. For other *hadiths* stating that *Shirk* is an unforgiveable sin, see *Sahih Muslim*, Vol. 7, Nos. 2565-2565R2, p. 174; *Sunan Abu Dawud*, Vol. 5, No. 4916, p. 319; and *Jami' At-Tirmidhi*, Vol. 4, No. 2023, p. 106.

468 *Tafsir Ahsanul-Bayan*, Vol. 1, p. 73.

9

Christ Was Not Crucified

> *Narrated Abu Hurairah: Allah's Messenger said, "The most perfidious (awful) name with Allah, on the Day of Resurrection, will be (that of) a man calling himself Malik Al-Amlak (king of the kings)."*[469]

An Imposter on the Cross

So now that we understand the unforgiveable sin of *Shirk*, and Muslim teachings about Christians in particular, let's look at what Muslims believe about Jesus Christ. Muslims simply say that Jesus was not crucified; instead, someone took his place on the cross. This is explicitly stated in the Koran:

Chapter 4, Verses 157-158

> *And because of their saying (in boast), "We killed Messiah 'Isa (Jesus), son of Maryam (Mary), the Messenger of Allah," - but they killed him not nor crucified him, but it appeared so to them [the resemblance of 'Isa (Jesus) was put over another man (and they killed that man)], and those who differ therein are full of doubts. They have no (certain) knowledge, they follow nothing but conjecture. For surely, they killed him not [i.e. 'Isa (Jesus), son of Maryam (Mary)]; But Allah raised him ['Isa (Jesus)] up*

---

[469] *Sahih Al-Bukhari*, Vol. 8, Book 78, No. 6205, p. 125. This *hadith* is also reported in *Sahih Muslim*, Vol. 6, Nos. 2143-2143R1, pp. 425-426; and *Jami' At-Tirmidhi*, Vol. 5, No. 2837, pp. 185-186.

(with his body and soul) to Himself (and he is in the heavens). And Allah is Ever All-Powerful, All-Wise.

Ibn Kathir provided the background for these verses:

> *Ibn Abi Hatim recorded that Ibn 'Abbas said, "Just before Allah raised 'Isa to the heavens, 'Isa went to his companions, who were twelve inside the house. When he arrived, his hair was dripping water and he said, 'There are those among you who will disbelieve in me twelve times after he had believed in me.' He then asked, 'Who volunteers that his image appear as mine, and be killed in my place. He will be with me (in Paradise)?' One of the youngest ones among them volunteered and 'Isa asked him to sit down. 'Isa again asked for a volunteer, and the young man kept volunteering and 'Isa asking him to sit down. Then the young man volunteered again and 'Isa said, 'You will be that man,' and the resemblance of 'Isa was cast over that man while 'Isa ascended to heaven from a hole in the house. When the Jews came looking for 'Isa, they found that young man and crucified him..."*[470]

Ibn Kathir pointed out that afterwards the Jews

> *boasted that they had killed 'Isa and some Christians accepted their false claim, due to their ignorance and lack of reason.*[471]

The *Tafsir Al-Jalalayn* provided a similar explanation:

> *The person killed and crucified was a companion of 'Isa who was made to look like him so that they thought it was*

---

470 *Tafsir Ibn Kathir*, Vol. 3, p. 28. A much briefer version of this is reported in *Tafsir Ahsanul-Bayan*, Vol. 1, p. 547.

471 *Tafsir Ibn Kathir*, Vol. 3, p. 27.

him. Those who argue about him ('Isa) are in doubt about it, about killing him, as one of them said when he saw the body of the person who had been killed, "It is the face of 'Isa but not his body. It is not him." Others said, "It is him." They have no real knowledge of it (his killing), just conjecture. They follow the supposition which they imagine to be the case. But they certainly did not kill him.[472]

The *Tafsir Ibn 'Abbas* said that the man who had been crucified in the place of Jesus was named Tatianos.[473]

And the modern *Tafsir Ahsanul-Bayan* pointed out that even today Christians are still divided on the issue of whether or not Jesus had actually been crucified.[474]

Ibn Kathir had an interesting explanation for what then happened with Christianity:

When Allah raised 'Isa to heaven, his followers divided into sects and groups. Some of them believed in what Allah sent 'Isa as, a servant of Allah, His Messenger, and the son of His female-servant. However, some of them went to the extreme over 'Isa, believing that he was the son of Allah. Some of them said that 'Isa was Allah Himself, while others said that he was one of a Trinity. Allah mentioned these false creeds in the Qur'an and refuted them. The Christians remained like this until the third century CE, when a Greek king called, Constantine, became a Christian for the purpose of destroying Christianity. Constantine was either a philosopher, or he

---

472 *Tafsir Al-Jalalayn*, p. 228.

473 *Tafsir Ibn 'Abbas*, p. 128.

474 *Tafsir Ahsanul-Bayan*, Vol. 1, p. 547.

> *was just plain ignorant. Constantine changed the religion of 'Isa by adding to it and deleting from it. He established the rituals of Christianity...So the religion of 'Isa became the religion of Constantine...Throughout this time, the Christians had the upper hand and dominated the Jews. Allah aided them against the Jews because they used to be closer to the truth than the Jews, even though both groups were and still are disbelievers, may Allah's curse descend on them.*[475]

Ibn Kathir also made an interesting observation. He wrote that those twelve companions in the house knew that Jesus ascended to Heaven from the house and that it was a substitute that was crucified.[476] The implication is that it was the Twelve Apostles in the house, which would mean that those Apostles then went out and knowingly preached a lie that spread across the world as the Christian religion. And of course, if there was no Crucifixion, there was no Resurrection, adding to the magnitude of the lie.

Jesus and His Disciples were Muslims

In Ibn Kathir's explanation for what happened to Christianity after the crucifixion, he touched on the claim that some of the followers of Jesus believed Jesus was only a *servant of Allah*. Ibn 'Abbas also mentioned this

---

475 *Tafsir Ibn Kathir*, Vol. 2, p. 171. Although these claims of Ibn Kathir are inaccurate, it is important to remember, as was earlier pointed out, that the *Tafsir Ibn Kathir* is influential in the Muslim world because

> *is the most popular interpretation of the Qur'an in the Arabic language, and the majority of the Muslims consider it to be the best source based on Qur'an and Sunnah.*

Tafsir Ibn Kathir, Vol. 1, p. 5.

476 Ibid., Vol. 3, p. 27.

in claiming that Jesus' followers split into three groups after the crucifixion of the substitute:

> *One group, Al-Ya'qubiyyah (Jacobites), said, 'Allah remained with us as long as He willed and then ascended to heaven.' Another group, An-Nasturiyyah (Nestorians), said, 'The son of Allah was with us as long as he willed and Allah took him to heaven.' Another group, Muslims, said, 'The servant and Messenger of Allah remained with us as long as Allah willed, and Allah then took him to Him.' The two disbelieving groups cooperated against the Muslim group and they killed them. Ever since that happened, Islam was then veiled until Allah sent Muhammad.'*[477]

So here we discover that there were already *Muslims* among the followers of Jesus; these early *Muslims* knew that Jesus was just a *servant and Messenger of Allah*, and therefore they were "believers." But the remainder of Jesus' followers were disbelievers, and they suppressed these early *Muslims* from the time of the crucifixion until the arrival of Muhammad.

The Koran provides the basis for Ibn 'Abbas' explanation, because it states that the disciples of Jesus proclaimed they were Muslim:

Chapter 5, Verse 111

> *And when I (Allah) inspired Al-Hawariyyun [the disciples of 'Isa (Jesus)] to believe in Me and My Messenger, they said: "We believe. And bear witness that we are Muslims."*

And why shouldn't they have been Muslim? In the first place, the Koran specifically states that Jesus was not the Son of God (e.g. 4:171, 5:72,

---

[477] Ibid., pp. 28-29.

9:30, 19:35, and 112:3). Instead, the Koran states that Jesus was one of the Messengers of Allah (e.g. 3:49, 3:53, 4:171, 5:75, 61:6 and 66:12), and a "slave" of Allah (e.g. 4:172, 19:30, 21:26, and 43:59). This status was even announced by Jesus while he was a baby in his cradle:

Chapter 19, Verses 29-30

> *Then she pointed to him* [Jesus]. *They said, "How can we talk to one who is a child in the cradle?" He ['Isa (Jesus)] said: "Verily, I am a slave of Allah, He has given me the Scripture and made me a Prophet.*[478]

And Muhammad said that Jesus was "Allah's slave and His Messenger."[479]

The Koran states that Jesus even proclaimed the coming of Muhammad:

Chapter 61, Verse 6

> *And (remember) when 'Isa (Jesus), son of Maryam (Mary), said: "O Children of Israel! I am the Messenger of Allah to you, confirming the Taurat [(Torah) which came] before me, and giving glad tidings of a Messenger to come after me, whose name shall be Ahmad." But when he (Ahmad, i.e. Muhammad) came to them with clear proofs, they said: "This is plain magic."*

Ibn Kathir explained this verse:

> *'Isa, peace be upon him, is the last and final Messenger from among the Children of Israel. He remained among*

---

478 The Koran provides other examples of Jesus speaking coherently as a baby: e.g. 3:46, 5:110, and 19:23-26 (at his birth). Muhammad also said that Jesus spoke while in his cradle - see *Sahih Al-Bukhari*, Vol. 4, Book 60, No. 3436, p. 405.

479 *Sahih Al-Bukhari*, Vol. 4, Book 60, No. 3435, p. 404.

the Children of Israel for a while, conveying the good news of the coming of Muhammad, whose name is also Ahmad, the Last and Final Prophet and Messenger.[480]

Jesus will Return to Earth

Both Christians and Muslims believe that Jesus will return to earth. However, Islam teaches a radically different reason for that return. Let's start with the following verse in the Koran:

Chapter 4, Verse 159

> *And there is none of the people of the Scripture (Jews and Christians) but must believe in him ['Isa (Jesus), son of Maryam (Mary), as only a Messenger of Allah and a human being] before his ['Isa (Jesus) or a Jew's or a Christian's] death (at the time of the appearance of the angel of death). And on the Day of Resurrection, he ['Isa (Jesus)] will be a witness against them.*

This verse means that Jews and Christians only have up until *the point of death* to believe that Jesus was just a Messenger of Allah and a human being. Some Islamic scholars believed that *the point of death* pertained to the death of the individual Christian or Jew; but the *Tafsir Ibn Kathir*, *Tafsir Ahsanul-Bayan*, and *Tafsir Ibn 'Abbas* explained that the Jews and Christians only have up until the point of Jesus' actual death, after he returns and fights the final battle, to so believe.[481]

---

[480] *Tafsir Ibn Kathir*, Vol. 9, p. 618.

[481] Ibid., Vol. 3, p. 29; *Tafsir Ahsanul-Bayan*, Vol. 1, p. 549; and *Tafsir Ibn 'Abbas*, p. 128.

And it is interesting to note that most of the authoritative Islamic commentators stated that 4:159 also meant that Jesus would kill all of the Jews and Christians, and leave only Muslims on the earth.[482]

After his death, Jesus would be resurrected to testify against the Jews and Christians. And why would Jesus testify against them? Here is what Muhammad said would happen when Jesus first returned:

> *Imam Ahmad recorded that Abu Hurayrah said that the Prophet said, The Prophets are paternal brothers; their mothers are different, but their religion is one. I, more than any of mankind, have more right to 'Isa, son of Maryam, for there was no Prophet between him and I. He will descend, and if you see him, know him. He is a well-built man, (the color of his skin) between red and white. He will descend while wearing two long, light yellow garments. His head appears to be dripping water, even though no moisture touched it. He will break the cross, kill the pig, and banish the Jizyah and will call the people to Islam. During his time, Allah will destroy all religions except Islam and Allah will destroy Al-Masih Ad-Dajjal (the False Messiah). Safety will then fill the earth...'Isa will remain for forty years and then will die, and Muslims will offer the funeral prayer for him.*[483]

---

482 *Tafsir Ahsanul-Bayan*, Vol. 1, p. 549.

483 *Tafsir Ibn Kathir*, Vol. 3, pp. 31-32. For a shorter version of this narrative, see *Sahih Al-Bukhari*, Vol. 4, Book 60, No. 3448, pp. 411-412; and *Sunan Abu Dawud*, Vol. 4, No. 4324, pp. 528-529.

Muhammad also said that when the Muslims were lined up for battle against the False Messiah and the prayer was called, Jesus would "descend and lead them in prayer." See *Sahih Muslim*, Vol. 8, No. 2897, p. 338; and *Tafsir Ibn Kathir*, Vol. 3, p. 33.

And Muhammad said that Jesus would descend close to the "white minaret" to the east of Damascus, with his hands on the wings of two angels.[484]

So what would happen during those forty years after Jesus returned? Allah would destroy all religions except Islam. And Jesus would be breaking the cross of Christianity and calling the people to Islam.

And, according to Muhammad, Jesus would also be judging mankind by the laws of the Koran:

> *Narrated Abu Hurairah: Allah's Messenger said, "How will you be when the son of Maryam (Mary) ['Isa (Jesus)] descends amongst you, and he will judge people by the law of the Qur'an and not by the law of the Gospel."*[485]

---

[484] *Sahih Muslim*, Vol. 8, No. 2937, p. 357; *Tafsir Ahsanul-Bayan*, Vol. 1, p. 548, and *Tafsir Ibn Kathir*, Vol. 3, p. 37. Ibn Kathir explained the "white minaret":

> *In our time, in the year seven hundred and forty-one* [circa 1340 AD], *a white minaret was built in the Umayyad Masjid (in Damascus) made of stone, in place of the minaret that was destroyed by a fire which the Christians were suspected to have started. May Allah's continued curses descend on the Christians until the Day of Resurrection. There is a strong feeling that this minaret is the one that 'Isa will descend on...*

Tafsir Ibn Kathir, Vol. 3, p. 38.

[485] *Sahih Al-Bukhari*, Vol. 4, Book 60, No. 3449, p. 412. For longer versions of this *hadith*, see *Sahih Al-Bukhari*, Vol. 3, Book 34, No. 2222, pp. 235-236; and Vol. 4, Book 60, No. 3448, pp. 411-412. Muhammad provided an interesting perspective on the approach Jesus would apparently take:

> *Narrated Abu Hurairah: The Prophet said, "'Isa (Jesus), the son of Maryam (Mary) seeing a man stealing, asked him, 'Did you steal?' He said, 'No, by Allah, except Whom there is no other Ilah (God). La ilaha illallah (none who has the right to be*

But what about Jesus banishing the *Jizyah*? Sheikh 'Umar Barakat ibn al-Sayyid provided an interesting explanation:

> *...After his final coming, nothing but Islam will be accepted from them, for taking the poll tax is only effective until Jesus' descent (upon him and our Prophet be peace), which is the divinely revealed law of Muhammad. The coming of Jesus does not entail a separate divinely revealed law, for he will rule by the law of Muhammad.*[486]

So Barakat explained that there would no longer be a need for the *Jizyah* because after Jesus descended back to earth, only conversion to Islam would be accepted from the Jews and Christians.

Conclusion

Since Muslims say that Jesus was not crucified, a Muslim looking at a crucifix would see only an imposter hanging on the cross. For a Muslim, this imposter would then represent a religion based on a lie and originally spread across the world by those knowing it was a lie. But Muslims also believe that Jesus will return to the earth and make things right.

As the modern *Tafsir Ahsanul-Bayan* summed it up:

> *...Muslims believe unanimously that 'Isa is alive in al-barzakh, that he descend* [sic] *to the earth before the Day*

> *worshipped but Allah).' 'Isa said, 'I believe in Allah and deny (or suspect) my eyes.'"*

Sahih Al-Bukhari, Vol. 4, Book 60, No. 3444, p. 409.

[486] *Reliance of the Traveller*, o9.8. Barakat was a noted Shafi'i scholar who wrote the commentary for *Reliance of the Traveller*.

of Resurrection, that he will kill the Dajjal and wipe out all of the religions except Islam...[487]

[487] *Tafsir Ahsanul-Bayan*, Vol. 1, p. 550. *Al-Barzakh* is the interval between death and resurrection.

10

Sharia Law and Women

I think the reason so many women support Sharia is because they have a very different understanding of sharia than the common perception in Western media. The majority of women around the world associate gender justice, or justice for women, with sharia compliance.

Dalia Mogahed, President Barack Obama's adviser on Muslim affairs, October 4, 2009

Introduction

Sharia Law is Islamic Sacred Law, and it is based largely on two foundations. The first is the Koran. The second foundation consists of the actions, examples, and teachings of Muhammad (the *Sunnah*). Does compliance with this law ensure "justice for women" as President Obama's adviser on Muslim affairs maintained? To answer that question we need to look at some of the relevant teachings of the major schools of Islamic Sacred Law.

The Muslim world is divided mainly between Sunni and Shia. The Sunni make up 80-85% of the world's Muslims, while the Shia make up 10-13%. There are four major Sunni schools. They are listed below with the percentage of their adherents in the Sunni world and where these adherents can largely be found (there is some overlap):

1. Hanafi - 45% (the oldest, and considered the most liberal)
   Pakistan, Turkey, Afghanistan, Iraq, Syria, India
   *Founded by Imam Abu Hanifah al-Nu'man ibn Thabit (c. 699-769)

2. Shafi'i - 28% Egypt, Yemen, Indonesia, Malaysia
*Founded by Imam Muhammad ibn Idris al-Shafi'i (c. 767-821)

3. Maliki - 15% Egypt, Kuwait, North Africa
*Founded by Imam Malik ibn Anas al-Asbahi (c. 712-795)

4. Hanbali - 2% (the most conservative) Saudi Arabia
* Founded by Imam Ahmad ibn Hanbal (c. 780-855)

The major Shia school is the Jafari, founded by Imam Ja'far ibn Muhammad al-Sadiq (c. 702-765); its adherents are located mainly in Iran.

An examination of some of the teachings of these schools will allow us to determine what kind of justice women would actually receive under Sharia Law.

General Impact

Sharia Law impacts a woman's life at birth. According to the Shafi'i and Hanbali schools, if the newborn baby is a male, it is recommended that two *shahs* (a one-year old sheep or a two year old goat) be slaughtered; if the newborn baby is a female, it is recommended to slaughter only one *shah*.[488] On the other hand, the Maliki and Hanafi schools state that one sheep is to be slaughtered whether it is a boy or a girl.[489]

In the Shafi'i school even the urine of a baby girl is to be treated differently:

> *The urine of a baby boy who has fed on nothing but human milk can be purified from clothes by sprinkling*

---

488 *Reliance of the Traveller*, j15.2; and *The Mainstay Concerning Jurisprudence*, p. 123.

489 *Al-Muwatta of Imam Malik ibn Anas*, 26.2.7; and *The Kitab al-Athar of Imam Abu Hanifah*, p. 477, n. 2053.

enough water on the spot to wet most of it, though it need not flow over it. The urine of a baby girl must be washed away as an adult's is [with a thorough washing].[490]

Muhammad himself established this belief:

Lubabah bint Al-Harith narrated: "Al-Husain bin 'Ali was with the Messenger of Allah on his lap (or chest), and he urinated on him. I told him (the Prophet): 'Wear another garment, and give me your Izar so that I may wash it.' He said: 'One needs to wash only for the urine of a girl, and sprinkle water for the urine of a boy.'"[491]

Sharia-based differentiation between men and women continues throughout the woman's life:

1. According to the four major Sunni schools, the indemnity for the death or injury of a woman is one-half of that paid for a man.[492]

2. The Shafi'i and Hanbali schools consider it offensive and objectionable for a woman to visit a grave.[493]

3. According to the Maliki school, if a man kisses a woman before he

---

490 *Reliance of the Traveller*, e14.9.

491 *Sunan Abu Dawud*, Vol. 1, No. 375, p. 236; also see Nos. 376-377, p. 237; *Sunan Ibn Majah*, Vol. 1, No. 522, pp. 365-366, and Nos. 525-527, pp. 366-368; and *Jami' At-Tirmidhi*, Vol. 1, No. 71, pp. 97-98.

492 *Reliance of the Traveller*, o4.9; *The Mainstay Concerning Jurisprudence*, p. 287; *Al-Muwatta of Imam Malik ibn Anas*, 43.6; and *The Kitab al-Athar of Imam Abu Hanifah*, 182.579 and 209.650.

493 *Reliance of the Traveller*, g5.9; and *The Mainstay Concerning Jurisprudence*, p. 72.

engages in his prayers, he is considered impure and must do *wudu'* (ritual washing) before praying.[494]

4. The major schools agree that when witnesses are needed concerning property matters, it is preferable to find two men; but if you cannot find two men, then find one man and two women.[495] This is based on Chapter 2, Verse 282 of the Koran:

> *...And get two witnesses out of your own men. And if there are not two men (available), then a man and two women, such as you agree for witnesses, so that if one of them (two women) errs, the other can remind her...*

So two women are needed so that they can help each other remember. And in terms of witnessing, consider the following:

a. According to the Shafi'i school, when testimony "concerns things which men do not typically see," if two men cannot be found, then one man and two women, or four women can provide testimony.[496]

b. According to the Hanbali school, in cases involving a challenge to the credibility of a witness, only the testimony of two men will do.[497]

c. If the man claims to be married to a woman and she denies

---

494 *Al-Muwatta of Imam Malik ibn Anas*, 2.16.66-68.

495 *Encyclopedia of Islamic Law*, pp. 373-374; *Reliance of the Traveller*, o24.7; and *The Mainstay Concerning Jurisprudence*, p. 335.

496 *Reliance of the Traveller*, o24.10.

497 *The Mainstay Concerning Jurisprudence*, p. 338.

the claim, or vice versa, the major schools agree that acceptable proof of marriage requires the testimony of "two just men." Evidence from women in this matter is acceptable only to the Hanafi school; however, the Hanafis require the evidence to be from "two just women" in conjunction with that from a "just man."[498]

d. Adding insult to injury, Muhammad told a group of Muslim women

> *"...I have not seen anyone more deficient in intelligence and religion than you. A cautious sensible man could be led astray by some of you." The women asked, "O Allah's Messenger! What is deficient in our intelligence and religion?" He said, "Is not the witness (evidence) of two women equal to the witness of one man?" They replied in the affirmative. He said, "This is the deficiency in her intelligence"...*[499]

e. Muhammad even said that it required the freeing of two female slaves to equal the virtue of freeing one male slave:

> *Abu Umamah, and other than him from the Companions of the Prophet, narrated that the Prophet said: "Any Muslim man who frees a Muslim man, then it is his salvation from the Fire* [of Hell] - *each of his limbs suffices for a limb of himself. And any Muslim man that*

---

[498] *Encyclopedia of Islamic Law*, p. 405.

[499] *Sahih Al-Bukhari*, Vol. 1, Book 6, No. 304, p. 210. For other versions of this *hadith* where Muhammad tells women they are deficient in intelligence, see: *Sahih Al-Bukhari*, Vol. 2, Book 24, No. 1462, pp. 314-315; and Vol. 3, Book 52, No. 2658, p. 477; and *Sunan Abu Dawud*, Vol. 5, No. 4679, p. 200.

frees two Muslim women, they are his salvation from the Fire - each of their limbs suffices for a limb of himself."[500]

5. The major schools agree that when a woman is in the presence of a strange man (basically any male other than a family member), it is obligatory for her to cover her whole body except for her face and hands.[501]

6. The major schools also agree that while it is permissible for a man to look at the face and hands of a female stranger, it is impermissible for him to touch her, except in an emergency. However, the Hanafi school states that shaking hands with "an old woman who has no sex appeal" is permissible "with the assurance of absence of a sexual motive."[502]

7. Imam Malik, founder of the Maliki school, when asked if a man should greet a woman, replied

> *As for an old woman, I do not disapprove of it. As for a young woman, I do not like it.*[503]

8. The liberal Hanafi school has an interesting approach to *shubhat*, a

---

500 *Jami' At-Tirmidhi*, Vol. 3, No. 1547, pp. 318-319. At-Tirmidhi stated,

> *In this Hadith is the proof that freeing males is more virtuous for a man than freeing females...*

Ibid., p. 319.

501 *Encyclopedia of Islamic Law*, p. 71.

502 Ibid., p. 74.

503 *Al-Muwatta of Imam Malik ibn Anas*, 53.1.2.

“mistake of act” in which a man has intercourse with a woman who is, unbeknownst to him, actually unlawful to him:

> *...where a man hires a woman for some work and then fornicates with her, or hires her for fornication and does so, the two will not be penalized for fornication, because of his ignorance that his hiring her does not include this act. Accordingly, if she is working in a business establishment or a factory and the proprietor of such establishment copulates with her believing this to be one of the benefits which accrue to him as a result of his hiring her, this act will not be termed fornication, but will be considered ‘a mistake’ and shall be a valid excuse for the proprietor in Imam Abu Hanifah’s opinion.*[504]

9. According to the Shafi’i and Hanbali schools, a woman cannot become an Islamic judge,[505] or, according to the Shafi'i school, even be the court secretary for that judge.[506] These are strictly male positions.

10. According to the four major Sunni schools, a menstruating woman is not allowed to do many things, including not being able to keep the fast or participate in the ritual prayers, not touching, reading, or reciting from the Koran, or even remaining in a mosque.[507]

---

504 *Encyclopedia of Islamic Law*, pp. 458-459. A similar approach is taken by the Hanafis in terms of intercourse with a slave woman that would otherwise be forbidden - see *The Kitab al-Athar of Imam Abu Hanifah*, 199.619-620.

505 *Reliance of the Traveller*, o22.1; and *The Mainstay Concerning Jurisprudence*, p. 325.

506 *Reliance of the Traveller*, o22.4.

507 *Encyclopedia of Islamic Law*, p. 39; *Reliance of the Traveller*, e10.7; and *The Mainstay Concerning Jurisprudence*, p. 31.

This physical condition of women was considered by Muhammad to be a "deficiency" in their religion, as he stated to a group of Muslim women

> *"...Isn't it true that a woman can neither offer Salat (prayers) nor observe Saum (fasting) during her menses?" The women replied in the affirmative. He said, "This is the deficiency in her religion."*[508]

11. However, there can be an advantage to being a woman if one is charged with apostasy. Instead of facing a death sentence for apostasy, as she would with the Shafi'i, Hanbali, and Maliki schools,[509] the liberal Hanafi school believes "that women should be forced to return to Islam by such punishment as beating or imprisonment."[510] Her imprisonment would last until she returned

---

508 *Sahih Al-Bukhari*, Vol. 1, Book 6, No. 304. p. 210. Different versions of this *hadith*, with the same message, are found in *Sahih Al-Bukhari*, Vol. 2, Book 24, No. 1462, pp. 314-315; and Vol. 3, Book 30, No. 1951, p. 109. On other occasions Muhammad said that Islam consisted of five things (The Five Pillars of Islam):

1. Proclamation of Faith (*Shahadah*): There is no God but Allah and Muhammad is his Messenger.
2. Five scheduled prayers daily
3. Alms/Charitable giving (*Zakat*)
4. Fasting
5. Pilgrimage to Mecca for those who are able (*Hajj*)

As we see, two of these Pillars are prayers and fasting. Consequently, through no fault of her own, a woman is excluded from 40% of Islam on a regular basis for most of her life, thus making her "deficient" in her religion.

509 *Reliance of the Traveller*, o8.1; *The Mainstay Concerning Jurisprudence*, p. 309; and *Al-Muwatta of Imam Malik ibn Anas*, 36.18.

510 *War and Peace in the Law of Islam*, p. 151.

to Islam or died.[511] But under the Jafari school "she will be imprisoned and beaten at the times of the prescribed prayer until she repents or dies,"[512] or she will be "condemned to perpetual imprisonment, and is to be beaten with rods at the hours of prayer."[513]

Praying in Mosques and Participating in Prayers[514]

The major schools agree that the call to the prescribed prayer (*Adhan*) is not valid if it is done by a woman.[515]

When it comes to praying in the mosque, when there are men, boys, and women present, there are to be prayer rows for each. The Hanafi school states that a woman cannot be between a man and the *imam* (prayer leader).[516] According to the Shafi'i school, the men are to be in the first row, the boys in the second, and the women in the third.[517] The Hanbali school takes it one step further, stating:

> *If the congregation consists of men, boys, hermaphrodites and women, the men should be lined up in the first row,*

---

511 *The Kitab al-Athar of Imam Abu Hanifah*, 186.591, and p. 347, n. 1650.

512 *Encyclopedia of Islamic Law*, p. 291.

513 *The Law of Apostasy in Islam*, p. 45.

514 See Chapter 18, *Muslim-Americans*, for information about Muslim women in American mosques.

515 *Encyclopedia of Islamic Law*, pp. 84-85.

516 *The Kitab al-Athar of Imam Abu Hanifah*, 36.115.

517 *Reliance of the Traveller*, f12.32.

the boys in the second, the hermaphrodites in the next, and the women in the last.[518]

This is based on the fact that Muhammad placed the women in the back during prayers:

> *It was reported from Musa bin Anas, who narrated from Anas that the Prophet led him and a woman among them (in the prayer), so he (the Prophet) made him (Anas) stand to his right, and the woman behind them.*[519]

---

518 *The Mainstay Concerning Jurisprudence*, p. 58.

519 *Sunan Abu Dawud*, Vol. 1, No. 609, pp. 372-373; This *hadith* was also reported in *Sahih Muslim*, Vol. 2, No. 660R1, p. 373. Similar *hadiths* are reported in *Sahih Al-Bukhari*, Vol. 1, Book 10, No. 727, p. 410, and No. 874, p. 478; and *Sunan An-Nasa'i*, Vol. 1, Nos. 802-805, pp. 474-475. Also see *Sunan Abu Dawud*, Vol. 1, Nos. 610-612 and the comments, pp. 373-374; and No. 678 and comments, pp. 404-405, where Muhammad said

> *The best rows for men are the front ones, and the worst are the last ones. And the best rows for women are the last ones, and the worst are the front ones.*

This statement of Muhammad's was also reported in *Sahih Muslim*, Vol. 2, No. 440, pp. 268-269; *Jami' At-Tirmidhi*, Vol. 1, No. 224, pp. 246-247; *Sunan Ibn Majah*, Vol. 2, Nos. 1000-1001, p. 115; and *Sunan An-Nasa'i*, Vol. 1, No. 821, p. 484.

This is especially interesting when considered with what Muhammad said about the front prayer row:

> *Bara' bin 'Azib said: "I heard the Messenger of Allah say: 'Allah and the angels send blessings upon the first row.'"*

> *It was narrated that Abu Hurairah said: "The Messenger of Allah said: 'If they knew what (goodness) there is in the first row, they would cast lots for it.'"*

Sunan Ibn Majah, Vol. 2, Nos. 997 and 998, respectively, p. 114.

In a *sahih hadith* a Muslim woman talked about going to the mosque to listen to Muhammad; she said she

> *was in the front row meant for women and it was adjacent to the last row of men...*[520]

And the back row(s) could even be some distance behind the men's rows. This was illustrated in a *hadith* about when Muhammad was leading the Muslims in the Eclipse Prayer. During the prayer Muhammad

> *moved backward and the rows behind him also moved backward till we reached the extreme (Abu Bakr said: till he reached near the women)...*[521]

Some modern *hadith* commentaries took a practical approach to explaining the difference between the first and last rows:

> *The first row of the congregation is near to the Imam and it deserves a special Mercy of Allah and of the prayer of angels, because it is far from the noise and disturbance of latecomers, and because the people in the first row follow the Imam accurately. It is also far from the rows of the women, so the mind is not disturbed and interrupted; therefore it is stated as the best one.*

Jami' At-Tirmidhi, Vol. 1, Comments to No. 224, p. 247. And:

> *The reason why the back rows of women have been regarded as the best is that these rows are away from the possibility of mingling with men. That is also the reason why women's praying at home is better than their praying at the mosque.*

Sunan Ibn Majah, Vol. 2, Comments to No. 1000, p. 115.

520 *Sahih Muslim*, Vol. 8, No. 2942R1, p. 365.

521 Ibid., Vol. 3, No. 904R2, p. 36.

Improper placement of men and women can even affect the validity of the prayer. Some Jafaris believe that if a man and a woman perform a prescribed prayer when the woman is either in front of or beside the man, without a screen or the proper distance between them, the prayer of both would be invalid. The Hanafis state that the prescribed prayer would be invalid if, among other things,

1. The woman is in front of or beside the man with no screen at least a cubit high between them.

2. The woman "has sex appeal" and her "shanks and ankles are adjacent" to the man's.

However, the Shafi'is, Hanbalis, and most Jafaris believe that in situations like this, even though the manner of performance is disapproved, the prescribed prayer itself is nevertheless valid.[522]

The Shafi'i school states that it is really better for women to pray at home than participate in the congregational prayers at the mosque; and it

> *is offensive for an attractive or young woman to come to the mosque to pray, though not offensive for women who are not young or attractive when this is unlikely to cause temptation.*[523]

The idea of women praying at home was actually encouraged by Muhammad:

> *Ibn 'Umar reported that the Messenger of Allah said: "Do not prevent your women from (going to) the Masajid* [mosque]- *but their houses are better for them.*[524]

---

[522] *Encyclopedia of Islamic Law*, p. 82. Also see *The Kitab al-Athar of Imam Abu Hanifah*, 43.137.

[523] *Reliance of the Traveller*, f12.4.

[524] *Sunan Abu Dawud*, Vol. 1, No. 567, p. 349.

The Shafi'i school also believes that attractive women should not be part of the group for the Eclipse Prayer, the Drought Prayer, or the Prayer on the Two 'Eids.[525] And the liberal Hanafi school is "not pleased" by the idea of women attending the Prayer of the Two 'Eids, "except for old women beyond child-bearing age."[526]

The Friday Prayer (*Jum'ah/Jumu'a*) "is the finest of prayers."[527] There is a consensus among the major schools that attendance at the Friday Prayer is obligatory for men, but not for women;[528] for this prayer it is preferred for women to pray at home.[529] And the Shafi'is and Hanbalis believe that for the Friday Prayer to be valid there must be at least 40 men in attendance.[530] However, some say it can be held with as few as three males present.[531] The number of women in attendance appears to have no effect on the validity of the Friday Prayer.

---

525 *Reliance of the Traveller*, f20.3, f21.2, and f19.4, respectively.

526 *The Kitab al-Athar of Imam Abu Hanifah*, 58.204.

527 *Reliance of the Traveller*, f18.1.

528 *Encyclopedia of Islamic Law*, p. 103; *The Mainstay Concerning Jurisprudence*, p. 62; and *Salaat: the Islamic Prayer from A to Z*, p. 113. Muhammad said

> *The Friday prayer in congregation is an obligation on every single Muslim, except for four: An owned slave, a woman, a child, and a sick person.*

See *Sunan Abu Dawud*, Vol. 1, No. 1067, p. 624.

529 *Salaat: the Islamic Prayer from A to Z*, p. 113.

530 *Reliance of the Traveller*, f18.7 (e); and *The Mainstay Concerning Jurisprudence*, p. 62.

531 *Salaat: the Islamic Prayer from A to Z*, p. 113.

When it comes to praying the Prayer Over The Dead, the Shafi'is state that the obligation to do so "is fulfilled if a single Muslim male prays over the deceased." However, the obligation

> *is not fulfilled by a prayer of women alone when there is a male available, though if there is no one besides women, they are obliged to pray and their prayer fulfills the obligation.*[532]

Marriage - Introduction

What should a Muslim man look for in a woman? Muhammad said

> *The best women* [sic] *is she who when you look at her, she pleases you, when you command her she obeys you, and when you are absent, she protects her honor and your property.*[533]

And in the *hadith* below, Muhammad and some of the early Muslim rulers showed that the woman was completely uninvolved in the choice of whom she was to marry. 'Umar (who became the second Caliph) wanted to marry off his daughter, Hafsa. He offered her to Uthman (who became the third Caliph) and then to Abu Bakr (the first Caliph to succeed Muhammad). Muhammad then "demanded" her hand, and she was married to Muhammad. However, Abu Bakr later assured 'Umar that he would have taken her if Muhammad had changed his mind. All with no input from Hafsa:

> *Narrated 'Abdullah bin 'Umar: 'Umar bin Al-Khattab said, "When (my daughter) Hafsa bint 'Umar lost her husband... I met 'Uthman bin 'Affan and suggested that he should marry Hafsa*

---

532 *Reliance of the Traveller*, g4.1.

533 *Tafsir Ibn Kathir*, Vol. 2, p. 443.

> *saying, 'If you wish, I will marry Hafsa bint 'Umar to you.' On that, he said, 'I will think it over.' I waited for a few days and then he said to me, 'I am of the opinion that I shall not marry at present.' Then I met Abu Bakr and said, 'If you wish, I will marry you Hafsa bint 'Umar.' He kept quiet and did not give me any reply and I became more angry with him than I was with 'Uthman. Some days later, Allah's Messenger demanded her hand in marriage and I married her to him. Later on, Abu Bakr met me and said, 'Perhaps you were angry with me when you offered me Hafsa for marriage and I gave no reply to you?' I said, 'Yes.' Abu Bakr said, 'Nothing prevented me from accepting your offer except that I learnt that Allah's Messenger had referred to the issue of Hafsa; and I did not want to disclose the secret of Allah's Messenger, but had he (i.e. the Prophet) given her up I would surely have accepted her.'"*[534]

So even the daughter of a future caliph was considered nothing more than a piece of property by Muhammad and the early Muslim leaders. Now let's see what Sharia Law itself has to say about marriage.

Marriage - Coercion and Consent

The five major schools are in agreement that the ability to enter into a contract of marriage requires the qualities of sanity and adulthood, unless the contract is concluded by a guardian.

The Hanafis believe that a marriage contract is valid even if there is coercion; the Shafi'i, Maliki, Hanbali, and Jafari schools consider free consent a requirement for that contract.[535] However, there is an interesting approach to the idea of the free consent of a virgin. In the Shafi'i school:

---

534 *Sahih Al-Bukhari*, Vol. 5, Book 64, No. 4005, p. 205.

535 *Encyclopedia of Islamic Law*, p. 401.

Whenever the bride is a virgin, the father or father's father may marry her to someone without her permission, though it is recommended to ask her permission if she has reached puberty. A virgin's silence is considered as permission.[536]

This is also reflected in the Hanbali school:

The father is entitled to give his minor children, male and female, and his virgin daughters, in marriage without their consent. In the case of the adult virgin, seeking her consent is recommended. As for his adult sons, and his widowed or divorced daughters, he is not entitled to give them in marriage without their consent..the consent of the virgin is indicated by silence...[537]

That silence is considered as consent from a virgin is also affirmed in the Hanafi[538] and the Maliki schools, and the Malikis believe that virgin daughters can also be married off without any consultation.[539]

It might appear unusual that the silence of a virgin is considered consent, but it was Muhammad who made that declaration:

Narrated Abu Hurairah: The Prophet said, "...a virgin should not be given in marriage except after her permission." The people asked, "O Allah's Messenger!

---

536 *Reliance of the Traveller*, m3.13 (2).

537 *The Mainstay Concerning Jurisprudence*, p. 201.

538 *The Kitab al-Athar of Imam Abu Hanifah*, 118.405.

539 *Al-Muwatta of Imam Malik ibn Anas*, 28.2.4, 6-7.

How can we know her permission?" He said, "Her silence (indicates her permission)."[540]

Marriage - Prepubescent Marriage

Another unusual concept for Western minds is the idea of prepubescent boys and girls being married, even to each other. This is acceptable under Sharia Law. And, in terms of girls, it is acknowledged in a verse of the Koran which deals with the '*iddah*, the prescribed waiting period for a woman before she can marry again after a divorce or the death of her husband:

Chapter 65, Verse 4

> *And those of your women as have passed the age of monthly courses, for them the 'Iddah (prescribed period), if you have doubt (about their periods), is three months; and for those who have no courses [(i.e. they are still immature) their 'Iddah (prescribed period) is three months likewise...*[541]

---

540 *Sahih Al-Bukhari*, Vol. 7, Book 67, No. 5136, p. 58. For similar *hadiths* about a virgin's silence meaning her consent, see: *Sahih Al-Bukhari*, Vol. 9, Book 89, No. 6946, p. 62; *Sahih Muslim*, Vol. 4, Nos. 1419-1421R2, pp. 352-353; *Sunan Abu Dawud*, Vol. 2, No. 2092, p. 524, and Nos. 2098-2099, p. 527; and *Jami' At-Tirmidhi*, Vol. 2, Nos. 1107-1108, pp. 477-478. Muhammad also said that the silence of an orphan girl indicated her consent - see *Sunan An-Nasa'i*, Vol. 4, No. 3263, p. 121, and No. 3272, p. 125; and *Sunan Abu Dawud*, Vol. 2, No. 2100, p. 527.

541 This is reiterated when 65:4 of the Koran was mentioned in *Sahih Al-Bukhari*, Vol. 7, Book 67, Chapter 39, p. 57:

> *And the 'Idda for the girl before puberty is three months (in the above Verse).*

And the example was set by Muhammad. Although you might still find Muslims who deny this, at about age 50 Muhammad married Aisha when she was only six years old, and he consummated the marriage when she was nine.[542] Aisha talked about the day her marriage was consummated in Medina:

> *The Messenger of God came to our house and men and women of the Ansar gathered around him. My mother came to me while I was being swung on a swing between two branches and got me down. Jumaymah, my nurse, took over and wiped my face with some water and started leading me. When I was at the door, she stopped so I could catch my breath. I was then brought [in] while the Messenger of God was sitting on a bed in our house. [My mother] made me sit on his lap and said, "These are your relatives. May God bless you with them and bless them with you!" Then the men and women got up and left. The Messenger of God consummated his marriage with me in my house when I was nine years old.*[543]

Aisha also stated that she took her dolls with her when she went to Muhammad's house as a nine-year-old bride, and her playmates would come to the house and play.[544]

---

542 See n. 83 for documentation and comments about Aisha's ages.

543 *The History of al-Tabari: The Last Years of the Prophet*, pp. 130-131. For similar narrations from Aisha, see *Sahih Al-Bukhari*, Vol. 5, Book 63, No. 3894, pp. 139-140; *Sunan Abu Dawud*, Vol. 5, Nos. 4933-4937, pp. 327-328; *Sunan Ibn Majah*, Vol. 3, No. 1876, p. 76, where at the time Aisha was "with some of my friends"; and *Sahih Muslim*, Vol. 4, No. 1422, p. 354, where Aisha said she was playing on the swing "along with my playmates."

544 *Sahih Muslim*, Vol. 4, No. 1422R2, p. 355, and Vol. 7, No. 2440, p. 101; *Sahih Al-Bukhari*, Vol. 8, Book 78, No. 6130, pp. 88-89; *Sunan Abu Dawud*, Vol. 5, No. 4931, p. 326; and *Sunan Ibn Majah*, Vol. 3, No. 1982, p. 133. One of Aisha's dolls was a horse with two wings made of cloth - see *Sunan Abu Dawud*, Vol. 5, No. 4932, p. 326.

Muhammad is considered the timeless standard of good conduct for Muslims, and Muhammad's example was followed. In the *hadith* collection of Al-Bukhari, a Muslim talked about a very young grandmother:

> *Al-Hasan bin Salih said, "I saw a neighbouress of mine who became a grandmother at the age of twenty-one."*[545]

The footnote for this *hadith* explained:

> *This woman attained puberty at the age of nine and married to give birth to a daughter at ten; the daughter had the same experience.*

Also, consider the following specific examples from the Shafi'i school:

1. *A guardian may not marry his prepubescent daughter to someone for less than the amount typically received as marriage payment by similar brides, nor marry his prepubescent son to a female who is given more than the amount typically received."*[546]

2. After a divorce, a *waiting period* [before marrying again] *is obligatory for a woman divorced after intercourse, whether the husband and wife are prepubescent, have reached puberty, or one has and the other has not.*[547]

3. In terms of establishing paternity, one of the conditions is that "the husband is at least nine and a half years old."[548] He is not legally considered the child's father if he is under that age.[549] (For the

---

545 *Sahih Al-Bukhari*, Vol. 3, Book 52, Chapter 18, p. 487.

546 *Reliance of the Traveller*, m8.2.

547 Ibid., n9.2.

548 Ibid., n10.2 (c).

Hanbalis, the minimum age to establish paternity is ten years old.[550])

And according to the Hanafi school

> *Abu Hanifah informed us from Hammad that Ibrahim said, "If a man divorces his wife and she is a girl and she is not menstruating, let her reckon her 'iddah by months.*[551]

In this statement by Abu Hanifah, "girl" is defined as someone who "has not reached puberty and does not menstruate."[552]

Marriage - Temporary Marriage

Temporary marriage was initially lawful during the time of Muhammad. It was allowed because the Muslim warriors would be away from their wives for extended periods of time during *holy fighting*:

> *Narrated 'Abdullah: We used to participate in the holy fighting carried on by the Prophet and we had no women (wives) with us. So we said (to the Prophet), "Shall we castrate ourselves?" But the Prophet forbade us to do that and thenceforth he allowed us to marry a woman (temporarily) by giving her even a garment (as Mahr), and then he recited: '"O you who believe! Make not unlawful the Tayyibat (all that is good as regards foods,*

---

549 Ibid., n10.3 (3).

550 *The Mainstay Concerning Jurisprudence*, p. 248.

551 *The Kitab al-Athar of Imam Abu Hanifah*, 138.466.

552 Ibid., p. 269, n. 1372.

things, deeds, beliefs, persons) which Allah has made lawful for you..."[553]

So Muslim warriors were allowed to alleviate the stress of being away from their wives by giving gifts to women for "temporary marriages." Muhammad said these marriages should last for at least three nights.[554]

Here is how it worked:

> *Sabra Juhanni reported: that Allah's Messenger (SAW) temporary* [sic] *permitted temporary marriage for us. So I and another man went out and saw a woman of Bani 'Amer, who was like a young long-necked she-camel. We presented ourselves to her (for contracting temporary marriage), where-upon she said: What dower would you give me? I said: My cloak. And my companion also said: My cloak. And the cloak of my companion was better than*

---

[553] *Sahih Al-Bukhari*, Vol. 6, Book 65, No. 4615, p. 111. A similar *hadith* is reported in *Sahih Muslim*, Vol. 4, No. 1404, p. 342. A shorter version of this *hadith*, from a different narrator, was reported in *Sahih Al-Bukhari*, Vol. 7, Book 67, No. 5071, p. 23. *Mahr* is the wedding gift or dowry a husband gives his new wife. The last four lines of this *hadith* are from 5:87 of the Koran.

The translator for the *Sahih Muslim* collection used in this book had an interesting explanation for this situation:

> *In these expeditions the muslims* [sic] *had been long separated from their wives, and at the same time all of them had not, by that time, learnt the habit of complete sex control. They were thus hard pressed and the Holy prophet* [sic] *(SAW) had to grant them some concession in the spirit in which a person who is driven to extreme hunger is allowed to eat carrion, blood, and the flesh of the swine...*

Sahih Muslim, Vol. 4, p. 346, n.1.

[554] *Sahih Al-Bukhari*, Vol. 7, Book 67, No. 5119, pp. 46-47.

> *my cloak, but I was younger than he. So when she looked at the cloak of my companion she liked it, and when she cast a glance at me I looked more attractive to her. She then said: Well, you and your cloak are sufficient for me. I remained with her for three nights, and then Allah's Messenger (SAW) said: He who has any such woman with whom he had contracted temporary marriage, he should let her off.*[555]

Instead of a garment, "a handful of dates or flour" could also be given.[556]

Muhammad later outlawed temporary marriages, a decision followed by the four major Sunni schools; however, the Jafari school believes that temporary marriages are still legal and will be so "until the Day of Judgment."[557]

---

555 *Sahih Muslim*, Vol. 4, No. 1406, p. 343.

556 Ibid., No. 1405R3, p. 342.

557 *Encyclopedia of Islamic Law*, p. 461. There are *sahih hadiths* stating that temporary marriage was not actually prohibited until it was forbidden by 'Umar, the second Caliph - see *Sahih Muslim*, Vol. 4, Nos. 1405R2-1405R3, p. 342, and No. 1405R4, p. 343. The translator of *Sahih Muslim* explained that Muhammad had originally forbidden temporary marriages "on the eve of the Conquest of Khaibar",

> *but as there were no elaborate means of communication, its prohibition could not be conveyed to all the muslims* [sic] *who had been living far away. Thus there was the necessity of the pronouncement of its prohibition again and again on different occasions. Hadrat 'Umar made vigorous efforts to convey it to every quarter, and imposed punishment of stoning upon those who committed this offence as is done in the case of fornication.*

The translator pointed out that only Muhammad was "authorised to declare any act illegal." See *Sahih Muslim*, Vol. 4, p. 346, n. 1.

Marriage - Role of the Guardian

Muhammad said

> *Any woman who marries without the permission of her guardian - then her marriage is void"...*[558]

The five major schools agree that the guardian is authorized to contract marriage on behalf of his minor or insane ward – whether male or female. The Shafi'i and Jafari schools believe that only the father and the paternal grandfather can contract a marriage on behalf of a minor, while the Malikis and Hanbalis limit that right to the father. On the other hand, the Hanafi school extends it to other male relatives, including a brother or an uncle.[559]

With regard to a virgin, adult female, the Shafi'i, Maliki and Hanbali schools are in agreement that the guardian has the sole authority over her marriage; but if she has been previously married, the guardian's authority is contingent on her consent. The Hanafis consider a sane, grown-up female as competent to choose her own husband, regardless of being a virgin or not; the role for the guardian here, and also with regard to non-virgins in the Shafi'i school, is to object and request an annulment from a judge if the female marries someone not her equal. Most of the Jafaris believe that "a sane girl of full age, on maturing" is capable of deciding her own marriage, whether she is a virgin or not.[560]

---

558 *Sunan Abu Dawud*, Vol. 2, No. 2083, p. 520.

559 *Encyclopedia of Islamic Law*, pp. 424-425.

560 Ibid., pp. 423-424; *Reliance of the Traveller*, m3.13 (1) and m3.15; and *The Kitab al-Athar of Imam Abu Hanifah*, 131.442.

Marriage - "Protecting" the Wife

A man asked Muhammad

> *"O Messenger of Allah! What are the rights that our wives have over us?" He replied: "That you feed her when you eat, and clothe her when you wear clothes, and that you avoid hitting her in the face, or disgracing her, and that you avoid abandoning her except at home."*[561]

Sharia Law does provide some "protection" for the wife:

1. According to the Shafi'is, "A guardian may not marry his prepubescent daughter to someone for less than the amount typically received as marriage payment by similar brides..."[562]

2. All the major schools agree it is unlawful for her to be married to anyone besides a Muslim male.[563] This is stated in Chapter 2, Verse 221 of the Koran:

   > *...And give not (your daughters) in marriage to Al-Mushrikun till they believe (in Allah Alone)...*[564]

---

[561] *Sunan Abu Dawud*, Vol. 2, No. 2142, p. 550. This was reported with similar wording in *Tafsir Ibn Kathir*, Vol. 2, p. 445.

[562] *Reliance of the Traveller*, m8.2.

[563] Ibid., m6.7 (5); *Encyclopedia of Islamic Law*, p. 416; and *The Mainstay Concerning Jurisprudence*, p. 210.

[564] It is interesting to note that this verse actually starts out with the prohibition against Muslim men marrying non-Muslim women:

> *And do not marry Al-Mushrikat (idolatresses) till they believe (worship Allah Alone)...*

3. All of the major schools also agree that her husband can have only three other wives.[565] The basis for this is Chapter 4, Verse 3 of the Koran:

> *And if you fear that you shall not be able to deal justly with the orphan girls then marry (other) women of your choice, two or three, or four...*[566]

But once she is married, Sharia Law gives her husband a tremendous amount of control over her. As Muhammad said:

> *If I were to command anyone to prostrate before anyone, I would have commanded the wife to prostrate before her husband, because of the enormity of his right upon her.*[567]

In the first instance, the new bride loses control of any personal finances she might have:

However, this verse was later abrogated by 5:5 which allowed Muslim men to marry Jewish and Christian women – see *Tafsir Ibn Kathir*, Vol. 1, pp. 611-612; and Vol. 3 pp. 104-105. The prohibition of Muslim women being married to non-Muslims is also mentioned in 60:10 of the Koran.

[565] *Reliance of the Traveller*, m6.10; *Encyclopedia of Islamic Law*, p. 413; *The Mainstay Concerning Jurisprudence*, p. 203; *Al-Muwatta of Imam Malik ibn Anas*, 29.29.76; and *The Kitab al-Athar of Imam Abu Hanifah*, 134.457.

[566] *Tafsir Ibn Kathir*, Vol. 2, pp. 374-375; *Tafsir Ahsanul-Bayan*, Vol. 1, p. 418; *Tafsir Al-Jalalayn*, p. 174; and *Tafsir Ibn 'Abbas*, p. 99. It is interesting to note that 33:50 of the Koran exempted only Muhammad from this limitation of four wives – see *Tafsir Ibn Kathir*, Vol. 7, p. 724; *Tafsir Al-Jalalayn*, p. 907; *Tafsir Ahsanul-Bayan*, Vol. 4, pp. 401-402; and *Tafsir Ibn 'Abbas*, p. 551.

[567] *Tafsir Ibn Kathir*, Vol. 2, p. 444. Similar versions of this *hadith* are mentioned in *Sunan Abu Dawud*, Vol. 2, No. 2140, pp. 549-550; *Jami' At-Tirmidhi*, Vol. 2, No. 1159, pp. 528-529; and *Sunan Ibn Majah*, Vol. 3, No. 1853, p. 63.

> *It was narrated from 'Amr bin Shu'aib, from his father, from his grandfather, that the Messenger of Allah said: "It is not permissible for a woman to give a gift from her wealth, once her husband has marital authority over her."*[568]

But there are larger concerns for the new wife.

Marriage - Beating Wives

The husband is allowed to beat his wives. This is stated in the Koran:

Chapter 4, Verse 34

> *Men are the protectors and maintainers of women, because Allah has made one of them to excel the other...As to those women on whose part you see ill conduct, admonish them (first), (next) refuse to share their beds, (and last) beat them (lightly, if it is useful)...*[569]

---

568 *Sunan An-Nasa'i*, Vol. 4, No. 3787, p. 415.

569 Al-Wahidi provided the context for the "revelation" of this verse:

> *...It happened Sa'd hit his wife on the face because she rebelled against him. Then her father went with her to see the Prophet, Allah bless him and give him peace. He said to him: 'I gave him my daughter in marriage and he slapped her.' The Prophet, Allah bless him and give him peace, said: 'Let her have retaliation against her husband.' As she was leaving with her father to execute retaliation, the Prophet, Allah bless him and give him peace, called them and said: 'Come back; Gabriel has come to me,' and Allah, exalted is He, revealed this verse. The Messenger of Allah, Allah bless him and give him peace, said: 'We wanted something while Allah wanted something else, and that which Allah wants is good.' Retaliation was then suspended."*

Al-Wahidi's Asbab al-Nuzul, p. 72.

In his authoritative *tafsir*, Ibn Kathir explained that such a beating was to be neither "violent" nor "severe."[570] The *Tafsir Al-Jalalayn* explained that the husband could beat his wife, "but not hard if the other courses of action do not work."[571]

The modern *Tafsir Ahsanul-Bayan* explained it this way:

> *In case a woman is disobedient, she should be counseled first to reform and mend her ways. If she does not reform, beds should be separated. This is the second step, enough for a woman of sound understanding. In case this fails to have any effect on her, then the man may thrash her providing this thrashing is not cruel or wild, which is the wont of the ignorant and the rustic.*[572]

---

570 *Tafsir Ibn Kathir*, Vol. 2, p. 446.

571 *Tafsir Al-Jalalayn*, p. 188.

572 *Tafsir Ahsanul-Bayan*, Vol. 1, p. 452. On the same page this modern commentary also pointed out:

> *This verse gives two reasons for man's domination and ascendancy over woman. One is his physical strength and mental prowess, giving him distinctive superiority over woman. This is natural and inborn. The second is acquired. Allah has tasked man to earn wealth and maintain her. Woman is free from this responsibility. Because of her physique, her natural weakness, and to protect her natural modesty, woman has been kept away from the din and clatter of public life and economic activities. This verse is clear textual evidence from the Qur'an, an absolute and incontrovertible proof, negating her right to domination, rule, or leadership.*

And Muhammad himself said "to beat them [wives] but not with severity."[573] And why not "with severity"? On another occasion, while giving a sermon, Muhammad said this about the treatment of women:

> *It is not wise for anyone of you to lash his wife like a slave, for he might sleep with her the same evening.*[574]

The authority to beat one's wives appeared to have been widely exercised in the early Muslim community, as Muhammad's young wife Aisha noted:

> *'Aishah said that the lady (came), wearing a green veil (and complained to her ('Aishah) of her husband and showed her a green spot on her skin caused by beating)...so when Allah's Messenger came, 'Aishah said, "I have not seen the women suffering as the believing* [Muslim] *women. Look! Her skin is greener than her clothes!"*[575]

And Aisha herself was also a recipient. One time, when it was her turn among the wives to have Muhammad spend the night with her, she secretly followed Muhammad when he left her bed. Aisha said that when she later confessed to Muhammad that she had followed him, "He struck me on the chest which caused me pain..."[576]

---

573 *The Life of Muhammad*, p. 651. For additional reports about Muhammad stating that wives could be beaten, see *The History of al-Tabari: The Last Years of the Prophet*, p. 113; and *Jami' At-Tirmidhi*, Vol. 2, No. 1163, p. 531.

574 *Sahih Al-Bukhari*, Vol. 6, Book 65, No. 4942, p. 392. A similar statement by Muhammad is reported in *Jami' At-Tirmidhi*, Vol. 6, No. 3343, p. 78:

> *One of you should not lash his wife as a slave is lashed, for perhaps he will lay with her at the end of the day.*

575 *Sahih Al-Bukhari*, Vol. 7, Book 77, No. 5825, p. 392.

576 *Sahih Muslim*, Vol. 3, No. 974R1, p. 72. This was also reported in *Sunan An-Nasa'i*, Vol. 3, No. 2039, p. 127.

And because Muhammad was sad on one occasion, 'Umar, who became the second Caliph, used the story of slapping a woman to make Muhammad laugh. This led to the slapping of two of his wives, Aisha and Hafsa, who happened to be present, with no objections from Muhammad:

> ['Umar] *found Allah's Apostle (SAW) sitting sad and silent with his wives around him. He (Hadrat 'Umar) said: I would say something which would make the Holy Prophet (SAW) laugh, so he said: Messenger of Allah, I wish you had seen (the treatment meted out to) the daughter of Kharija when you asked me some money* [sic], *and I got up and slapped her on the neck. Allah's Messenger (SAW) laughed and said: They* [Muhammad's wives] *are around me as you see, asking for extra money. Abu Bakr (Allah be pleased with him) then got up, went to 'Aisha (Allah be pleased with her) and slapped her on the neck, and 'Umar stood up before Hafsa and slapped her saying: You ask Allah's Messenger (SAW) which he does not possess* [sic].[577]

The idea of beating wives is also codified in two sections of Sharia Law in the Shafi'i school:

1. *If she commits rebelliousness, he keeps from sleeping with her without words, and may hit her, but not in a way that injures her, meaning he may not break bones, wound her, or cause blood to flow. He may hit her whether she is rebellious only once or whether more than once...*[578]

2. *If keeping from her is ineffectual, it is permissible for him to hit*

---

[577] *Sahih Muslim*, Vol. 4, No. 1478, p. 408. Abu Bakr was Aisha's father; 'Umar was Hafsa's father.

[578] *Reliance of the Traveller*, m10.12.

> *her if he believes that hitting her will bring her back to the right path...His hitting her may not be in a way that injures her...*[579]

The Hanbali school also states that a husband "is entitled to beat" his wife, but "without inflicting severe pain."[580] And in that school's Book of Oaths (*Kitab al-Aiman*), examples are given of how oaths are to be construed. One of those examples is:

> *If he swears that he will surely beat his wife, with the intention of causing her pain, his oath is not kept except by a beating that causes her pain. If he swears that he will surely beat her with ten lashes, but he combines them and beats her with a single blow, his oath is not kept.*[581]

Muhammad provided an apt conclusion to this section:

> *A man should not be asked why he beats his wife...*[582]

Marriage - The Price of Maintenance

But on a more positive note, relatively speaking, Sharia Law does require the husband to support his wife. The major schools agree that a wife's "maintenance" is obligatory with regard to food, clothing and housing.[583]

---

579 Ibid., m10.12 (4) (c).

580 *The Mainstay Concerning Jurisprudence*, p. 223.

581 Ibid., p. 271.

582 *Sunan Ibn Majah*, Vol. 3, No. 1986, p. 135. For a similar report see *Sunan Abu Dawud*, Vol. 2, No. 2147, pp. 552-553.

583 *Encyclopedia of Islamic Law*, p. 483.

However, the Shafi'i school does qualify this in terms of clothing: a wife is "entitled to the kind of clothing that is customary in town for dressing oneself."[584] But the Shafi'is believe that if the husband

> *gives her clothing for a season, and it wears out before the end of the season, he is not obliged to furnish new clothing, though if it lasts beyond the season, he is nevertheless obliged to provide new clothing for each new season.*[585]

If there is a dispute between the husband and wife over whether or not the husband has been paying his wife's maintenance, the Hanafi, Shafi'i, and Hanbali schools say that the wife's word is to be accepted with the burden of proof being on the husband; however, the Jafari and Maliki schools state that if the husband is living with the wife, then his word will be accepted.[586]

It is interesting to note that if the husband states that he has not paid maintenance to her because she is not entitled to it "due to her not surrendering herself to him [for sex]," all of the schools agree that the husband's word will be accepted because maintenance is not required until after she so surrenders herself.[587] As the Shafi'i school succinctly explains:

> *The husband is only obliged to support his wife when she gives herself to him or offers to, meaning she allows him full enjoyment of her person and does not refuse him sex at any time of the night or day.*[588]

---

584 *Reliance of the Traveller*, m11.5.

585 Ibid., m11.7.

586 *Encyclopedia of Islamic Law*, p. 488.

587 Ibid., pp. 488-489.

588 *Reliance of the Traveller*, m11.9.

The Shafi'is go even further by stating that it "is obligatory for a woman to let her husband have sex with her immediately" when he asks her, they are at home, and "she can physically endure it"; and a "husband possesses full rights to enjoy his wife's person in what does not physically harm her."[589] For the Shafi'is it is not enough that the wife allows her husband "free access," she must also go to him and "expressly" say, "I surrender myself to you."[590]

The Hanbali school simply states

> *The husband's rightful claim on his wife is her submission and obedience to him in lovemaking, whenever he wishes, so long as she has no valid excuse.*[591]

As Muhammad himself said,

> *When a man calls his wife to fulfill his need, then let her come, even if she is at the oven.*[592]

The major schools agree that a disobedient wife is not entitled to continued maintenance. All of the major schools except for the Hanafis agree that a wife is disobedient if she "does not allow her husband free access to her person without any legal and reasonable excuse." The Hanafis state that

---

[589] Ibid., m5.1 and m5.4.

[590] *Encyclopedia of Islamic Law*, pp. 477-478.

[591] *The Mainstay Concerning Jurisprudence*, p. 220.

[592] *Jami' At-Tirmidhi*, Vol. 2, No. 1160, p. 529. A variation of this was reported in *Sunan Ibn Majah*, Vol. 3, No. 1853, p. 63:

> *"...The Messenger of Allah said: '...No woman can fulfill her duty towards Allah until she fulfills her duty towards her husband. If he asks her (for intimacy) even if she is on her camel saddle, she should not refuse.'"*

although the wife denies herself to her husband (an unlawful act), if she confines herself to her husband's home and does not leave it without his permission, she is still obedient in terms of receiving maintenance.[593]

What about maintenance if the wife is a minor and the husband is an adult? Except for the Hanafis, all of the major schools state that the minor wife is not entitled to maintenance.[594] For the Hanafis there are three different categories of female minors in terms of determining whether or not she should receive maintenance:

1. A minor wife who is not of any use for service or sociability shall not be entitled to maintenance.

2. A minor wife who is of use for service or for sociability alone, but not for intercourse, shall not be entitled to maintenance.

3. A minor wife with whom intercourse is possible enjoys the rights to maintenance of an adult wife.[595]

So for the liberal school of Sharia Law, a female minor is only guaranteed food, clothing and housing if she is capable of engaging in intercourse.

If the wife is an adult, capable of intercourse, and the husband is a minor, incapable of intercourse, the Hanafi, Shafi'i, and Hanbali schools state that her maintenance is still obligatory. For the Malikis and some of the Jafaris, her maintenance is not obligatory because a minor husband is free of such obligations.[596]

---

593 *Encyclopedia of Islamic Law*, p. 477.

594 Ibid., p. 478.

595 Ibid.

596 Ibid., and *The Kitab al-Athar of Imam Abu Hanifah*, 167.519.

There is another way by which a wife can lose her maintenance: all of the schools agree that a wife is considered disobedient if she leaves her husband's home without his permission.[597] And according to the Shafi'i and Hanbali schools, if the wife goes out with her husband's permission, but for her own needs, her husband is not obligated to provide any support for that particular venture.[598]

When it comes to the husband's obligations for the medical expenses of his wife, there "is no mention of medicine and medical treatment in the Quran and the Traditions."[599] Consequently, the schools are of mixed minds in addressing this issue. The Shafi'i school states that the husband "is not obliged to pay for his wife's cosmetics, doctor's fees, the purchase of medicine for her, and similar expenses."[600] The Jafari school states that if she is ill, the wife is not entitled to claim medicine from her husband. However, Sayyid Abu al-Hasan, a Jafari scholar, qualified that by stating that if the medicine was "of common use and needed for common ailments," then such medicine was considered as maintenance; but he further stated that medicine which was for "difficult cures and uncommon ailments, which require expensive treatment," was not considered as maintenance, and it was not the husband's "duty" to provide them to his wife.[601] And the Hanafis say that it is not obligatory for the husband to provide medicine for his wife if they are going through a "period of dispute."[602]

---

597 *Encyclopedia of Islamic Law*, p. 479.

598 *Reliance of the Traveller*, m11.9 (2); and *The Mainstay Concerning Jurisprudence*, p. 220.

599 *Encyclopedia of Islamic Law*, p. 484.

600 *Reliance of the Traveller*, m11.4.

601 *Encyclopedia of Islamic Law*, pp. 484-485.

602 Ibid., p. 484.

Inheritance

Originally, according to 2:240 of the Koran, when a husband died he was supposed to leave a year's worth of maintenance for his wives:

> *And those of you who die and leave behind wives should bequeath for their wives a year's maintenance and residence without turning them out...*

However, this requirement of one year's worth of maintenance was later abrogated by 4:12 of the Koran: [603]

> *In that which your wives leave, your share is a half if they have no child...In that which you leave, their (your wives) share is a fourth if you leave no child...*

A required year's worth of maintenance was replaced by a fixed, but lesser, share. Consequently, all the major schools are in agreement that when it comes to inheritance, a wife will generally receive only half of that which her husband receives.[604] And the major schools also acknowledge the Koran's injunction that if there is more than one wife involved, all of the wives will divide the one portion for the woman between themselves.[605]

Chapter 4, Verse 11 of the Koran also applied this idea to the inheritance of children:

---

603 *Tafsir Ibn Kathir*, Vol. 1, p. 676; *Tafsir Al-Qurtubi*, p. 623; *Tafsir Al-Jalalayn*, p. 91; *Tafsir Ahsanul-Bayan*, Vol. 1, p. 221; Tafsir *Ibn 'Abbas*, p. 50.; and *Sunan An-Nasa'i*, Vol. 4, No. 3573, p. 310.

604 *Encyclopedia of Islamic Law*, pp. 294 and 334.

605 Ibid., p. 335; *Reliance of the Traveller*, L6.0 in general, and especially L6.3 and L6.4; and *The Mainstay Concerning Jurisprudence*, p. 175. This is also stated in *Tafsir Ibn Kathir*, Vol. 2, p. 395.

Allah commands you as regards your children's (inheritance): to the male, a portion equal to that of two females...

Divorce

In terms of divorce, under Sharia Law the husband is in control. The major schools are in agreement that the husband is the divorcer and the wife is the divorcee, the recipient of the divorce.[606]

In the Maliki school, if there is a dispute about whether or not a divorce has taken place, the wife can bring a witness who states that a divorce had taken place. But if the husband swears an oath that it did not happen, there is no divorce; as Imam Malik said, "The right to make an oath only belongs to the husband..."[607]

In the Hanafi school, if the husband writes a letter to his wife intending that they be divorced, "she is divorced from the moment he writes it"; if he notes in the letter that she is not divorced until the letter reaches her, she is then divorced upon receipt of the letter.[608]

According to the Jafari school, a divorce requires the husband to say in Arabic, when possible, "you are divorced" or "so and so is divorced" or "she is divorced"; this must be properly recited, without conditions, in front of two male witnesses. Female witnesses do not suffice.[609]

---

606 *Encyclopedia of Islamic Law*, p. 501.

607 *Al-Muwatta of Imam Malik ibn Anas*, 36.4.7.

608 *The Kitab al-Athar of Imam Abu Hanifah*, 157.498.

609 *Encyclopedia of Islamic Law*, pp. 504, and 505-506.

The other four major schools "allow divorce in any manner in which there is an indication of it," allow conditions to be placed (such as, "If you speak to your father you are divorced"), and do not require witnesses.[610]

In the Shafi'i school divorcing one's wife can even be conditionally whimsical, with no involvement at all required of the wife:

> *When the husband makes a divorce conditional on another person's act, such as by saying, "If So-and-so enters the house, you are divorced," and the person enters before or after he knows it is a condition, whether remembering it or not, then if the person named is not someone who would mind if they were divorced, then the wife is divorced. But if the person knows it is a condition and enters forgetfully, then if he is someone who would mind if they were divorced, the wife is not divorced.*[611]

According to the Jafari school, the husband cannot give the wife the option of initiating the divorce.[612] However according to the other four major schools, the husband can authorize the wife or someone else to initiate the divorce.[613]

The Hanafi school has an interesting approach to the wife being allowed to initiate the divorce. When the wife is offered that initiative by her husband, she is allowed that option

> *as long as she is still sitting [with her husband] and does not take up some other activity. If she takes up some other*

---

610 Ibid., pp. 504-505.

611 *Reliance of the Traveller*, n4.6.

612 *Encyclopedia of Islamic Law*, p. 503.

613 Ibid., p. 505; *Reliance of the Traveller*, n1.3 and n3.3 (3); and *The Kitab al-Athar of Imam Abu Hanifah*, 171.530-536.

> *activity or stands up from sitting with him, her choice is obviated.*[614]

Along this line, the Shafi'i school states that

> *when a husband tells his wife, "Divorce yourself," then if she immediately says, "I divorce myself," she is divorced, but if she delays, she is not divorced unless the husband has said, "Divorce yourself whenever you wish."*[615]

The four major Sunni schools also allow a wife to request a "divorce for consideration" (*al-khul*) in which she pays her husband to divorce her; if both parties agree, it is a valid divorce.[616] These four schools also agree that the husband can arrange a "divorce for consideration" with a stranger:

> *Therefore, if a stranger asks the husband to divorce his wife for a sum which he undertakes to pay, and the husband divorces her, the divorce is valid even if the wife is unaware of it and on coming to know does not consent.*[617]

The Jafaris do not consider such a divorce involving a stranger to be valid; however, they believe that, with the wife's permission, a stranger can act as an agent to ask the husband for a "divorce for consideration" and then act as guarantor for that consideration.[618]

---

614 *The Kitab al-Athar of Imam Abu Hanifah*, 171.531.

615 *Reliance of the Traveller*, n1.3.

616 *Encyclopedia of Islamic Law*, pp. 511-514; *Reliance of the Traveller*, n5.0; *The Mainstay Concerning Jurisprudence*, p. 224; *Al-Muwatta of Imam Malik ibn Anas*, 29.11 and 29.12; and *The Kitab al-Athar of Imam Abu Hanifah*, 168.520.

617 *Encyclopedia of Islamic Law*, p. 512.

618 Ibid.

The four Sunni schools state that if a divorced woman has custody of a child from the previous marriage, she loses her right to that custody if she then marries a man who is unrelated to that child; however, if the man is related to the child, the woman retains custody.[619] The Jafaris believe that when a woman remarries, she automatically loses custody of a child from the previous marriage.[620]

Annulment

In terms of an annulment of the marriage, there are situations where the wife can take the initiative. One such situation is impotency on the part of the husband. The five major schools give the wife the right to annul the marriage under this condition.[621] The Shafi'i, Hanbali and Hanafi schools say she has this right even if her husband is capable of having intercourse with other woman. However, the Jafari school believes that if the husband is capable of having intercourse with other women, the wife does not have a right to such an annulment.[622] If the husband denies that he is impotent, the major schools agree that the burden of proof is on the wife. And if the husband takes an oath that he is not impotent, and there is no evidence to the contrary, then her claim is dismissed.[623]

---

[619] Ibid., p. 471; *Reliance of the Traveller*, m13.4; *The Mainstay Concerning Jurisprudence*, p. 250; and *The Kitab al-Athar of Imam Abu Hanifah*, 226.706.

[620] *Encyclopedia of Islamic Law*, p. 471.

[621] Ibid., p. 428.

[622] Ibid., pp. 428-429.

[623] Ibid., pp. 429-430.

Death

Even in death, Sharia Law relegates a woman to a subordinate status. For example, according to the liberal Hanafi school, the body of a man is to be placed closer to the *imam* than the body of a woman.[624] In the Shafi'i school, if there are several bodies to be buried, the closest body to the *imam* should be an adult male, then a boy, then a woman; and if bodies are brought successively, the first one brought is placed closest to the *imam*, although a woman's body "should be placed further from the *imam* than that of a male brought subsequently."[625] It is simply considered *Sunnah* to place a body of a male closer to the imam than the body of a female.[626]

In terms of an after-life, women seemed to have one sure way of getting to paradise:

> *It was narrated from Musawir Al-Himyari from his mother that she heard Umm Salamah say: "I heard the Messenger of Allah say: 'Any woman who dies when her husband is pleased with her, will enter Paradise.'"*[627]

However, on another occasion Muhammad said that when dead, women had a greater chance of going to Hell:

> *Narrated 'Imran bin Husain: The Prophet said, "I looked at Paradise and found poor people forming the majority of*

---

[624] *The Kitab al-Athar of Imam Abu Hanifah*, 72.245-247.

[625] *Reliance of the Traveller*, g4.5.

[626] *Sunan Abu Dawud*, Vol. 3, No. 3193, p. 602. Also see *Sunan An-Nasa'i*, Vol. 3, Nos. 1979-1980, pp. 98-99. *Sunnah* means the examples, ways, and teachings of Muhammad that have become rules to be followed by Muslims.

[627] *Sunan Ibn Majah*, Vol. 3, No. 1854, p. 64.

its inhabitants; and I looked at Hell and saw that the majority of its inhabitants were women."[628]

And women had less of a chance of getting into Paradise:

Imran b. Husain reported that Allah's Messenger (may peace be upon him) said: Amongst the inmates of Paradise the women would form a minority.[629]

Conclusion

Under Sharia Law a woman is generally regarded as subordinate to the men around her, deficient in her intelligence and religion, and someone for whom men can make important decisions with few objections allowed from her. For her husband she is a tightly controlled sex object whom he can hit, and she is dependent on her husband for the necessities of life and easily subject to divorce should he so decide. It is curious that some considered this treatment to be "justice for women."

As Muhammad so succinctly put it:

Treat women well, for they are [like] domestic animals with you and do not possess anything for themselves.[630]

---

628 *Sahih Al-Bukhari*, Vol. 4, Book No. 59, No. 3241, p. 290. For similar statements by Muhammad about women in Hell, see: *Sahih Muslim*, Vol. 8, Nos. 2736-2737, p. 253; and *Jami' At-Tirmidhi*, Vol. 5, No. 2613, p. 24.

629 *Sahih Muslim*, Vol. 8, No. 2738, p. 253.

630 *The History of al-Tabari: The Last Years of the Prophet*, p. 113. This statement was made by Muhammad during his Farewell Pilgrimage to Mecca about three months before he died. Ibn Ishaq reported Muhammad's statement as

Lay injunctions on women kindly, for they are prisoners with you having no control of their persons.

It should also come as no surprise that in terms of promoting "gender equality," a 2011 annual report of 135 countries ranked 22 Muslim-majority countries among the bottom 35 (of those 22, Islam was the official religion in 12). Of the remaining 13 at the bottom, six of those countries had Muslim populations ranging from 19.6% to 50%. In contrast, of the countries in the top 35, 18 had Muslim populations too small to number; of the remaining 17 at the top, 13 had Muslim populations of less than 6%.[631]

See *The Life of Muhammad*, p. 651. Another version, in which Muhammad said that women were "but like captives with you," can be found in *Jami' At-Tirmidhi*, Vol. 5, No. 3087, p. 396.

[631] For the ranking of countries see *The Global Gender Gap Report 2011*, World Economic Forum, November 2011, pp. 8-9. The report is accessible at: http://www3.weforum.org/docs/WEF_GenderGap_Report_2011.pdf.

The Global Gender Gap Index was started by the World Economic Forum in 2006

> *as a framework for capturing the magnitude and scope of gender-based disparities and tracking their progress. The Index benchmarks national gender gaps on economic, political, education- and health-based criteria, and provides country rankings...*

See the website at http://www.weforum.org/reports/global-gender-gap-report-2011, accessed July 27, 2012.

The percentage of Muslims in a country's population was obtained from *The World Fact Book*, published on-line by the Central Intelligence Agency. This fact book is located at https://www.cia.gov/library/publications/the-world-factbook/index.html and was accessed on July 30, 2012.

Here is the ranking by country, with the percentage of the Muslim population, or Islam is the "Official" religion of the country; (-) indicates the Muslim population is too small to number:

Top 35

Iceland-1 (-), Norway-2 (1.8%), Finland-3 (-), Sweden-4 (-), Ireland-5 (-), New Zealand-6 (-), Denmark-7 (2%), Philippines-8 (5%), Lesotho-9 (-), Switzerland-10 (4.3%), Germany-11 (3.7%), Spain-12 (-), Belgium-13 (-), South Africa-14 (1.5%), Netherlands-15 (5.8%), United Kingdom-16 (2.7%), United States-17 (0.6%), Canada-18 (1.9%), Latvia-19 (-), Cuba-20 (-), Trinidad and Tobago-21 (5.8%), Bahamas-22 (-), Australia-23 (1.7%), Burundi-24 (10%), Costa Rica-25 (-), Mozambique-26 (17.9%), Nicaragua-27 (-), Argentina-28 (-), Uganda-29 (12.1%), Luxembourg-30 (-), Sri Lanka-31 (7.6%), Namibia-32 (-), Barbados-33 (-), Austria-34 (4.2%), Portugal-35 (-).

Bottom 35

Maldives-101 (Official), Cambodia-102 (2.1%), United Arab Emirates-103 (Official), Suriname-104 (19.6%), Kuwait-105 (Official), Zambia-106 (Muslim/Hindu 24-49%), Korea, Rep.-107 (-), Tunisia-108 (Official), Fiji-109 (6.3%), Bahrain-110 (81.2%), Qatar-111 (77.5%), Guatemala-112 (-), India-113 (13.4%), Mauritania-114 (Official), Burkina Faso-115 (60.5%), Ethiopia-116 (33.9%), Jordan-117 (Official), Lebanon-118 (59.7%), Cameroon-119 (20%), Nigeria-120 (50%), Algeria-121 (Official), Turkey-122 (99.8%), Egypt-123 (90%), Syria-124 (90%), Iran, Islamic Rep.-125 (Official), Nepal-126 (4.2%), Oman-127 (Ibadhi Muslim 75%, Sunni/Shia and Hindu 25%), Benin-128 (24.4%), Morocco-129 (Official), Côte d'Ivoire-130 (38.6%), Saudi Arabia-131 (Official), Mali-132 (90%), Pakistan-133 (Official), Chad-134 (53.1%), Yemen-135 (Official).

11

Whom Your Right Hands Possess

Narrated 'Aisha:..the hand of Allah's Messenger did not touch any woman's hand except the hand of the woman that his right hand possessed (i.e., his captives or his lady-slaves).[632]

Women Captives and the Koran

The unenviable status of a Muslim woman under Sharia Law pales in comparison to the status of a non-Muslim woman captured by Muslims during battle. Such a captive falls under the category of those "whom your right hands possess."[633] She then becomes a slave to her Muslim captor and it becomes "legal" for him to have intercourse with her. This is authorized by Chapter 4, Verse 24 of the Koran, which begins by stating

> *Also (forbidden are) women already married, except those (slaves) whom your right hands possess. Thus has Allah ordained for you...*

Ibn Kathir explained the meaning of this verse:

---

632 *Sahih Al-Bukhari*, Vol. 9, Book 93, No. 7214, p. 203.

633 The use of the phrase "whom your right hands possess" in reference to captured women and/or slave girls is found in both the Koran (e.g. 4:3, 4:24-25, 23:6, 24:31, 33:50, 33:52, and 70:30) and the *hadiths*, where it was used by Muhammad (e.g., *Sunan Ibn Majah*, Vol. 3, No. 1920, p. 101; *Sunan Abu Dawud*, Vol. 4, No. 4017, p. 381; and *Jami' At-Tirmidhi*, Vol. 5, No. 2769, p. 141). The phrase was also used by some Muslims in general (e.g., *Sahih Al-Bukhari*, Vol. 7, Book 67, No. 5159, p. 69; and *Sunan An-Nasa'i*, Vol. 4, No. 3384, p. 185).

> *The Ayah* [verse] *means, you are prohibited from marrying women who are already married, (except those whom your right hands possess) except those whom you acquire through war, for you are allowed such women after making sure they are not pregnant. Imam Ahmad recorded that Abu Sa'id Al-Khudri said, "We captured some women from the area of Awtas who were already married, and we disliked having sexual relations with them because they already had husbands. So, we asked the Prophet about this matter, and this Ayah was revealed...Consequently we had sexual relations with these women.*[634]

This was also reported in *Sahih Muslim* in a chapter titled:

> *It Is Permissible To Have Sexual Intercourse With A Captive Woman After She Is Purified (Of Menses Or Delivery) In Case She Has A Husband, Her Marriage Is Abrogated After She Becomes Captive*[635]

---

634 *Tafsir Ibn Kathir*, Vol. 2, p. 422. This situation regarding what to do with the captured women from Awtas, with the same conclusion, was also reported in *Al-Wahidi's Asbab al-Nuzul*, p. 71; *Sunan Abu Dawud*, Vol. 2, No. 2155, pp. 555-556; *Jami' At-Tirmidhi*, Vol. 2, No. 1132, pp. 502-503; and Vol. 5, Nos. 3016-3017, pp. 331-332; and *Sunan An-Nasa'i*, Vol. 4, No. 3335, p. 155.

A modern commentary pointed out that this became a *permanent principle*:

> *For a solution and as a permanent principle regarding war captives, particularly those who are given a female captive as their share from the spoils of war, even though her non-believer and polytheist husband is alive; the recipient was allowed to have sexual intercourse with her after finding out the condition of her womb...*

Jami' At-Tirmidhi, Vol. 5, Comments to *Hadith* No. 3016, p. 331.

635 *Sahih Muslim*, Vol. 4, Nos. 1456-1456R4, pp. 386-387. The translator pointed out that the phrase *those whom your right hands possess* "denotes slave

In the *Tafsir Al-Jalalayn*, the phrase *slaves whom your right hands possess* is stated as *those you have taken in war as slaves*. And this *tafsir* explained that,

> *You may have relations with them if they have husbands in the Abode of War after istibra' (the waiting period to ascertain whether they are pregnant).*[636]

The modern *Tafsir Ahsanul-Bayan* explained 4:24 this way:

> *The historical background of the verse is that when pagan women were captured by Muslims in battles, they disliked having intercourse with them because they had husbands. The Companions asked the Messenger of Allah about it. Thereupon, this verse was revealed. This verse allowed the Muslims to have intercourse with pagan women if they were captured in battles even if they had husbands, providing their wombs have been cleansed, that is, after one menses or, in case they are pregnant, after the delivery of the child.*[637]

---

girls, i.e. women who were captured in the holy war." He goes on to note that there is supposed to be a procedural delay to the raping of those captured women:

> *The Muslims are not permitted to have sexual intercourse indiscriminately after they are captured. They can do it only after they are properly delivered to their charge by the head of the Islamic State or someone else on his behalf.*

Ibid., p. 387, n. 1. So instead of the Muslim warriors "indiscriminately" raping captured women, the warriors are allowed to rape only those specific women who have been "properly delivered" to them.

636 *Tafsir Al-Jalalayn*, p. 185. This explanation was also mentioned in the *Tafsir Ibn 'Abbas*, p. 103.

637 *Tafsir Ahsanul-Bayan*, Vol. 1, pp. 441-442.

The commentary about this verse in the *Tafsir Ahsanul-Bayan* continued under a section titled *Problem of slave women.* The commentary stated that slavery had originated "from two main causes." The first was "an unending cycle of tribal warfare" which "gave rise to a continual flow of captives."

> *...The second source was Islamic wars. Women captured in these wars were distributed among Muslim soldiers who kept them as slave girls. In the absence of any international covenant governing these captives, keeping them as slaves was the only solution possible, since leaving them would result in a great deal of corruption in public life. Married Muslim women are prohibited. And so are unbelieving women, except for those who are captured by Muslims, after their wombs have become clear.*[638]

It is interesting to note that this modern *tafsir* identified "Islamic wars" as one of the two main causes of slavery. And it reiterated that Muslim warriors were given slave girls from among the women captives, who, after a specified waiting period, could be legally raped by their new Muslim owners.

And, although a Muslim was limited to no more than four wives, there were no limitations on the number of slave girls he could possess.[639]

---

638 Ibid., p. 442.

639 From the commentaries on 33:50 of the Koran: *Tafsir Ibn Kathir*, Vol. 7, p. 724; *Tafsir Ibn 'Abbas*. p. 551; *Tafsir Ahsanul-Bayan*, Vol. 4, p. 402; and *Tafsir Al-Jalalayn*, p. 907. The lack of limits on the number of slave girls is also noted by the Hanafi School, which states that "one may collect as many slave women as one wishes," without "reckoning the number even if it exceeds a thousand." See *The Kitab al-Athar of Imam Abu Hanifah*, 134.457 and n. 1347, p. 263.

Women Captives and Sharia Law

It is interesting to note that the founders of the four major Sunni schools of Sharia Law agreed that

> *when a married woman becomes a prisoner of war without her husband, her contract of marriage with her husband ends, and her new master has the right to have sexual relations with her after the birth of a child if she is pregnant, or after waiting a while to confirm the status of her womb if she is not apparently pregnant.*[640]

The Hanafi school, the largest of these schools, stated it this way in an explanatory footnote while discussing what 4:24 said about married women taken in war:

> *Although the ayah literally says, "Those whom your right hands own," it refers here to slaves taken in war, since a man may not have sexual relations with one of his slave women who is in a legitimate marriage. Wives of combatants captured in war are automatically divorced and are thus not under this restriction.*[641]

The Shafi'i school stated:

> *When a child or a woman is taken captive, they become slaves by the fact of capture, and the woman's previous marriage is immediately annulled.*[642]

---

640 *Jami' At-Tirmidhi*, Vol. 2, Comments, p. 503.

641 *The Kitab al-Athar of Imam Abu Hanifah*, 114.390, n. 1217, p. 225.

642 *Reliance of the Traveller*, o9.13. Although this is a Shafi'i book of Sharia Law, the introduction to *Reliance of the Traveller* pointed out that in 1990, Dr. Taha Jabir al-Alwani, then-President of the Fiqh [Islamic Jurisprudence] Council of North America, and then-President of the International Institute of Islamic Thought located in Northern Virginia, said of this English translation (p. xviii):

Women Captives and Muhammad

Muhammad himself was quite involved in distributing women captives and allowing them to be raped. After the defeat of the Jewish Bani Qurayzah tribe, Muhammad divided up that tribe's "property, wives, and children" among the Muslims.[643] And after the defeat of the Jews at Khaybar, Muhammad had the women of Khaybar "distributed among the Muslims."[644]

Although on another occasion Muhammad did place some restrictions on his warriors:

> *Ruwaifi' bin Thabit Al-Ansari narrated: "A person stood up among us to deliver a sermon, and said: 'I only say to you what I heard the Messenger of Allah say on the Day of Hunain. He said: "It is not permissible for a man who believes in Allah and the Last Day that he discharges his water to a field that belongs to another" - meaning pregnant women, "and it is not permissible for a man who believes in Allah and the Last Day that he uses a slave*

> *There is no doubt that this translation is a valuable and important work, whether as a textbook for teaching Islamic jurisprudence to English-speakers, or as a legal reference for use by scholars, educated laymen, and students in this language...its aim is to imbue the consciousness of the non-Arabic-speaking Muslim with a sound understanding of Sacred Law...*

In 1991 this English translation was certified by the Islamic Research Academy of Al-Azhar University in Cairo, Egypt, to correspond "to the Arabic original," and it "conforms to the practice and faith of the orthodox Sunni Community" [my emphasis]. (p. xx)

643 *The Life of Muhammad*, p. 466.

644 Ibid., p. 511.

> *woman (sexually) until he confirms that she is free (of pregnancy)..."*[645]

Muhammad's attitude about how captured women could be treated was further shown in the glaring example of how Muhammad condoned the rape of female captives from the Mustaliq tribe. We can see that the only problem to be resolved in the *sahih hadith* below was whether or not the ransom the Muslims were expecting for these particular female captives would be affected if the captives were returned pregnant. In response to the question about whether the Muslim warriors should therefore engage in *coitus interruptus* with their rape victims, Muhammad, instead of prohibiting the rapes, merely said that *coitus interruptus* would not matter because every soul that was destined to be born would be born:

> *Abu Sirma said to Abu Sa'id Al Khudri (Allah he pleased with him): O Abu Sa'id, did you hear Allah's Messenger (SAW) mentioning al-'azl* [coitus interruptus]*? He said: Yes, and added: We went out with Allah's Messenger (SAW) on the expedition to the Bi'l-Mustaliq. We took captive some excellent Arab women. We desired them, for we were suffering from the absence of our wives, (but at the same time) we also desired ransom for them. So we decided to have sexual intercourse with them but by observing 'azl...But we said: We are doing an act whereas Allah's Messenger is amongst us; why not ask him? So we asked Allah's Messenger (SAW), and he said: It does not matter if you do not do it, for every soul that is to be born up to the Day of Resurrection will be born.*[646]

---

645 *Sunan Abu Dawud*, Vol. 2, No. 2158, pp. 556-557.

646 *Sahih Muslim*, Vol. 4, No. 1438, p. 373. For similar *hadiths* about the captured Bani al-Mustaliq women, see *Sahih Al-Bukhari*, Vol. 3, Book 49, No. 2542, pp. 413-414; Vol. 5, Book 64, No. 4138, pp. 278-279; and Vol. 9, Book 97, No. 7409, pp. 303-304; and *Sunan Abu Dawud*, Vol. 2, No. 2172, pp. 564-565.

It was reported that *coitus interruptus* was one of the ten "characteristics" that Muhammad disliked - see *Sunan Abu Dawud*, Vol. 4, No. 4222, p. 474.

And Muhammad appeared to have no problem with even the general idea of raping female captives:

> *Narrated Abu Sa'id Al-Khudri: We got female captives in the war booty and we used to do coitus interruptus with them. So we asked Allah's Messenger about it and he said, "Do you really do that?" repeating the question thrice, "There is no person that is destined to exist but will come into existence, till the Day of Resurrection."*[647]

So according to Muhammad, there was no question about whether or not a woman captive would be raped by her Muslim captor; it was just a matter of when it would happen. And, as pointed out earlier, the only determining factor with regard to the timing was whether or not she was pregnant.

Muhammad even approved of Ali bin Abi Talib, his cousin and son-in-law, and the subsequent fourth caliph, having sex with a captured slave girl; and Muhammad said that Ali deserved even more than that:

> *Narrated Buraida: The Prophet sent 'Ali to Khalid to bring the Khumus (of the booty) and I hated 'Ali, and 'Ali had taken a bath (after a sexual act with a slave-girl from the Khumus). I said to Khalid, "Don't you see this (i.e., 'Ali)?" When we reached the Prophet I mentioned that to him. He said, "O Buraida! Do you hate 'Ali?" I said, "Yes." He said, "Don't hate him, for he deserves more than that from the Khumus."*[648]

---

647 *Sahih Al-Bukhari*, Vol. 7, Book 67, No. 5210, p. 97. For similar *hadiths* see *Sahih Al-Bukhari*, Vol. 3, Book 34, No. 2229, p. 239; and Vol. 8, Book 82, No. 6603, p. 319.

648 *Sahih Al-Bukhari*, Vol. 5, Book 64, No. 4350, p. 387. The *Khumus* is the one-fifth of the war booty given in Allah's Cause, a portion of which went to Muhammad.

It is interesting to note how Muhammad reacted when four Muslims complained to him about Ali doing this on another occasion:

> *'Imran bin Husain narrated that the Messenger of Allah dispatched an army and he put 'Ali bin Abi Talib in charge of it. He left on the expedition and he entered upon a female slave. So four of the Companions of the Messenger of Allah scolded him, and they made a pact saying: "[If] we meet the Messenger of Allah we will inform him of what 'Ali did."*[649]

When the army returned, the four Muslims took turns complaining to Muhammad about Ali's conduct. Muhammad became angry and said to them:

> *"What do you want from 'Ali?! Indeed 'Ali is from me, and I am from him, and he is the ally of every believer after me."*[650]

The modern commentary for this *hadith* explained that the phrase *'Ali is from me and I am from him* meant not only the family connection, but it was "also to emphasize" that Ali's "conduct and character resembles" that of Muhammad.[651]

And, in case there had been any question about the matter, the Koran specifically made women captives legal for Muhammad:

Chapter 33, Verse 50

> *O Prophet (Muhammad)! Verily, We have made lawful to you your wives, to whom you have paid their Mahr (bridal-money given by the husband to his wife at the time*

---

649 *Jami' At-Tirmidhi*, Vol. 6, No. 3712, p. 386.

650 Ibid., pp. 386-387.

651 Ibid., p. 387.

> *of marriage), and those (slaves) whom your right hand possesses - whom Allah has given to you...*

As Ibn Kathir explained this verse,

> *those (slaves) whom your right hand possesses whom Allah has given to you, means, 'the slave girls whom you took from the war booty are also permitted to you.' He* [Muhammad] *owned Safiyyah and Juwayriyah, then he manumitted them and married them, and he owned Rayhanah bint Sham'un An-Nadariyyah and Mariyah Al-Qibtiyyah, the mother of his son Ibrahim, upon him be peace; they were both among the prisoners, may Allah be pleased with them.*[652]

The *Tafsir Al-Jalalayn* presented the first part of the verse in this manner:

> *O Prophet, We have made lawful for you: your wives to whom you have given dowries and any slavegirls you own from the booty Allah has allotted you - from among those unbelievers you have captured, such as Safiyya and Juwayriyya...*[653]

The *Tafsir Ibn 'Abbas* explained this verse in the following manner:

> *(O Prophet! Lo! We have made lawful unto thee thy wives unto whom thou hast paid their dowries, and those whom thy right hand possesseth) Maria the Copt (of those whom Allah hath given thee as spoils of war...*[654]

---

[652] *Tafsir Ibn Kathir*, Vol. 7, p. 720.

[653] *Tafsir Al-Jalalayn*, p. 907.

[654] *Tafsir Ibn 'Abbas*, p. 551.

The *Tafsir Ahsanul-Bayan* explained about the slaves:

> *The reference is to his slave girls who were four in number: Safiyah, Juwairiyah, Raihanah and Mariya Al-Qibtiyyah (the Copt). As for the first two (Safiyah and Juwairiyah), he set them free and later married them. Raihanah and Mariyah remained with him as slave-girls.*[655]

There is another verse of the Koran that specifically addressed the issue of slave girls for Muhammad:

Chapter 33, Verse 52

> *It is not lawful for you (to marry other) women after this, nor to change them for other wives even though their beauty attracts you, except those (slaves) whom your right hand possesses. And Allah is Ever a Watcher over all things.*

Some Muslim scholars believed that this verse was "revealed" after 33:50 and during the period when Muhammad had nine wives at one time; others said any restrictions in this verse pertaining to wives was actually abrogated by 33:50.[656] Nevertheless, here we have a second verse saying that Muhammad could have as many slave girls as he liked.[657]

---

655 *Tafsir Ahsanul-Bayan*, Vol. 4, p. 402.

656 *Tafsir Ibn Kathir*, Vol. 8, pp. 21-22.

657 Ibid., Vol. 8, p. 22 (*He was forbidden to marry more women...except for those whom his right hand possessed (slave women).*); *Tafsir Ahsanul-Bayan*, Vol. 4, p. 405 (*This ban did not apply to keeping slave-girls.*); and *Tafsir Al-Jalalayn*, p. 908 (*...any you own as slaves - who are still lawful for you*).

Conclusion

Among the many claims you hear is that Islam does not allow slavery and women are treated well under Islam. With this chapter we have seen that the Koran itself allows the enslavement of women war captives and the legal rape of those captives. Lest there be any doubt, we have the examples and teachings of Muhammad to support such treatment. And remember, Muhammad speaks for Allah and is still considered the timeless standard for good conduct by a Muslim.

12

The Pact of 'Umar

Introduction

As Islam expanded after Muhammad's death, many of the conquered lands were inhabited by Jews and Christians who, instead of converting to Islam, accepted second class status as *Dhimmis* and paid the *Jizyah* (as required by 9:29 of the Koran). This led to the necessity of creating a procedure for how the Muslims were to deal with large populations of *Dhimmis*.

The Pact of 'Umar was reportedly a treaty between 'Umar, the second Caliph, and the conquered Christians of Syria, circa 637. And although Jews were not specifically mentioned in the Pact, it was nevertheless generally considered a model for how Muslims were to deal with both Jewish and Christian populations. One can find various versions of this Pact. The version used here is found in the *Tafsir Ibn Kathir*.

Ibn Kathir wrote about the Pact of 'Umar in a section titled *Paying Jizyah is a Sign of Kufr* [disbelief] *and Disgrace*, which was part of Ibn Kathir's explanation of the meaning of 9:29 of the Koran. As we saw in Chapter 5, *The Religion of Peace*, 9:29 consists of Allah's orders to the Muslims to fight against the Jews and Christians

> *until they pay the Jizyah with willing submission, and feel themselves subdued.*

Ibn Kathir said that because of this,

> *Muslims are not allowed to honor the people of Dhimmah or elevate them above Muslims, for they are miserable, disgraced and humiliated.*[658]

---

658 *Tafsir Ibn Kathir*, Vol. 4, p. 406.

Ibn Kathir then quoted Muhammad:

> *Do not initiate the Salam* [greeting] *to the Jews and Christians, and if you meet any of them in a road, force them to its narrowest alley.*[659]

With this as an introduction, Ibn Kathir then wrote the following about the Pact of 'Umar:

The Pact of 'Umar

> *This is why the Leader of the faithful 'Umar bin Al-Khattab, may Allah be pleased with him, demanded his well-known conditions be met by the Christians, these conditions that ensured their continued humiliation, degradation and disgrace.*
>
> *The scholars of Hadith narrated from 'Abdur-Rahman bin Ghanm Al-Ash'ari that he said, "I recorded for 'Umar bin Al-Khattab, may Allah be pleased with him, the terms of the treaty of peace he conducted with the Christians of Ash-Sham* [Syria]*:*
>
> *'In the Name of Allah, Most Gracious, Most Merciful. This is a document to the servant of Allah 'Umar, the Leader of the faithful, from the Christians of such and such city. When you (Muslims) came to us we requested safety for ourselves, children, property and followers of our religion. We made a condition on ourselves that we will neither erect in our areas a monastery, church, or a sanctuary for a monk, nor restore any place of worship that needs restoration nor use any of them for the purpose of enmity against Muslims. We will not prevent any Muslim from resting in our churches whether they come by day or night, and we will open the doors [of our houses of worship] for the wayfarer and passerby. Those Muslims who come as guests, will enjoy boarding and food for three days. We will not*

659 Ibid.

allow a spy against Muslims into our churches and homes or hide deceit [or betrayal] against Muslims. We will not teach our children the Qur'an, publicize practices of Shirk, invite anyone to Shirk or prevent any of our fellows from embracing Islam, if they choose to do so. We will respect Muslims, move from the places we sit in if they choose to sit in them. We will not imitate their clothing, caps, turbans, sandals, hairstyles, speech, nicknames and title names, or ride on saddles, hang swords on the shoulders, collect weapons of any kind or carry these weapons. We will not encrypt our stamps in Arabic, or sell liquor. We will have the front of our hair cut, wear our customary clothes wherever we are, wear belts around our waist, refrain from erecting crosses on the outside of our churches and demonstrating them and our books in public in Muslim fairways and markets. We will not sound the bells in our churches, except discretely, or raise our voices while reciting our holy books inside our churches in the presence of Muslims, nor raise our voices [with prayer] at our funerals, or light torches in funeral processions in the fairways of Muslims, or their markets. We will not bury our dead next to Muslim dead, or buy servants who were captured by Muslims. We will be guides for Muslims and refrain from breaching their privacy in their homes.'

When I gave this document to 'Umar, he added to it, "We will not beat any Muslim. These are the conditions that we set against ourselves and followers of our religion in return for safety and protection. If we break any of these promises that we set for your benefit against ourselves, then our Dhimmah (promise of protection) is broken and you are allowed to do with us what you are allowed of people of defiance and rebellion.'"[660]

This leaves us still looking for that common heritage, common linkages, and common pieces of respectful dialogue.

---

660 Ibid., pp. 406-407.

13

Why 5 Daily Prayers?

The Prophet said, "O Lord, my followers are weak in their bodies, hearts, hearing and constitution, so lighten our burden."[661]

Making Things Easier

The number of daily prayers required for a Muslim was determined by Allah when Muhammad made his "Night Journey" from Mecca to the seven levels of Heaven. He was accompanied by the angel *Jibril* (Gabriel) and rode on *Al-Buraq*, a white, horse-like animal, smaller than a mule and bigger than a donkey.

Jibril took Muhammad to each level of Heaven. On the first level of Heaven Muhammad was introduced to Adam. He went to the second level and met *Isa* (Jesus) and *Yahya* (John). On the third level he met *Yusuf* (Joseph). On the fourth level he met a prophet named *Idris*.[662] On the fifth level he met *Harun* (Aaron). On the sixth level he met *Musa* (Moses). On the seventh level he met *Ibrahim* (Abraham) and was shown *Al-Bait-ul-Ma'mur* (Allah's House). It was here that Muhammad received the command from Allah that Muslims were to actually pray fifty times a day. Muhammad accepted this, started to descend,

---

661 *Sahih Al-Bukhari*, Vol. 9, Book 97, No. 7517, p. 371.

662 *Idris* was mentioned as a prophet and *man of truth* in 19:56 of the Koran. He was also mentioned as "among the patient" in 21:85. The *Tafsir Al-Jalalayn* said that *Idris* was the great-grandfather of Noah - see p. 656. The *Tafsir Ahsanul-Bayan* explained that *Idris* was the first prophet after Adam, and the father or grandfather of Noah; *Idris* was also "he who stitched garments first." See *Tafsir Ahsanul-Bayan*, Vol. 3, pp. 421-422.

and then Musa stopped him and asked, "O Muhammad! What did your Lord enjoin upon you?" The Prophet replied, "He enjoined upon me to perform fifty Salat (prayers) in a day and a night." Musa said, "Your followers cannot do that. Go back so that your Lord may reduce it for you and for them." So the Prophet turned to Jibril (Gabriel) as if he wanted to consult him about that issue. Jibril (Gabriel) told him of his opinion, saying, "Yes, if you wish." So ascended with him [Jibril (Gabriel)] to the Irresistible and said while he was in his place, "O Lord, please lighten our burden as my followers cannot do that." So Allah deducted for him ten Salat (prayers) whereupon he returned to Moses who stopped him again and kept on sending him back to his Lord till the enjoined Salat (prayers) were reduced to only five Salat (prayers).[663]

But Moses was worried that even five prayers a day would be too much of a burden for Muhammad's followers, who Moses said were weaker than the Jews:

O Muhammad! By Allah! I tried to persuade my nation, Bani Isra'el to do less than this, but they could not do it and gave it up. However, your followers are weaker in body, heart, sight and hearing, so return to your Lord so that he may lighten your burden.[664]

After discussing the matter, Muhammad and *Jibril* returned to Allah.

The Prophet said, "O Lord, my followers are weak in their bodies, hearts, hearing and constitution, so lighten our burden." On that the Irresistible said, "O Muhammad...The Word that comes from Me does not

---

663 *Sahih Al-Bukhari*, Vol. 9, Book 97, No. 7517, pp. 370-371.

664 Ibid., p. 371.

change, so it will be as I enjoined on you in the Mother of the Book." Allah added, "Every good deed will be rewarded as ten times so it is fifty Salat (prayers) in the Mother of the Book (in reward) but you are to perform only five (in practise).'[665]

On being advised of this, Moses actually urged Muhammad to try one more time to get a reduction in the number of prayers, but Muhammad declined.[666]

So instead of fifty, the Muslims are required to pray only five times a day because, as Muhammad told Allah, the Muslims needed to have a lighter "burden" of prayer.

Making Things Easier in Battle

It is interesting to note that this lightening of the burden also happened in the Koran with regard to another matter. The below verse ordered Muslims to stand and fight their enemies even if the Muslims were outnumbered 10-to-1:

Chapter 8, Verse 65

> *O Prophet (Muhammad)! Urge the believers to fight. If there are twenty steadfast persons amongst you , they will overcome two hundred, and if there be a hundred steadfast persons they will overcome a thousand of those*

---

665 Ibid.

666 There are other reports of Muhammad's Night Journey and the prayer requirement, e.g.: *Sahih Al-Bukhari*, Vol. 1, Book 8, No. 349, pp. 237-239; and Vol. 4, Book 59, No. 3207, pp. 272-275; *Sahih Muslim*, Vol. 1, Nos. 162, and 163-164, pp. 113-119; *Sunan An-Nasa'i*, Vol. 1, Nos. 449-452, pp. 262-269; The *Life of Muhammad*, pp. 181-187; and *The Sealed Nectar*, pp. 178-183.

who disbelieve, because they (the disbelievers) are a people who do not understand.

This caused consternation among the Muslims because of the odds involved in this order to fight the disbelievers. As a result, the following verse was revealed that abrogated Verse 65 and ordered the Muslims to stand and fight only if the odds were not greater than two-to-one:

Chapter 8, Verse 66

> *Now Allah has lightened your (task), for He knows that there is weakness in you. So, if there are of you a hundred steadfast persons, they shall overcome two hundred, and if there are a thousand of you, they shall overcome two thousand with the Leave of Allah. And Allah is with As-Sabirun (the patient).*

Consequently, if the odds were greater than two-to-one against the Muslims, they were not obligated to fight.[667]

So when it came to prayer and combat, Allah lightened the task for his believers.

---

[667] *Tafsir Ibn Kathir*, Vol. 4, pp. 352-353; *Tafsir Ahsanul-Bayan*, Vol. 2, pp. 312-313; *Tafsir Al-Jalalayn*, pp. 392-393; *Tafsir Ibn 'Abbas*, p. 225; and *Sahih Al-Bukhari*, Vol. 6, Book 65, No. 4653, pp. 137-138.

14

Nature of Paradise

Muhammad said the gates of Paradise were only open on Monday and Thursday, and it was on these two days that the deeds of people would be presented to Allah; but those who associated anything with Allah (*Shirk*) would not be admitted to Paradise.[668] However, some of the Muslims would be very lucky, because Muhammad said that 70,000 of them would enter Paradise without even having to account for their lives.[669]

So what is the nature of this Paradise? As we will see, it is a Paradise of sensual pleasures.

Physical Description

Muhammad provided the details about the physical description of Paradise. He said that there were one hundred levels of Paradise, and the distance between two levels was either one hundred years or "like what is between the heavens and the earth."[670]

---

[668] *Sahih Muslim*, Vol. 7, Nos. 2565-2565R2, p. 174. This was also mentioned in *Sunan Abu Dawud*, Vol. 5, No. 4916, p. 319; and *Jami' At-Tirmidhi*, Vol. 4, No. 2023, p. 106.

[669] *Sahih Al-Bukhari*, Vol. 7, Book No. 77, No. 5811, p. 387; and Vol. 8, Book No. 81, No. 6541, pp. 293-294. Although one narrator said the actual number mentioned by Muhammad could have been 700,000 - see *Sahih Al-Bukhari*, Vol. 8, Book No. 81, No. 6543, pp. 294-295.

[670] *Jami' At-Tirmidhi*, Vol. 4, Nos. 2529-2530, pp. 518-519.

There were pavilions with women in Paradise:

> *Narrated 'Abdullah bin Qais: Allah's Messenger said, "In Paradise there is a pavilion made of a single hollow pearl, sixty miles wide, in each corner of which there are wives who will not see those in the other corners; and the believers will visit and enjoy them.*[671]

And Muhammad said these pavilions were 30 miles in height.[672]

Muhammad said there was a river in Paradise named *Al-Kauthar*, the banks of which were made of tents of hollow pearls;[673] although in another narration he said the banks were made of gold.[674] The river bed was made of rubies and pearls.[675] This river was so wide that it took a month to cross it, its water was whiter than milk, and whoever drank from it would never be thirsty again.[676]

There were even oceans:

> *Hakim bin Mu'awiyah narrated from his father, that the Prophet said: "Indeed in Paradise there is a sea of water, and a sea of honey, and a sea of milk, and a sea of wine, then the rivers shall split off afterwards.*[677]

---

671 *Sahih Al-Bukhari*, Vol. 6, Book No. 65, No. 4879, p. 335.

672 Ibid., Vol. 4, Book No. 59, No. 3243, p. 291.

673 Ibid., Vol. 6, Book No. 65, No. 4964, p. 411.

674 *Jami' At-Tirmidhi*, Vol. 6, No. 3361, p. 92.

675 *Sunan Ibn Majah*, Vol. 5, No. 4334, p. 420.

676 *Sahih Al-Bukhari*, Vol. 8, Book No. 81, No. 6579, p. 310. A somewhat similar description is given in 47:15 of the Koran.

677 *Jami' At-Tirmidhi*, Vol. 4, No. 2571, p. 554.

Muhammad said that every tree in Paradise had a trunk of gold.[678] He told Muslims not to wear silk or use silver or gold plates or cups - those were for the disbelievers in this world and for the Muslims in Paradise.[679] And according to 18:31 of the Koran, the inhabitants of Paradise would wear bracelets of gold, green garments of thick fine silk, and recline on raised thrones.

Food and drink would be plentiful, but with no ill effects:

> *Jabir b. Abdullah reported that Allah's Messenger (may peace be upon him) said that the inmates of Paradise would eat therein and they would also drink, but they would neither void excrement, nor suffer catarrh, nor pass water, and their eating (would be digested) in the form of belching and their sweat would be musk and they would glorify and praise Allah as easily as you breathe.*[680]

And clothes would never wear out nor youth decline:

> *Abu Huraira reported that Allah's Apostle (may peace be upon him) had said: He who would get into Paradise (would enjoy such an everlasting) bliss that he would neither become destitute, nor would his clothes wear out, nor his youth would decline.*[681]

---

678 Ibid., No. 2525, p. 515.

679 *Sahih Al-Bukhari*, Vol. 7, Book No. 70, No. 5426, pp. 210-211.

680 *Sahih Muslim*, Vol. 8, No. 2835R2, p. 311.

681 Ibid., No. 2836, p. 311.

Beautiful Virgin Wives

Muhammad said that each Muslim male would receive two beautiful wives from among the *Hur*[682] in Paradise:

> *Narrated Abu Hurairah: Allah's Messenger said, "The first group (of people) who will enter Paradise will be (glittering) like the moon on a full-moon night. They will neither spit therein nor blow their noses nor relieve nature. Their utensils therein will be of gold and their combs of gold and silver; in their censers the aloeswood will be used, and their sweat will smell like musk. Everyone of them will have two wives; the marrow of the bones of the wives' legs will be seen through the flesh out of excessive beauty...*[683]

And

> *Narrated Abu Hurairah: The Prophet said, "...everyone will have two wives from the Hur, (who will be so beautiful, pure and transparent that) the marrow of the bones of their legs will be seen through the bones and the flesh."*[684]

And these two wives were especially a reward for one who died as a martyr fighting in Allah's Cause:

---

682 *Hur*: "Very fair females created by Allah as such not from the offspring of Adam, with intense black irises of their eyes and intense white scleras." See *Sahih Al-Bukhari*, Vol. 9, Glossary, pp. 410-411. They are also referred to as *Al-Huril-'Ayn*, *Al-Hoor Al-'lyn*, and *Houris*.

683 *Sahih Al-Bukhari*, Vol. 4, Book No. 59, No. 3245, p. 292.

684 Ibid., No. 3254, p. 295.

He [the martyr]*was brought to the apostle and laid behind him and covered by his shepherd's cloak. The apostle, who was accompanied by a number of his companions, turned towards him and then turned away. When they asked him why, he said, 'He has with him now his two wives from the dark-eyed houris.' 'Abdullah b. Abu Najih told me that he was told that, when a martyr is slain, his two wives from the dark-eyed houris pet him, wiping the dust from his face, saying the while, 'May God put dust on the face of the man who put dust on your face, and slay him who slew you!'*[685]

The Koran further describes these women in paradise:

1. Chapter 55, Verse 56

Wherein both will be Qasirat-ut-Tarf [chaste females (wives) restraining their glances, desiring none except their husbands], with whom no man or jinni has had Tamth [sexual intercourse] *before them.*

Ibn Kathir explained:

> *Wherein will be, meaning on these couches or beds, Qasirat At-Tarf, chaste females, wives restraining their glances, desiring none except their husbands, seeing them as the most beautiful men in Paradise...Allah said, whom never deflowered a human before nor Jinn, meaning they are delightful virgins of comparable age who never had sexual intercourse with anyone, whether from mankind or Jinns, before their husbands.*[686]

---

685 *The Life of Muhammad*, p. 519.

686 *Tafsir Ibn Kathir*, Vol. 9, p. 400. *Jinns* (*Jaann, Jinniyy*) were beings created from fire by Allah.

2. Chapter 56, Verses 34-37

And on couches or thrones raised high. Verily, We have created them (maidens) of special creation. And made them virgins. Loving (their husbands only), (and) of equal age.

Ibn Kathir explained these verses:

> *The Ayat describe the women who will be on the beds and couches... Verily, We have created them, meaning, in the other life, after they became old in this life, they were brought back while virgin, youthful, being delightfully passionate with their husbands, beautiful, kind and cheerful.*[687]

The *Tafsir Al-Jalalayn* noted that these verses referred to "houris who were created without being born" and "whenever their husbands come to them, they find them virgins."[688]

3. Chapter 78, Verses 31-34

Verily, for the Muttaqun [pious Muslims], *there will be a success (Paradise); Gardens and vineyards, and young full-breasted (mature) maidens of equal age, and a full cup (of wine).*

The *Tafsir Ahsanul-Bayan* explained:

> *The idea is that these maidens will have swelling bosoms, an index of their voluptuous beauty.*[689]

---

687 Ibid., pp. 428-429.

688 *Tafsir Al-Jalalayn*, p. 1161.

689 *Tafsir Ahsanul-Bayan (Part 30)*, p. 24.

Ibn Kathir wrote:

> *...meaning wide-eyed maidens with fully developed breasts. Ibn 'Abbas, Mujahid and others have said.."This means round breasts. They meant by this that the breasts of these girls will be fully rounded and not sagging, because they will be virgins, equal in ages. This means that they will only have one age."*[690]

And the Tafsir Ibn' Abbas stated that the *maidens* were *maidens for companions*, 33 years of age.[691]

The beautiful female virgins waiting in Paradise are mentioned in additional verses of the Koran: e.g. 37:48-49, 38:52, 44:54, 52:20, 55:70-76, and 56:22-24.

And if you met a certain requirement, you could actually have your choice of the beautiful women of Paradise:

> *It was narrated from Sahl bin Mu'adh bin Anas, from his father, that the Messenger of Allah said: "Whoever restrains his anger when he is able to implement it, Allah will call him before all of creation on the Day of Resurrection, and will give him his choice of any houri that he wants.*[692]

---

690 *Tafsir Ibn Kathir*, Vol. 10, pp. 333-334. Ibn Kathir stated that some scholars said this "one age" was 33 - see *Tafsir Ibn Kathir*, Vol. 9, p. 430. The reason for this age was that it "is the average age of youthfulness, beauty and perfect physical built" - see Abdul-Halim ibn Muhammad Nassar As-Salafi, *Description of Paradise in the Glorious Qur'an* (Riyadh, Kingdom of Saudi Arabia: Darussalam, 2010), p. 207.

691 *Tafsir Ibn 'Abbas*, p. 834.

692 *Sunan Ibn Majah*, Vol. 5, No. 4186, p. 331. The commentary for this *hadith* pointed out:

And not only was the Muslim male to be given beautiful wives in Paradise, he was to be given sexual prowess:

> *Anas narrated that the Prophet said: "The believer shall be given in Paradise such and such strength in intercourse." It was said: "O Messenger of Allah! And will he be able to do that ?" He said: "He will be given the strength of a hundred."*[693]

There was a similar report from a different narrator:

> *Abu Al-Qasim At-Tabarani recorded that Abu Hurayrah said that the Messenger of Allah was asked, "O Allah's Messenger! Will we have sexual intercourse with our wives in Paradise?" He said, "The man will be able to have sexual intercourse with a hundred virgins in one day."*[694]

> *In Paradise, every man will get beautiful women, but whoever controls his anger and avoids being unjust to people, then for him is a special reward. Such a person is allowed to select beautiful women of Paradise for himself.*

693 *Jami' At-Tirmidhi*, Vol. 4, No. 2536, p. 523. The commentary for this *hadith* pointed out:

> *All the bounties bestowed upon the people of Paradise will be endless with no fear of their dwindling or diminishing. No weakness, therefore, shall occur for the male partners after having conjugal relations umpteen times with their consorts.*

Ibid., p. 524

Muhammad's statement about *the strength of a hundred* was also reported in *Tafsir Ibn Kathir*, Vol. 9, p. 429.

694 *Tafsir Ibn Kathir*, Vol. 9, p. 429.

It is evident that each Muslim male will have at least two wives in Paradise. But there were reports that he could actually have seventy-two wives. This idea of seventy-two wives has been questioned by, among others, Irshad Manji, then-Director of the Moral Courage Project, New York University:

> *I don't see any of it is in the Koran for the pledge of seventy-two virgins. This notion of seventy-two virgins actually comes from a mistranslation, uh, with the real translation being seventy-two raisins.*[695]

Ms. Manji is correct about one thing: the Koran does not mention seventy-two virgins. However, here is the *hadith* that not only affirms the promised reward, but also shows that the subject has nothing to do with raisins:

> *Al-Miqdam bin Ma'diykarib narrated that the Messenger of Allah said: "There are six things with Allah for the martyr: He is forgiven with the first flow of blood (he suffers), he is shown his place in Paradise, he is protected from punishment in the grave, secured from the greatest terror, the crown of dignity is placed upon his head - and its gems are better than the world and what is in it - he is married to seventy-two wives among Al-Huril-'Ayn of Paradise, and he may intercede for seventy of his closest relatives."*[696]

---

[695] *ABC Television 20/20 Special - Islam: Questions and Answers* (aired October 1, 2010).

[696] *Jami' At-Tirmidhi*, Vol. 3, No. 1663, p. 410. This *hadith* is also reported in *Description of Paradise in the Glorious Qur'an*, pp. 186-187, and 202. Raisins are dried grapes, and in this book the author, As-Salafi, has a section discussing grapes in Paradise, but he makes no mention of Manji's contention - see Ibid., pp. 231-232.

And it was reported in another *hadith* from a different narrator:

> *Abu Sa'eed Al-Khudri narrated that the Messenger of Allah said: "The least of the people of Paradise in position is the one with eighty thousand servants and seventy-two wives...*[697]

So it would appear that the Muslim male will be given the sexual stamina to have daily intercourse with one hundred virgins in Paradise. As luck would have it, however, he will apparently only be given between two and seventy-two virgins.

Beautiful Immortal Boys Serving Wine

Muhammad said that although Muslims were forbidden to drink wine in "this world," they could drink wine in Paradise.[698] However, the Koran stated that this wine would not cause headaches or intoxication (e.g. 37:47 and 56:19). And it is interesting to note that a number of verses in the Koran state that this wine would be served by beautiful, immortal boys:

1. Chapter 52, Verses 23-24

> *There they shall pass from hand to hand a (wine) cup, free from any Laghw (dirty, false, evil vain talk between them), and free from sin (because it will be lawful for them to drink). And there will go round boy-servants of theirs, to serve them as if they were preserved pearls.*

---

[697] *Jami' At-Tirmidhi*, Vol. 4, No. 2562, p. 548. At-Tirmidhi noted that this *hadith* was strange (*gharib*) because it was known only from the narration of Rishdin bin Sa'd - see Ibid., p. 549.

[698] See, for example, *Sahih Muslim*, Vol. 6, No. 2003R4, p. 348; *Jami' At-Tirmidhi*, Vol. 3, No. 1861, p. 547, *Sunan Ibn Majah*, Vol. 4, Nos. 3373-3374, p. 378; *Sunan Abu Dawud*, Vol. 4, No. 3679, p. 226; and *Tafsir Ibn Kathir*, Vol. 3, p. 261.

Ibn Kathir explained about the *boy-servants*:

> *This is a description of the servants and aids, the believers will have in Paradise. Their servants will be beautiful, graceful in appearance, clean and neat as well-preserved pearls.*[699]

The *Tafsir Al-Jalalayn* noted that the "beauty and fineness" of these servants was like that of "hidden pearls."[700]

2. Chapter 56, Verses 17-18

Immortal boys will go around them (serving), with cups, and jugs, and a glass of flowing wine,

Ibn Kathir said that these "immortal boys" would "never grow up, get old or change in shape."[701]

The *Tafsir Ibn 'Abbas*, explained that these "immortal youths" were "the children of the disbelievers who are made servants for the people of Paradise."[702] However, the more accepted interpretation among Muslim scholars is that these boys were created by Allah especially for this purpose.[703]

---

699 *Tafsir Ibn Kathir*, Vol. 9, p. 292.

700 *Tafsir Al-Jalalayn*, p. 1130.

701 *Tafsir Ibn Kathir*, Vol. 9, p. 418.

702 *Tafsir Ibn 'Abbas*, p. 735. This belief among some scholars of Islam was also pointed out in *Description of Paradise in the Glorious Qur'an*, p. 311.

703 *Description of Paradise in the Glorious Qur'an*, pp. 311-312.

3. Chapter 76, Verse 19

And round about them will (serve) boys of everlasting youth. If you see them, you would think them scattered pearls.

Ibn Kathir explained that this verse meant

> *...young boys from the boys of Paradise will go around serving the people of Paradise, everlasting youth, meaning in one state forever which they will be never changing from, they will not increase in age...when you see them dispersing to fulfill the needs of their masters, their great number, their beautiful faces, handsome colors, fine clothing and ornaments, you would think that they were scattered pearls. There is no better quality than this, nor is there anything nicer to look at than scattered pearls in a beautiful place.*[704]

The *Tafsir Al-Jalalayn* said that

> *Ageless youths - who never grow old...because of their beauty and how they are dispersed - you would think them scattered pearls - detached from a necklace or from a shell, or more beautiful still.*[705]

---

704 *Tafsir Ibn Kathir*, Vol. 10, p. 297.

705 *Tafsir Al-Jalalayn*, p. 1274.

And Muhammad said:

> *There is none from among the dwellers of Paradise who will not have a thousand boy-servants. Each of them will have a responsibility different from that of another.*[706]

Demographics in Paradise

The focus of Paradise seems to be on pleasing the Muslim men. What about the Muslim women? According to Muhammad, their prospects were not good:

> *Imran b. Husain reported that Allah's Messenger (may peace be upon him) said: Amongst the inmates of Paradise the women would form a minority.*[707]

And where was the final destination for most women?

> *Narrated 'Imran bin Husain: The Prophet said, "I looked at Paradise and found poor people forming the majority of its inhabitants; and I looked at Hell and saw that the majority of its inhabitants were women."*[708]

Perhaps this is why the Koran and the *hadiths* are relatively silent about the rewards in Paradise waiting specifically for Muslim women.

---

706 *Description of Paradise in the Glorious Qur'an*, p. 309.

707 *Sahih Muslim*, Vol. 8, No. 2738, p. 253.

708 *Sahih Al-Bukhari*, Vol. 4, Book No. 59, No. 3241, p. 290. For similar statements by Muhammad about women making up the majority in Hell, see: *Sahih Muslim*, Vol. 8, Nos. 2736-2737, p. 253; and *Jami' At-Tirmidhi*, Vol. 5, No. 2613, p. 24.

The author of *Description of Paradise in the Glorious Qur'an* provided this male-oriented plea to Allah:

> *Therefore, it is expected of whoever hears these great descriptions* [of Paradise] *to endeavour and not to leave any stone unturned in ensuring that he attains Paradise. He should also know that it is only those who suppress their anger who will be given the privilege of choosing from Al-Hoor Al-'lyn, as it is authentically established in the Sunnah...We beseech Allah to bestow upon us honor and success out of His infinite Mercy and not to deprive us of Al-Hoor Al-'lyn in Paradise of Bliss* [sic].[709]

---

[709] Comments by the author of *Description of Paradise in the Glorious Qur'an*, pp. 215-216.

15

Suicide or Paradise?

Narrated 'Umar bin Al-Khattab: I heard Allah's Messenger saying, "The reward of deeds depends upon the intentions and every person will get the reward according to what he has intended..."[710]

Introduction

Suicide is a major sin in Islam. So did the Muslims who hijacked the civilian airplanes on September 11, 2001, commit suicide as they crashed those airplanes into the buildings and the field? And when a Muslim kills himself and others by detonating the explosives he is wearing, or that are in a vehicle he is driving, is he really a "suicide bomber," as many in the non-Muslim world say? Are these acts of suicide, or can there be a justification in Islam for such actions in which a Muslim intentionally kills himself?

Suicide

First we need to gain a better understanding of how suicide is viewed in Islam. The following verses in the Koran are often referred to when pointing out that Islam condemns suicide:

---

[710] *Sahih Al-Bukhari*, Vol. 1, Book 1, No. 1, p. 45. For reports from other narrators that Muhammad said that people will be judged by their intentions, see, for example, *Sunan Ibn Majah*, Vol. 5, Nos. 4229-4230, p. 353.

Chapter 4, Verses 29-30

> *O you who believe! Eat not up your property among yourselves unjustly except it be a trade amongst you, by mutual consent. And do not kill yourselves (nor kill one another). Surely, Allah is Most Merciful to you. And whoever commits that through aggression and injustice, We shall cast him into the Fire, and that is easy for Allah.*

The first part of these verses refers to usury and acquiring property illegally. The third sentence is relevant to our inquiry. Ibn Kathir explained that this sentence meant that one should not kill oneself "by committing Allah's prohibitions, falling into sin..."[711]

The *Tafsir Al-Jalalayn* noted

> *...do not kill yourselves by committing what will lead to your destruction in this world or the Next. Allah is Most Merciful to you in forbidding you to do that.*[712]

The *Tafsir Ibn 'Abbas* provided some qualifiers:

> *...(and kill not one another) without justified right. (Lo! Allah is ever Merciful unto you) when He forbade you to kill one another without such a justification.*[713]

The *Tafsir Ahsanul-Bayan* provided an interesting addition:

> *This may also mean suicide, a major sin, and any other sin if it leads to perdition, <u>and killing a Muslim, the latter because the Muslims as a whole are like a single body,</u>*

---

711 *Tafsir Ibn Kathir*, Vol. 2, p. 432.

712 *Tafsir Al-Jalalayn*, p. 186.

713 *Tafsir Ibn 'Abbas*, p. 105.

<u>and hence killing him is like killing oneself.</u> [my emphasis][714]

One also finds numerous *hadith*s in which Muhammad said that those who committed suicide would go to Hell, even those who had previously fought bravely, e.g.:

1. *Narrated Jundub: Allah's Messenger said, "Amongst the nations before you there was a man who got a wound, and growing impatient (with its pain), he took a knife and cut his hand with it and the blood did not stop till he died. Allah said, 'My slave hurried to bring death upon himself so I have forbidden him (to enter) Paradise.'"*[715]

2. *Narrated Abu Hurairah: The Prophet said, "Whoever purposely throws himself from a mountain and kills himself, will be in the (Hell) Fire falling down into it and abiding therein perpetually forever; and whoever drinks poison and kills himself with it, he will be carrying his poison in his hand and drinking it in the (Hell) Fire wherein he will abide eternally forever; and whoever kills himself with an iron weapon, will be carrying that weapon in his hand and stabbing his abdomen with it in the (Hell) Fire wherein he will abide eternally forever."*[716]

3. *Narrated Sa'd bin Sahl As-Sa'idi: "The Prophet looked at a man fighting against Al-Mushrikun... and he was one of the most competent persons fighting on behalf of the Muslims. The Prophet said, "Let him who wants to look at a man from the dwellers of the (Hell) Fire look at this (man)." Another man followed him and*

---

714 *Tafsir Ahsanul-Bayan*, Vol. 1, p. 447. This view of Muslims as a single body was also reflected in the comments of Muslim scholar Sa'id bin Jubayr when discussing 5:32 in Chapter 6, *The Religion of Peace, Redux*.

715 *Sahih Al-Bukhari*, Vol. 4, Book 60, No. 3463, p. 417.

716 Ibid., Vol. 7, Book 76, No. 5778, p. 370.

kept on following him till he (the fighter) was injured and, seeking to die quickly, he placed the tip of the blade of his sword between his breasts and leaned over it till it passed through his shoulders (i.e. committed suicide). The Prophet added, "A person may do deeds that seem to the people as the deeds of the people of Paradise while in fact, he is from the dwellers of the (Hell) Fire; similarly a person may do deeds that seem to the people as the deeds of the people of the (Hell) Fire while in fact, he is from the dwellers of Paradise. Verily, the (results of) deeds done depend upon the last actions."[717]

A similar *hadith,* narrated by Abu Hurairah, dealt with the suicide of another brave Muslim warrior, about whom Muhammad had earlier said he was from the dwellers of Hell Fire. This warrior was badly wounded during the battle of Khaybar and consequently killed himself with an arrow from his own quiver. Muhammad referred to him as a wicked man.[718]

And Muhammad would not pray for someone who had committed suicide.[719]

Martyrdom in Allah's Cause

It would appear that the Islamic understanding and condemnation of suicide is similar to the common understanding and condemnation among many non-Muslims in the West. However, this chapter started out with a quote from Muhammad about how deeds would be rewarded based on the

---

717 *Sahih Al-Bukhari,* Vol. 8, Book 81, No. 6493, pp. 270-271. For a longer version of this *hadith* see *Sahih Al-Bukhari,* Vol. 5, Book 64, No. 4203, pp. 317-318.

718 Ibid., Vol. 5, Book 64, No. 4204, pp. 318-319.

719 *Sahih Muslim,* Vol. 3, No. 978, p. 75; *Sunan Ibn Majah,* Vol. 2, No. 1526, pp. 408-409; and *Sunan Abu Dawud,* Vol. 3, No. 3185, pp. 598-599.

intentions of the person. And in the following *hadith*, Muhammad applied this specifically to the idea of dying while fighting in the Cause of Allah (*Al-Jihad*):[720]

> *It was reported from 'Abdullah bin 'Amr, may Allah be pleased with him, who said: "O Messenger of Allah! Inform me about Al-Jihad and military expeditions." He said: "O 'Abdullah bin 'Amr! If you fight with endurance seeking from Allah your reward, Allah will resurrect you showing endurance and seeking your reward from Allah, and if you fight showing off, seeking to acquire much (of worldly gains), Allah will resurrect you with your showing off seeking to acquire much. O 'Abdullah bin 'Amr, with whatever intention you fight or are killed, Allah will resurrect you in that condition."*[721]

And what did it mean to fight in the Cause of Allah? Muhammad explained:

> *Narrated Abu Musa: A man came to the Prophet and asked, "O Allah's Messenger! What kind of fighting is in Allah's Cause? (I ask this), for some of us fight because of being enraged and angry and some for the sake of their pride and haughtiness." The Prophet raised his head (as the questioner was standing) and said, "He who fights that Allah's Word (i.e. Allah's Religion of Islamic Monotheism) should be superior, fights in Allah's Cause."*[722]

A warrior killed while fighting in the Cause of Allah becomes a martyr and is guaranteed entrance into Paradise. This is stated in the following verse of the Koran:

---

720 For more information about *Al-Jihad*, see n. 30.

721 *Sunan Abu Dawud*, Vol. 3, No. 2519, p. 215.

722 *Sahih Al-Bukhari*, Vol. 1, Book 3, No. 123, p. 128.

Chapter 9, Verse 111

> *Verily, Allah has purchased of the believers their lives and their properties for (the price) that theirs shall be Paradise. They fight in Allah's Cause, so they kill (others) and are killed. It is a promise in truth which is binding on Him in the Taurat (Torah) and the Injil (Gospel) and the Qur'an. And who is truer to his covenant than Allah? Then rejoice in the bargain which you have concluded. That is the supreme success.*

In a section titled *Allah has purchased the Souls and Wealth of the Mujahidin in Return for Paradise*, Ibn Kathir explained that in this verse

> *Allah states that He has compensated His believing servants for their lives and wealth - if they give them up in His cause - with Paradise.*[723]

This promise of Paradise in exchange for dying while fighting in Allah's Cause was also noted in the *Tafsir Al-Jalalayn*, *Tafsir Ibn 'Abbas*, and *Al-Wahidi's Asbab al-Nuzul*.[724]

The *Tafsir Ahsanul-Bayan* further explained:

> *This is a special favor of Allah for the believers. He gave them Paradise in exchange for their lives and property...These words have been addressed to the Muslims. But the Muslims can only rejoice in it if they agree to this bargain, meaning when they do not shrink*

---

723 *Tafsir Ibn Kathir*, Vol. 4, p. 520. *Mujahidin* are those Muslim warriors engaging in *jihad* and fighting for the Cause of Allah.

724 *Tafsir Al-Jalalayn*, p. 431; *Tafsir Ibn 'Abbas*, p. 246; and *Al-Wahidi's Asbab al-Nuzul*, pp. 129-130.

back from sacrificing their lives and wealth in the cause of Allah.[725]

So for Muslims there is one guaranteed way to get to Paradise: become a martyr by dying while fighting in Allah's Cause. Muhammad said this way of dying was so honorable that the martyr would be willing to leave Paradise itself to repeat the experience; and those who had no desire for *Jihad*, and did not die as martyrs, were hypocrites and deficient. These teachings are illustrated in a number of *hadiths*:

1. *Narrated Abu Hurairah: The Prophet said, "Allah assigns for a person who participates in (holy battles) in Allah's Cause and nothing causes him to do so except belief in Allah and in His Messengers, that he will be recompensed by Allah either with a reward, or booty (if he survives) or will be admitted to Paradise (if he is killed in the battle as a martyr)." The Prophet added: "Had I not found it difficult for my followers, then I would not remain behind any Sariya (an army-unit) going for Jihad and I would have loved to be martyred in Allah's Cause and then made alive, and then martyred and then made alive, and then again martyred in His Cause."*[726]

2. *Narrated Anas bin Malik: The Prophet said, "Nobody who dies and finds good from Allah (in the Hereafter) would wish to come back to this world, even if he were given the whole world and whatever is in it, except the martyr who, on seeing the superiority of martyrdom, would like to come back to the world and get killed again (in Allah's Cause)."*[727]

---

[725] *Tafsir Ahsanul-Bayan*, Vol. 2, p. 414.

[726] *Sahih Al-Bukhari*, Vol. 1, Book 2, No. 36, pp. 72-73. This *hadith* is found in a chapter titled *Al-Jihad (holy fighting in Allah's Cause) is a part of faith*. The footnote for this chapter title provides virtually the same definition of *Al-Jihad* as is mentioned in n. 30 of this book.

[727] *Sahih Al-Bukhari*, Vol. 4, Book 56, No. 2795, p. 51. Muhammad also said that a martyr would wish to leave Paradise and

3. *Imam Ahmad recorded that Anas said that the Messenger of Allah said, "A man from among the people of Paradise will be brought and Allah will ask him, "O son of Adam! How did you find your dwelling?" He will say, "O Lord, it is the best dwelling." Allah will say, "Ask and wish." The man will say, "I only ask and wish that You send me back to the world so that I am killed ten times in Your cause," because of the honor of martyrdom he would experience..."*[728]

4. *It has been narrated on the authority of Abu Huraira that the Messenger of Allah (may peace be upon him) said: One who died but did not fight in the way of Allah nor did he express any desire (or determination) for Jihad died the death of a hypocrite.*[729]

5. *Narrated Samura: The Prophet said, "Last night two men came to me (in a dream) and made me ascend a tree and then admitted me into a better and superior Dar (abode, dwelling place, house, etc.) better of which I have never seen. One of them said, 'This Dar is the Dar of martyrs.'"*[730]

The importance of *jihad* and the reward for the martyr exerted a strong influence on the Muslim warriors:

---

return to the world so that he may be martyred ten times because of the honour and dignity he receives (from Allah).

Ibid., No. 2817, p. 63.

728 *Tafsir Ibn Kathir*, Vol. 2, p. 209.

729 *Sahih Muslim*, Vol. 6, No. 1910, p. 289. Muhammad also said that meeting Allah in such a state indicated the Muslim had "a defect" or "a deficiency." See, respectively, *Jami' At-Tirmidhi*, Vol. 3, No. 1666, p. 412; and *Sunan Ibn Majah*, Vol. 4, No. 2763, p. 47.

730 *Sahih Al-Bukhari*, Vol. 4, Book 56, No. 2791, p. 49.

1. *The tradition has been narrated on the authority of 'Abdullah b. Qais. He heard it from his father who, while facing the enemy, reported that the Messenger of Allah (may peace be upon him) said: Surely, the gates of Paradise are under the shadows of the swords. A man in a shabby condition got up and said: Abu Musa, did you hear the Messenger of Allah (may peace be upon him) say this? He said: Yes. (The narrator said): He returned to his friends and said: I greet you (A farewell greeting). Then he broke the sheath of his sword, threw it away, advanced with his (naked) sword towards the enemy and fought (them) with it until he was slain.*[731]

2. A Bedouin converted to Islam and during one of the battles had been away caring for some livestock. He was upset when he returned and received a share of the prisoners taken in battle:

> *...He took it and brought it to the Prophet and said: "What is this?" He said: "I allocated it to you." He said: "It is not for this that I followed you. Rather I followed you so that I might be shot here - and he pointed to his throat - with an arrow and die and enter Paradise." He said: "If you are sincere toward Allah, Allah will fulfill your wish." Shortly after that they got up to fight the enemy, then he*

---

[731] *Sahih Muslim*, Vol. 6, No. 1902, p. 285. This *hadith* is also reported in *Jami' At-Tirmidhi*, Vol. 3, No. 1659, pp. 407-408; the comment about this latter *hadith* explained:

> *The Hadith tells us that one of the paths leading straight to Paradise is to take part in Jihad and confront the enemy fearlessly, under the shadow of swords and other weapons.*

Muhammad's statement that Paradise was under the shades/shadows of swords was also reported in *Sahih Al-Bukhari*, Vol. 4, Book 56, No. 2818, p. 63 (in a chapter titled *Paradise is under the blades of swords (Jihad in Allah's Cause)*; *Sahih Muslim*, Vol. 5, No. 1742, p. 166; and *Sunan Abu Dawud*, Vol. 3, No. 2631, p. 272.

was brought to the Prophet; he had been shot by an arrow in the place he had pointed to. The Prophet said: "Is it him?" They said: "Yes." He said: "He was sincere toward Allah and Allah fulfilled his wish." Then the Prophet shrouded him in his own cloak and put him in front of him and offered the (funeral) prayer for him. During his supplication he said: "O Allah, this is Your slave who went out as a emigrant (Muhajir) for Your sake and was killed as a martyr; I am a witness to that."[732]

3. *Narrated Al-Bara': A man whose face was covered with an ironmask (i.e. clad in armour) came to the Prophet and said, "O Allah's Messenger! Shall I fight or embrace Islam first?" The Prophet said, "Embrace Islam first and then fight." So he embraced Islam, and was martyred. Allah's Messenger said, "A little work, but a great reward. [He did very little (after embracing Islam), but he will be rewarded in abundance]."*[733]

4. And at the Battle of Badr a Muslim warrior actually took off his armor, at Muhammad's suggestion, before he attacked the enemy:

'Auf b. Harith...said 'O apostle of God, what makes the Lord laugh with joy at His servant?' He answered, 'When he plunges into the midst of the enemy without mail.' 'Auf drew

[732] *Sunan An-Nasa'i*, Vol. 3, No. 1955, pp. 83-84.

[733] *Sahih Al-Bukhari*, Vol. 4, Book 56, No. 2808, p. 58. For other narrations involving different warriors, but with the same comments by Muhammad, see *Sahih Muslim*, Vol. 6, No. 1900, p. 284, and *The Sealed Nectar*, p. 188. For a *hadith* about a warrior at the battle of Uhud who accepted Islam before the battle and went to Paradise after he died of his wounds, but with no comments from Muhammad, see *Sunan Abu Dawud*, Vol. 3, No. 2537, p. 226. As he lay dying he was asked why he fought. He replied, "Out of anger of Allah and His Messenger."

off the mail-coat that was on him and threw it away; then he seized his sword and fought the enemy till he was slain.[734]

5. *Narrated Jabir bin 'Abdullah: On the day (of the battle) of Uhud, a man came to the Prophet and said, "Can you tell me where I will be if I should get martyred?" The Prophet replied, "In Paradise." The man threw away some dates he was carrying in his hand, and fought till he was martyred.*[735]

6. Ibn Ishaq related a similar story but said it took place during the Battle of Badr:

> *Then the apostle went forth to the people and incited them saying, 'By God in whose hand is the soul of Muhammad, no man will be slain this day fighting against them with steadfast courage advancing not retreating but God will cause him to enter Paradise.' 'Umayr b. al-Humam brother of B. Salima was eating some dates which he had in his hand. 'Fine, Fine!' said he, 'is there nothing between me and my entering Paradise save to be killed by these men?' He flung the dates from his hand, seized his sword, and fought against them till he was slain...*[736]

And one did not have to fight long in Allah's Cause to achieve martyrdom:

---

734 *The Life of Muhammad*, p. 300. This was also reported in *The History of al-Tabari: The Foundation of the Community*, pp. 55-56.

735 *Sahih Al-Bukhari*, Vol. 5, Book 64, No. 4046, p. 231.

736 *The Life of Muhammad*, p. 300. This was also reported in *Sahih Muslim*, Vol. 6, No. 1901, pp. 284-285; *Tafsir Ibn Kathir*, Vol. 4, p. 352; and *The History of al-Tabari: The Foundation of the Community*, p. 55. 'Umayr was only sixteen years old, and as he flung the dates away he called out, "These (the dates) are holding me back from Paradise." See *The Sealed Nectar*, p. 265.

> *It was reported from Mu'adh bin Jabal that he heard the Messenger of Allah say: "Whoever fights in the cause of Allah as long as the time between two milkings of a she-camel, Paradise is guaranteed for him. And whoever asks Allah with sincerity in his soul to be killed, and then dies, or is killed, he will have the reward of a martyr."* [my emphasis][737]

Even getting wounded in Allah's Cause was rewarded in Paradise:

> *Narrated Abu Hurairah: Allah's Messenger said, "By Him in whose Hands my soul is! Whoever is wounded in Allah's Cause - and Allah knows well who gets wounded in His Cause - will come on the Day of Resurrection with his wound having the colour of blood but its smell will be the smell of musk (perfume).*[738]

So we can see from these examples the significance of intentions. Even though these Muslim warriors intentionally sought death, the fact that they did so while fighting in Allah's Cause guaranteed their entrance into Paradise. Because of their intentions, these were not acts of suicide, but rather acts of martyrdom.

This was aptly summed up by Omar Ahmad, then-Chairman of the Board of Directors for the Council on American-Islamic Relations (CAIR), when speaking about suicide bombers to a youth session at a conference of the Islamic Association for Palestine on November 25, 1999:

---

737 *Sunan Abu Dawud*, Vol. 3, No. 2541, p. 229. The comment for this *hadith* pointed out that a "she-camel once milked is given a few minutes' respite before being milked again." A version of this *hadith* was also reported by Abu Hurairah in *Jami' At-Tirmidhi*, Vol. 3, No. 1650, pp. 401-402; the comment for this latter *hadith* said the interval between milkings was so short that it was referred to as "hiccups of the she-camel."

738 *Sahih Al-Bukhari*, Vol. 4, Book 56, No. 2803, p. 55. On another occasion Muhammad said that the color of the martyr's blood would be "saffron." See *Jami' At-Tirmidhi*, Vol. 3, No. 1657, p. 407.

Someone in Islam is allowed to fight...Fighting for freedom, fighting for Islam - that is not suicide. They kill themselves for Islam.[739]

Conclusion

So when considering the actions of *jihadists* on "suicide" missions, we must keep in mind the importance of their intentions. Were they going against the commands of the Koran and the teachings of Muhammad, and killing themselves because they were uncomfortable or in pain? Or were they following the commands of the Koran and the teachings of Muhammad, and asking for death in order to become martyrs in Allah's Cause? And also perhaps anticipating the reward of seventy-two wives from among the beautiful women of Paradise.

...the highest rank there is, that one fights in the cause of Allah and dies in the process, with his face covered in dust and blood.[740]

---

[739] Steven Emerson, *American Jihad: The Terrorists Living Among Us* (New York: The Free Press, 2002), pp. 200-201. The conference was held in Chicago, IL.

[740] Statement by Ibn Kathir in *Tafsir Ibn Kathir*, Vol. 2, p. 354.

16

Changing Islam?

AIFD's mission is derived from a love for America and a love of our faith of Islam. Dr. Jasser and the board of AIFD believe that Muslims can better practice Islam in an environment that protects the rights of an individual to practice their faith as they choose...The purest practice of Islam is one in which Muslims have complete freedom to accept or reject any of the tenants or laws of the faith no different than we enjoy as Americans in this Constitutional republic.[741]

Introduction

Can Islam be changed to allow for the freedom of speech to criticize Muhammad and/or Islam itself? Can changes be made to allow the free movement of Muslims between religions, or even to allow Muslims to completely abandon religion? Can Muslims be allowed the freedom to accept or reject any of the verses in the Koran or any of the teachings of Muhammad? Unfortunately, the obstacles appear insurmountable.

The First Obstacle - the Koran

Muslims believe the Koran is the infallible, pure word of Allah, eternal and perfect. These verses from the Koran clearly state that it is the Word of Allah:

---

[741] From the American Islamic Forum for Democracy (AIFD) website at http://www.aifdemocracy.org/about/, accessed July 10, 2012. AIFD is a Muslim-American organization founded by Dr. M. Zuhdi Jasser. The organization believes in the founding principles of the United States Constitution and the separation of mosque and state.

1. Chapter 10, Verse 37

And this Qur'an is not such as could ever be produced by other than Allah (Lord of the heavens and the earth), but it is a confirmation of (the Revelation) which was before it [i.e. the Taurat (Torah), and the Injil (Gospel)], and a full explanation of the Book (i.e. the laws decreed for mankind) - wherein there is no doubt - from the Lord of the 'Alamin (mankind, jinn, and all that exists).

According to the modern *Tafsir Ahsanul-Bayan*, this verse meant:

> *The Qur'an is an exposition of that which is decreed by Allah for mankind, of the lawful and the unlawful, the fair and the unfair, and so on. There is no doubt over what it relates about past or future events. All of these things prove that it is a revelation from Allah, Who knows the past as well as the future.*[742]

Ibn Kathir explained this verse meant:

> *The Qur'an has a miraculous nature that cannot be imitated. No one can produce anything similar to the Qur'an...The eloquence, clarity, precision and grace of the Qur'an cannot be but from Allah. The great and abundant principles and meanings within the Qur'an...cannot be but from Allah.*[743]

He also pointed out that with regard to the Torah and the Gospel, the Koran

---

742 *Tafsir Ahsanul-Bayan*, Vol. 2, pp. 457-458.

743 *Tafsir Ibn Kathir*, Vol. 4, p. 606.

confirms these books...It shows the changes, perversions and corruption that have taken place within these Books.[744]

2. Chapter 4, Verse 105

Surely, We have sent down to you (O Muhammad) the Book (this Qur'an) in truth that you might judge between men by that which Allah has shown you (i.e. has taught you through Divine Revelation), so be not a pleader for the treacherous.

Ibn Kathir said this verse showed that the Koran "truly came from Allah and its narrations and commandments are true."[745]

The Koran cannot be changed:

Chapter 15, Verse 9

Verily, We, it is We Who have sent down the Dhikr (i.e. the Qur'an) and surely We will guard it (from corruption).

The footnote for this verse in *The Noble Qur'an* pointed out that, as opposed to the *Taurat* and the *Injil*, the Koran had not changed and would not change:

This verse is a challenge to mankind and everyone is obliged to believe in the miracles of this Qur'an. It is a clear fact that more than 1400 years have elapsed and not a single word of this Qur'an has been changed, although the disbelievers tried their utmost to change it in every way, but they failed miserably in their efforts. As it is

---

744 Ibid.

745 Ibid., Vol. 2, pp. 573-574.

> *mentioned in this holy Verse: "We will guard it." By Allah! He has guarded it. On the contrary, all the other holy Books [the Taurat (Torah), the Injil (Gospel)] have been corrupted in the form of additions or subtractions or alterations in the original text.*[746]

Ibn Kathir simply pointed out:

> *Then Allah, may He be exalted, stated that He is the One Who revealed the Dhikr to him, which is the Qur'an, and He is protecting it from being changed or altered.*[747]

The *Tafsir Al-Jalalayn* stated this verse meant the Koran would be preserved "from alteration, distortion, additions, or deletions."[748]

The *Tafsir Ibn 'Abbas* said this verse meant that the Koran was to be guarded

> *from satans such that they do not add or diminish from it anything nor change its judgements.*[749]

And the modern *Tafsir Ahsanul-Bayan* explained:

> *That is, it is our job to keep the Qur'an safe from the vagaries of time and from alterations and tampering. As a result of this divine pledge, the Qur'an remains exactly as it was originally. While some people have tried to distort its meanings, its words remain the same as they were revealed the first day...just as the Qur'an has been*

---

[746] *The Noble Qur'an*, n. 1, p. 349. *Dhikr* means "Remembrance of Allah."

[747] *Tafsir Ibn Kathir*, Vol. 5, p. 382.

[748] *Tafsir Al-Jalalayn*, p. 548.

[749] *Tafsir Ibn 'Abbas*, p. 321.

preserved from tampering, the sayings of the Messenger of Allah have also been preserved from alteration and modification until the Last Hour. This has contributed greatly to the correct exposition of Islam. That is, the Qur'an and the sayings and lifework of the Messenger of Allah help communicate the message of Islam in its pristine purity to mankind at large.[750]

And the Koran prohibits picking and choosing among its verses:

Chapter 2, Verse 85

...Then do you believe in a part of the Scripture and reject the rest? Then what is the recompense of those who do so among you, except disgrace in the life of this world, and on the Day of Resurrection they shall be consigned to the most grievous torment. And Allah is not unaware of what you do.

The *Tafsir Ahsanul-Bayan* explained the *grievous torment* part of this verse:

That is the punishment of those who obey some laws of Allah and disobey others. Instead of honor, they are condemned to ignominy and dishonor in this world, and to terrible chastisement in the Hereafter. This leads us to infer that Allah demands of us to obey all His laws and commandments without distinction. Obeying some of them while ignoring others is a crime according to Allah.[751]

The Koran states that the religion of Islam was perfected and finalized during the time of Muhammad:

---

750 *Tafsir Ahsanul-Bayan*, Vol. 3, p. 151.

751 Ibid., Vol. 1, p. 88.

Chapter 5, Verse 3

> *...This day, I have perfected your religion for you, completed My Favour upon you, and have chosen for you Islam as your religion...*

Ibn Kathir explained that this section of the verse meant Allah

> *has completed their religion* [Islam] *for them, and they, thus do not need any other religion or any other Prophet except Muhammad. This is why Allah made Muhammad the Final Prophet and sent him to all humans and Jinn. Therefore, the permissible is what he allows, the impermissible is what he prohibits, the Law is what he legislates and everything that he conveys is true and authentic and does not contain lies or contradictions.*[752]

The *Tafsir Al-Jalalayn* pointed out that Islam had been perfected "by finalising its rulings and obligations..."[753]

The *Tafsir Ibn 'Abbas* explained that Allah had "elucidated" to the Muslims

> *the prescriptions of your religion: the lawful and the unlawful, the commands and the prohibitions...*[754]

The Koran is the perfect, unchangeable word of Allah, and the Koran states that Islam was perfected and finalized during the time of Muhammad. So how can a Muslim reject any of the verses or change what is unchangeable and has been perfected?

---

752 *Tafsir Ibn Kathir*, Vol. 3, p. 93.

753 *Tafsir Al-Jalalayn*, p. 236.

754 *Tafsir Ibn 'Abbas*, p. 133.

The Second Obstacle - Muhammad

The Koran tells us that Muhammad spoke for Allah. And Muhammad said that anyone denying a verse of the Koran could be killed:

> *It was narrated from Ibn 'Abbas that the Messenger of Allah said: "Whoever denies a Verse of the Qur'an, it is permissible to strike his neck (i.e. execute him)..."*[755]

Muhammad also took a dim view of the idea of making changes to Islam. He said:

> *The most truthful speech is Allah's speech, and the best guidance is the guidance of Muhammad. The worst matters are the newly invented (in religion), every newly invented matter is an innovation, and every innovation is a heresy, and every heresy is in the Fire.*[756]

And Muhammad said that Allah "cursed him who accommodated an innovator (in religion)."[757]

Muhammad even said it was legal to kill a Muslim who introduced innovations and new ideas into Islam:

> *Narrated 'Abdullah: Allah's Messenger said, "The blood of a Muslim who confesses that La ilaha illallah (none has the right to be worshipped but Allah) and that I am the*

---

[755] *Sunan Ibn Majah*, Vol. 3, No. 2539, p. 455. The Shafi'i School of Sharia Law specifically states that it is apostasy to deny any verse of the Koran or to add a verse that does not belong to it - see *Reliance of the Traveller*, o8.7 (7). And, as was pointed out in n. 642, the law in *Reliance of the Traveller* "conforms to the practice and faith of the orthodox Sunni Community."

[756] *Tafsir Ibn Kathir*, Vol. 2, p. 588.

[757] *Sahih Muslim*, Vol. 6, No. 1978R2, p. 329.

> *Messenger of Allah, cannot be shed except in three cases:...(3) the one who turns renegade from Islam (apostate) and leaves the group of Muslims (by innovating heresy, new ideas and new things, etc. in the Islamic religion)."*[758]

And Muhammad talked about being in Paradise to greet the Muslims who died after him, and seeing some of those Muslims taken away because of changes they had made to Islam after he died:

> *...There will come to me some people whom I know and they know me, and then a barrier will be set up between me and them." Abu Sa'id Al-Khudri added that the Prophet further said, "I will say those people are from me (i.e. they are my followers). It will be said, 'You do not know what new changes and new things (heresies) they did after you.' Then I will say, 'Far removed (from mercy), far removed (from mercy), those who changed, did new things in (the religion) after me!'".*[759]

The Third Obstacle - It's Been Decided

The Koran said that if there was any dispute about religion among Muslims, they were to refer to the Koran and the *Sunnah* for the correct judgment; to do otherwise would be disbelief:

---

[758] *Sahih Al-Bukhari*, Vol. 9, Book 87, No. 6878, p. 20.

[759] Ibid., Book 92, No. 7050-7051, pp. 123-124. There are similar *hadiths* about the error and dire consequences of innovation in Islam - see *Sahih Al-Bukhari*, Vol. 3, Book 53, No. 2697, p. 505; Vol. 8, Book 81, No. 6576, p. 309, and Nos. 6582-6584, pp. 311-312; Vol. 9, Book 92, No. 7049, p. 123; *Sahih Muslim*, Vol.7, Nos. 2294-2295, p. 28; *Tafsir Ibn Kathir*, Vol. 3, p. 306; *Sunan An-Nasa'i*, Vol. 2, No. 905, p. 35; *Sunan Abu Dawud*, Vol. 5, No. 4607, pp. 161-162; and *Sunan Ibn Majah*, Vol. 1, No. 14, p. 81, and Nos. 42-46, pp. 99-104; Vol. 4, No. 3057, p. 211; and Vol. 5, No. 4306, pp. 400-401.

Chapter 4, Verse 59

> *O you who believe! Obey Allah and obey the Messenger (Muhammad), and those of you (Muslims) who are in authority. (And) if you differ in anything amongst yourselves, refer it to Allah and His Messenger, if you believe in Allah and in the Last Day. That is better and more suitable for final determination.*

Ibn Kathir explained this verse:

> *This is a command from Allah that whatever areas the people dispute about, whether major or minor areas of the religion, they are required to refer to the Qur'an and Sunnah for judgment concerning these disputes...Therefore, whatever the Book and Sunnah decide and testify to the truth of, then it, is the plain truth. What is beyond truth, save falsehood?...those who do not refer to the Book and Sunnah for judgment in their disputes, are not believers in Allah or the Last Day.*[760]

The *Tafsir Al-Jalalayn* noted that this approach was the way "to search out the right answer" and "better than dispute and speaking from mere opinion."[761]

The *Tafsir Ahsanul-Bayan* explained this verse in relationship to Muslim rulers, scholars and jurists:

> *Yes, of course, they shall be obeyed if their instructions are in accord with the commands of Allah and His Messenger. If they deviate, it is no longer obligatory for*

---

760 *Tafsir Ibn Kathir*, Vol. 2, pp. 498-499.

761 *Tafsir Al-Jalalayn*, p. 197.

> *the people to obey them. Rather, obeying them then is a major sin.*[762]

The Koran also said that Muslims are not allowed to disagree once Allah and Muhammad have *decreed* a matter:

Chapter 33, Verse 36

> *It is not for a believer, man or woman, when Allah and His Messenger, have decreed a matter that they should have any option in their decision. And whoever disobeys Allah and His Messenger, he had indeed strayed into a plain error.*

Ibn Kathir explained this verse quite simply:

> *This Ayah is general in meaning and applies to all matters, i.e., if Allah and His Messenger decreed a matter, no one has the right to go against that, and no one has any choice or room for personal opinion in this case.*[763]

Both the *Tafsir Al-Jalalayn* and the *Tafsir Ibn 'Abbas* agreed that this verse meant it was wrong for Muslims to disagree with what Allah and Muhammad had commanded.[764]

And the modern *Tafsir Ahsanul-Bayan* continued with this interpretation by stating that this verse

> *said in no unclear terms that it was not permissible for believers to have a say in a matter already decided by*

---

762 *Tafsir Ahsanul-Bayan*, Vol. 1, p. 472.

763 *Tafsir Ibn Kathir*, Vol. 7, p. 694.

764 *Tafsir Al-Jalalayn*, pp. 902-904; and *Tafsir Ibn 'Abbas*, p. 548.

Allah and His Messenger. Their duty is just to submit to Allah's will and His Prophet's, without demur.[765]

This warning about disagreeing with Allah and Muhammad was repeated in another verse:

Chapter 59, Verse 7

> *...And whatsoever the Messenger (Muhammad) gives you, take it; and whatsoever he forbids you, abstain (from it). And fear Allah; verily, Allah is Severe in punishment.*

Ibn Kathir explained the meaning of this verse:

> *...'whatever the Messenger commands you, then do it and whatever he forbids you, then avoid it. Surely, He only commands righteousness and forbids evil'...fear Allah by obeying His orders and refraining from His prohibitions. Surely, Allah is severe in punishment for those who defy Him and reject and disobey His commands as well as, those who commit what He forbids and prohibits.*[766]

And the Koran also said that anyone who contradicted and/or opposed Allah and Muhammad would go to the Fires of Hell:

---

765 *Tafsir Ahsanul-Bayan*, Vol. 4, p. 389.

766 *Tafsir Ibn Kathir*, Vol. 9, pp. 558-559. This idea was reinforced by Muhammad himself:

> *It was narrated that Abu Hurairah said: "The Messenger of Allah said, 'Whatever I have commanded you, do it, and whatever I have forbidden you, refrain from it.'"*

Sunan Ibn Majah, Vol. 1, No. 1, p. 73.

1. Chapter 4, Verse 115

And whoever contradicts and opposes the Messenger (Muhammad) after the right path has been shown clearly to him, and follows other than the believers' way, We shall keep him in the path he has chosen, and burn him in Hell - what an evil destination!

Under a section titled *The Punishment for Contradicting and Opposing the Messenger and Following a Path Other than That of the Believers*, Ibn Kathir explained that this verse referred to

> *whoever intentionally takes a path other than the path of the Law revealed to the Messenger, after the truth has been made clear, apparent and plain to him. Allah's statement, and follows other than the believers' way, refers to a type of conduct that is closely related to contradicting the Messenger. This contradiction could be in the form of contradicting a text (from the Qur'an or Sunnah) or contradicting what the Ummah* [Muslim community/nation] *of Muhammad has agreed on...Allah made the Fire the destination of such people in the Hereafter.*[767]

The *Tafsir Ahsanul-Bayan* took a similar approach:

> *Whoever opposes the Messenger of Allah and turns away from the way of the believers, after the guidance (of Allah) has become manifest to him, then he has in fact forsaken Islam. Allah has promised punishment in Hell for such people...Some scholars consider that the believers' way refers to a consensus (ijma'). Consensus*

[767] *Tafsir Ibn Kathir*, Vol. 2, pp. 580-582.

means a consensus of the Companions on a matter, and some say it means a consensus of all the contemporary scholars and jurists of Islam. Denying or refuting a consensus is disbelief according to the majority of scholars.[768]

2. Chapter 9, Verse 63

Know they not that whoever opposes and shows hostility to Allah and His Messenger, certainly for him will be the fire of Hell to abide therein. That is the extreme disgrace.

Ibn Kathir wrote that this verse

means, have they not come to know and realize that those who defy, oppose, wage war and reject Allah, thus becoming on one side while Allah and His Messenger on another side, certainly for him will be the fire of Hell to abide therein, in a humiliating torment, That is the extreme disgrace, that is the greatest disgrace and the tremendous misery.[769]

And Muhammad said the Fires of Hell were the destination for anyone who interpreted the Koran according to personal opinion:

Whoever explains the Qur'an with his opinion or with what he has no knowledge of, then let him assume his seat in the Fire.[770]

---

768 *Tafsir Ahsanul-Bayan*, Vol. 1, p. 518.

769 *Tafsir Ibn Kathir*, Vol. 4, p. 461.

770 *Tafsir Ibn Kathir*, Vol. 1, p. 33.

Conclusion

Can Islam be changed to allow Muslims the freedom of religion, or freedom from religion, that we know in the West? Can Muslims be allowed to pick and choose among the verses of the Koran and the teachings of Muhammad? Can Muslims be allowed to disagree with Allah and Muhammad? No, not according to the Koran and the teachings of Muhammad. For those Muslims who try, their eternal home will be in the Fires of Hell.

> *Just as it is obligatory to accept the commandments proven by the textual evidence from the Qur'an, and that it is utter disbelief to reject them, so are the commandments proven by the hadeeths of the Messenger of Allah. It is obligatory to act by them, and it is sheer disbelief to deny them.*[771]

---

771 *Tafsir Ahsanul-Bayan*, Vol. 1, pp. 622-623.

17

A Forum on Being an American Muslim

The cartoonist behind the recent "Everybody Draw Mohammed Day" cartoon has been drawn into hiding after a fatwa was issued for her death. Molly Norris of the Seattle Weekly has gone into hiding on the recent advice of the FBI after being declared a "prime target" for death by extremist cleric Anwar al-Awlaki in a June issue of "Inspire," an English language magazine. "The gifted artist is alive and well, thankfully," a Seattle Weekly reporter wrote Friday. "But on the insistence of top security specialists at the FBI, she is, as they put it, 'going ghost': moving, changing her name and essentially wiping away her identity.

Ethan Sacks, "'Everybody Draw Mohammed Day' cartoonist Molly Norris goes into hiding after radical cleric's fatwa," *New York Daily News*, September 19, 2010

A unique forum took place on October 7, 2010 in the Sheslow Auditorium of Drake University in Des Moines, Iowa. The forum was titled "What it means to be an American Muslim," and the four panelists and the moderator were all Muslim Americans:

Moderator: Dr. Mahmoud Hamad, Assistant Professor, Department of Politics and International Relations, Drake University

Luai Amro, Then-President of the Islamic Cultural Center of Des Moines

Bill Aossey, President of Midamar Corporation

Dr. M. Zuhdi Jasser, MD, Founder and President of the American Islamic Forum for Democracy

Dr. Saima Zafar, MD

The entire forum can be seen in eight parts on *YouTube*, starting with Part 1at *http://www.youtube.com/watch?v=kX5tHJnJ0hI&feature=related.*

An eye-opening moment in the forum came after the presentations by the panelists, when they were presented with an issue involving our First Amendment right to freedom of speech. This segment is at the beginning of Part 4 and can be found at:

http://www.youtube.com/watch?v=mrvNPo3sZ4A&feature=related[772]

This author was among the first to get up to ask a question of the panel. I said:

> *Molly Norris used to be the editorial cartoonist for the Seattle Weekly. She came up with the idea earlier this year of Everybody Draw Muhammad Day. Because of threats of death from people who said they were Muslims and from a particular Muslim, Anwar Al-Awlaki, and advice from the FBI, Molly Norris is now in hiding and has changed her name. What I would like to do is offer the panelists, being Muslims in America, the chance to show that the First Amendment has significance. I'd like, I'd like our panelists to go on record and say that everybody in the United States has the First Amendment right to criticize Muhammad and to draw a picture of Muhammad if they'd like. And two, to also, to also condemn anybody who says they're a Muslim who threatens death or physical harm to anybody exercising that First Amendment right.*

Dr. Hamad started saying "thank you" before I had ended the last sentence. I walked back to my seat expecting to hear an interesting panel discussion about the relationship between the First Amendment and the teachings of Islam. However, even before I had arrived at my seat the moderator had

---

772 Accessed July 25, 2012.

already gone on to the next person in line to ask a question. I sat down and quickly realized that my comments to the panel were not even going to be addressed.

A few minutes later we found out why Dr. Hamad had ignored my comments. Dr. Jasser had been asked a question about the separation of mosque and state. At the end of his response to that question, he said (at 7:10 on the Part 4 video):

> *Our moderator said that the question on Molly Norris is not relevant. I can't tell you how relevant I think it is. I think American Muslims should stand up*

Jasser got no further because at this point Dr. Hamad actually took the microphone out of Dr. Jasser's hand and said

> *As the moderator I am the one who decides.*

Dr. Hamad then went on with the forum. There was no comment about this from any of the other panelists.

The issue involving Molly Norris comes down to the question of which takes precedence in the United States: our Constitutional right to freedom of speech, or Islam's prohibition against doing anything that could be construed as criticizing or reviling Muhammad? Earlier in the forum Luai Amro had talked about the obligation for Muslim-Americans to say what they believed and to say who they really were; this was the panelists' opportunity to do both. It was unfortunate that the matter ended with the microphone being removed from Dr. Jasser's hand.

18

Muslim-Americans

The dream of opportunity for all people has not come true for everyone in America, but its promise exists for all who come to our shores -- and that includes nearly 7 million American Muslims in our country today...

President Barack Obama, speech in Cairo, Egypt, June 4, 2009

And, in fact, we have 5 million Muslims, which would make us larger than many other countries that consider themselves Muslim countries.

President Barack Obama, talking about Muslim-Americans in an interview with Anwar Iqbal, a Pakistani journalist, June 19, 2009.[773]

How Many Muslim-Americans?

It is time to find out more about Muslim-Americans in general. So let's begin by addressing the frequently stated claim that there are 7 million, or 5 million, Muslims in the United States. This is erroneous. A Pew Research Center study found that in 2007 there were 2.35 million Muslims in America; by 2011 that number had grown to only 2.75 million.[774] So

---

[773] http://archives.dawn.com/archives/99969. Accessed August 10, 2012. A two-part video of this interview is accessible at http://pakistaniat.com/2009/07/16/obama-anwar-iqbal-dawn/.

[774] *Muslim Americans: No Signs of Growth in Alienation or Support for Extremism*, Pew Research Center, August 30, 2011, p. 20. This report is

where did the claim of 7 million Muslim-Americans originate? This question was answered by a 2007 Pew Research Center study titled *Muslim Americans, Middle Class and Mostly Mainstream*. The study noted:

> *An ambitious 2001 survey led by researchers from Hartford Institute for Religious Research provided a basis for the frequently cited estimate of 6-7 million Muslim adults and children. The study, sponsored by the Council on American-Islamic Relations* [CAIR], *attempted to identify every mosque in the U.S. Leaders from a representative sample of mosques were then questioned about a host of issues, including the number of worshippers associated with each one. This study concluded that 2 million Muslims in the U.S. are involved with a mosque, at least tangentially. Based on this number, the authors surmise that "estimates of a total Muslim population of 6-7 million in America seem reasonable." Some critics speculated that mosque representatives may have inflated or otherwise misreported the number of people associated with the mosque, a tendency researchers have found among religious leaders in other faiths.*[775]

So now we know that the Muslims in America make up less than 1% of the United States population. Let's take a closer look at that Muslim community.

---

accessible at http://pewresearch.org/pubs/2087/muslim-americans-islamic-extremism-911-attacks-mosuqes.

[775] *Muslim Americans, Middle Class and Mostly Mainstream*, Pew Research Center, May 22, 2007, p. 13. This report is accessible at http://pewresearch.org/assets/pdf/muslim-americans.pdf.

"Suicide Bombing"

How do Muslim-Americans feel about "suicide bombing"? The trend is disturbing. In a multi-year study of the attitude of Muslim-Americans, the Pew Research Center asked the following question in 2007 and again in 2011:

> *Some people think that suicide bombing and other forms of violence against civilian targets are justified in order to defend Islam from its enemies. Other people believe that, no matter what the reason, this kind of violence is never justified. Do you personally feel that this kind of violence is often justified to defend Islam, sometimes justified, rarely justified, or never justified?*[776]

Surprisingly, in terms of percentages, three of the four responses were the same in both 2007 and 2011: *often justified*- 1%, *sometimes justified* - 7%, *rarely justified* - 5%.[777] The lack of change in these percentages appeared to support the claim in this study that there had been no growth in support for extremism among Muslim Americans.

However, the Muslim-American population had increased between 2007 and 2011. So here is the breakdown to those responses by the numbers:

Figure 1

	Often (1%)	*Sometimes (7%)*	*Rarely (5%)*	**Totals**
2007	23,500	164, 500	117,500	305,500
2011	27,500	192,500	137,500	357,500

---

[776] *Muslim Americans: No Signs of Growth in Alienation or Support for Extremism*, p. 115.

[777] Ibid., p. 65.

The totals show the number of Muslim-Americans who believed they could justify, to varying degrees, the use of suicide bombing and other forms of violence against civilian targets in defense of Islam. There was not only a consistent 13% of Muslim-Americans who so believed, but in the four year time period, due to population growth, over 50,000 Muslims in America were added to that category. This was a 17% increase in Muslim-American support for suicide bombing and violence against civilian targets in defense of Islam.

There was an additional disturbing observation about this in the 2007 Pew study: the difference in attitude about this kind of violence among young Muslim adults. Here is the percentage breakdown to the above question in 2007 by age groups:[778]

Figure 2

	Often	*Sometimes*	*Rarely*	**Totals**
18-29	2%	13%	11%	26%
30 or Older	6% (combined)		3%	9%

So we find that in 2007, 26% of those in the 18-29 age group could justify the use of suicide bombing and other forms of violence against civilian targets in defense of Islam. This was in stark contrast to the fact that only 9% of older Muslims could justify that kind of violence.

Now let's go from percentages to actual numbers. The 2007 Pew study showed that Muslims in the 18-29 age range made up 30% of the Muslim-American population, meaning there were 705,000 people in this age group;[779] 26% (from *Figure 2*) of that age group equals 183,300. As we

---

[778] *Muslim Americans, Middle Class and Mostly Mainstream*, pp. 53-54.

[779] Ibid., p. 16.

saw in *Figure 1*, in 2007 a total of 305,500 Muslim-Americans said they could justify the use of suicide bombing and other forms of violence in defense of Islam; so of that number, 183,300, or 60%, were in the 18-29 age range.

Unfortunately, the 2011 Pew study did not address the 18-29 age group in terms of this question. But if we assume that, in terms of the question, the percentages for this age group held from 2007 to 2011, as they did with the general Muslim-American population (*Figure 1*), there are some eye-opening results. In 2011 the 18-29 age group had increased from 30% to 36% of the Muslim-American population,[780] which meant there were now 990,000 in that particular age group. If the 26% shown in *Figure 2* held steady, that would mean that in 2011 there were now 257,400 Muslim-Americans in the 18-29 age group who could justify the use of suicide bombing and other forms of violence against civilian targets in defense of Islam. That would also mean their percentage of all those justifying such violence had grown from 60% in 2007 to 72% in 2011!

And with this possible increase in mind, let's consider another troubling statistic, this from 2008. Muslim-Americans were asked the following question:

> *Did you experience the following feelings during A LOT OF THE DAY yesterday? How about anger?*[781]

Here are the results, by age group, of those Muslim-Americans who responded "yes":

18-29: 26% **30-44: 20%** **45-64: 16%**

---

[780] *Muslim Americans: No Signs of Growth in Alienation or Support for Extremism*, p. 15.

[781] *Muslim Americans: A National Portrait*, The Muslim West Facts Project, November 2010, p. 120. The report is accessible at http://www.gallup.com/se/148820/muslim-americans-national-portrait.aspx.

Once again we find a disturbing concentration among the 18-29 age group. And it is interesting that this "anger" percentage for the 18-29 age group is the same as the percentage of that age group who could justify suicide bombing and other forms of violence in 2007.

View of Al-Qaeda

As with "suicide bombing," there are disturbing trends among Muslim-Americans with regards to Al-Qaeda. In 2007 and 2011 The Pew Research Center asked about the views that Muslims in America had concerning Al-Qaeda. Keep in mind that in 1998 Al-Qaeda declared war on the United States and on September 11, 2001, killed thousands on American soil. In 2004 Osama bin Laden even admitted that he had come up with the idea for the September 11th attack.

So here is the question that was asked in both studies:

> *Overall, do you have a favorable or unfavorable opinion of Al Qaeda?* ***[IF FAVORABLE, FOLLOW WITH:*** *And is that very favorable or only somewhat favorable?* ***IF UNFAVORABLE, FOLLOW WITH:*** *and is that very unfavorable or only somewhat unfavorable?].*[782]

Here are the results by percentages from the 2011 report, listed in a chart titled *Very Unfavorable Views of al Qaeda Increase:*[783]

---

[782] *Muslim Americans: No Signs of Growth in Alienation or Support for Extremism*, p. 117.

[783] Ibid., p. 66.

Figure 3

	Favorable	Somewhat Unfavorable	Very Unfavorable
2007	5%	10%	58%
2011	5%	11%	70%

These percentages showed that an unfavorable view of Al-Qaeda had definitely increased among Muslim-Americans, while the "favorable" view had apparently remained the same.

However, as before, we need to take into consideration the population increase from 2.35 to 2.75 million, and then look at the actual numbers. And for the purposes of this question, instead of just using the heading *Favorable*, we also need to look at the sub-categories actually used in the question: *Very Favorable* or *Somewhat Favorable*. Here are the percentages and numbers:[784]

Figure 4

	Very Favorable (1%)	Somewhat Favorable (4%)	Totals
2007	23,500	94,000	117,500

	Very Favorable (2%)	Somewhat Favorable (3%)	Totals
2011	55,000	82,500	137,500

784 Ibid., p. 117.

The significant findings in this 2011 study were not only that the number of Muslim-Americans with a generally favorable view of Al-Qaeda had increased by about 17%, but that the actual number of Muslim-Americans with a "very favorable" opinion about Al-Qaeda had more than doubled! And this was an opinion about an enemy who had killed thousands of Americans and against whom we had been fighting for many years! Unfortunately, these significant findings were largely ignored.

And, as with the question about "suicide bombing," the 2011 Pew study did not address the 18-29 age group's attitude about Al-Qaeda. It would have been interesting to see if the percentages had changed since 2007. In 2007, 5% of Muslim-Americans had a "favorable" view of Al-Qaeda. But that view was held by 7% of Muslim-Americans in the 18-29 age group; the other age groups mentioned only had "favorable" views of 2-4%.[785] Using the population numbers in the previous section, we find that in 2007 there were 49,350 Muslim-Americans in the 18-29 age group with a "favorable" view of Al-Qaeda. If the 7% figure held steady, that would mean that in 2011 there were now 69,300 in that age group with a "favorable" view of Al-Qaeda.

<u>American Mosques and their Religious Leaders (*Imams*)</u>

The number of mosques in the United States has increased from 1,209 in 2000 to 2,106 in 2011. Among the states with the largest number of mosques were New York (257), California (246), Texas (166), Florida (118), Illinois (109), and New Jersey (109). The states with the fewest number of mosques included Vermont (1), Hawaii (2), Montana (2), Alaska (3), New Hampshire (3), North Dakota (3), and Wyoming (3).[786]

---

785 *Muslim Americans, Middle Class and Mostly Mainstream*, p. 54.

786 *The American Mosque 2011: Basic Characteristics of the American Mosque, Attitudes of Mosque Leaders*, US Mosque Survey 2011, January 2012, pp. 5-6. This report is accessible at http://www.hartsem.edu/news/comprehensive-study-us-mosques.

As of 2011, 81% of all mosques in the United States had an imam, but only 44% of the imams were full-time and paid.[787] 66% of all these imams were born outside the United States, and 47% of these foreign-born imams arrived in the United States since 2000. 43% of the foreign-born imams came from the Arab world, 24% came from South Asia, and 14% came from Sub-Saharan Africa.[788]

As of 2011, 45% of all imams had a BA, MA or PhD in Islamic studies from an overseas university; only 3% of all imams had a MA or PhD in Islamic studies from an American university. The largest number of imams received their degrees in Egypt, and the vast majority of these came from Al-Azhar University. The next largest number received their degrees in Saudi Arabia, mostly from the Islamic University of Medina.[789] Neither one of these universities has a reputation for liberalism and/or modernizing Islam.

This background of many of the imams in the United States was probably a contributing factor in the results of a study that looked at the change between 2000 and 2011 in the approach American mosque leaders took to interpreting Islam. The study used the following four categories to measure that change:[790]

1. *Refer to Quran and Sunnah...and follow an interpretation that*

---

[787] *The American Mosque 2011: Activities, Administration and Vitality of the American Mosque*, US Mosque Survey 2011, May 2012, p. 12. This report is accessible at http://www.hartsem.edu/news/comprehensive-study-us-mosques-0.

[788] Ibid., p. 14.

[789] Ibid., p. 13.

[790] *The American Mosque 2011: Basic Characteristics of the American Mosque, Attitudes of Mosque Leaders*, pp. 18-19. For the actual report covering the 2000 time period, see *The Mosque in America: A National Portrait, A Report from the Mosque Study Project*, April 26, 2001. This report is accessible at http://www.cair.com/AmericanMuslims/ReportsandSurveys.aspx.

takes into account its purposes...and modern circumstances. (This would typically be a more flexible, liberal approach.)

2. *Refer to Quran and Sunnah and follow an interpretation that follows the opinions of the great scholars of the past.* (This approach is generally more conservative than the first category. In the 2000 study, instead of this category there was a category titled *Refer directly to the Quran and Sunnah and follow a literal interpretation.*)

3. *Follow a particular madhhab* (a traditional legal school of thought). (This approach tends to be traditional and fairly conservative in the practice of Islam.)

4. *Follow the salafi minhaj* (way of thought). (This is the most conservative approach and seeks to strictly follow the ways of the first three generations of Muslims.)

So of the four categories used for the study, only the first one allowed the application of modern circumstances and could be considered flexible and more liberal.

Here are the results presented in this study:

Figure 5

	2000	2011
1. Quran, Sunnah, Modern Circumstances	71%	56%
2a. Quran, Sunnah, Great Scholars	----	31%
2b. Quran, Sunnah, Literal Interpretation	21%	----
3. Follow a Particular Madhhab	6%	11%
4. Follow Salafi way	----	1%
5. None of Above	2%	1%

The results showed that there was a significant shift away from the more liberal approach found in Category 1. Including the one percentage point drop in *None of the Above*, what we see is a sixteen percentage point shift toward more conservative interpretations of Islam. It is interesting to note that in spite of this shift, in the *Major Findings* section of the study these results were presented this way:

> *The majority of mosque leaders (56%) adopt the more flexible approach of looking to interpretations of Quran and Sunnah (the normative practice of Prophet Muhammad) that take into account the overall purposes of Islamic Law and modern circumstances. Only 11% of mosque leaders prefer the more traditional approach of the classical legal schools of thought—madhhabs. A little over 1% of all mosque leaders follow the salafi way.*[791]

So those taking a quick look at the report summary would have no idea that there had been a sixteen percentage point shift toward the conservative approaches, and a related fifteen percentage point drop in support for *the more flexible approach*. They would instead come away with the impression that there was a majority trend in American mosques toward a more flexible, modern approach to Islam. It would be only by looking into the body of the report that one would find the authors stating that these results actually showed a general shift toward conservatism in interpreting Islam:

> *Apparently most of those in 2000 that chose "follow a literal interpretation" and a smaller number of those that chose "look to purposes"* [Category 1] *preferred in 2011 the category of "follow the great scholars." This again indicates the conservative nature of the "follow the great scholars of the past" response.*[792]

---

791 *The American Mosque 2011: Basic Characteristics of the American Mosque, Attitudes of Mosque Leaders*, p. 4.

792 Ibid., p. 19.

Praying with Women

The trend toward a conservative interpretation of Islam has also been reflected in designating where women are allowed to pray in a mosque. A 2001 study of mosques in America found that in 1994, women prayed behind a curtain in 52% of the mosques; by 2000, women prayed "behind a curtain or a partition or in another room" in 66% of the mosques.[793] The study specifically noted that, "The practice of having women pray behind a curtain or in another room is becoming more wide spread."[794]

This trend was reflected in the below results from the two previously mentioned Pew Research Center studies:[795]

Figure 6

Question: *When praying at a mosque women should pray*

	2007	2011
Separately from men (either in another area of the mosque or behind a curtain)	46%	48%
Behind men not separately (but with no curtain)	23%	25%
An area alongside men (but with no curtain)	21%	20%
Other/Don't Know	10%	8%

793 *The Mosque in America: A National Portrait, A Report from the Mosque Study Project*, p. 11.

794 Ibid.

795 *Muslim Americans, Middle Class and Mostly Mainstream*, p. 26; and *Muslim Americans: No Signs of Growth in Alienation or Support for Extremism*, p. 30.

We can see that support for keeping women generally separated from men has continued to increase.

Women also make up only a small percentage of those attending the Friday Prayer (*Jum'ah*), the weekly congregational prayer. In 2000 women made up 15% of those in attendance; in 2011 they had increased to only 18%.[796] A study of mosques noted that this was a problem not being addressed:

> *Women are still largely marginalized in mosques, as evidenced by the statistic that only 18% of Jum'ah attendance are women. The challenge of making mosques women friendly is not a call that has been answered by mosques.*[797]

However, this low attendance by women should come as no surprise. As we saw in Chapter 10, *Sharia Law and Women*, Muhammad said that the Friday Prayer was not obligatory for a woman, and it was actually better for women to pray at home. This could be a large factor in why the mosques have not become more *women friendly*.

Conclusion

Muslim-Americans still make up less than 1% of the United States population. However, among many of them there is a trend toward a more conservative approach to understanding and teaching Islam.

There is also a disturbing trend toward extremism and support for an enemy of the United States. Between 2007 and 2011 the Muslim-American population increased by about 17%. During that same time period the number of Muslim-Americans who could justify "suicide

---

796 *The American Mosque 2011: Activities, Administration and Vitality of the American Mosque*, p. 5.

797 Ibid., p. 24.

bombing" and other forms of violence, and who had a generally favorable view of Al-Qaeda, had also increased by about 17%. This would suggest a relatively solid core of support for these two issues among Muslim-Americans, which would grow in actual numbers as the Muslim-American population increases.

Of additional concern is the fact that while the percentage of Muslim-Americans who had a generally favorable view of Al-Qaeda had stayed the same, there had actually been a significant shift not accounted for by the population increase. Between 2007 and 2011 the population of Muslim-Americans had increased by only about 17%, but those with a "very favorable" view of Al-Qaeda had more than doubled!

These are troubling trends that must not be ignored.

19

Handling the Koran at Gitmo

Two hands will be used at all times when handling the Koran in manner [sic] *signaling respect and reverence.*

Department of Defense Memorandum, 19 JAN 03, 5.c.2

The Department of Defense (DOD) gives each detainee at the detention facility in Guantanamo Bay, Cuba (Gitmo), a Koran.[798] And who are these

---

[798] There is a tremendous amount of respect and deference shown to Islam at Gitmo. In addition to getting a Koran,

Surgical masks are provided to the detainees so they can keep the Koran off the floor and prevent guards from touching it.

It is also noteworthy that arrows are painted on the floors of the recreation yards and barracks so that the detainees will know the direction of Mecca when the call to prayer is sounded. And the guards actually put out cones and signs "during the detainees' prayer time, so they [the guards] remember to be quiet." For this and DOD photographs of the Gitmo detention facility as of April 5, 2006, see http://www.defense.gov/home/features/gitmo/facilities.html. Accessed on July 19, 2012.

Another DOD news release, dated June 29, 2005, gave further insight into how Islam was "respected" at Gitmo, and explained:

A loudspeaker at the camp signals the Muslim "call to prayer" five times a day - generally at 5:30 in the morning, 1 and 2:30 in the afternoon, and 7:30 and 9:30 at night, Mendez said.

Once the prayer call sounds, detainees get 20 minutes of uninterrupted time to practice their faith, he said. Those who choose to can take advantage of the prayer caps, beads and oil given to them as part of

detainees? An April 2004 DOD news release provided the following description:

> *Guantanamo detainees include many rank-and-file jihadists who took up arms against the U.S., as well as senior al Qaida operatives and leaders, and Taliban leaders.*[799]

> *their basic-issue items and pray toward the Muslim holy city of Mecca, in the direction designated by arrows painted in each detainee cell and all common areas.*
>
> *Detainees who display good behavior and abide by camp rules receive traditional Islam prayer rugs as well, Mendez said.*
>
> *The Joint Task Force Guantanamo Bay staff strives to ensure detainees aren't interrupted during the 20 minutes following the prayer call, even if they're not involved in religious activity, Mendez said.*
>
> *Staff members schedule detainee medical appointments, interrogations and other activities in accordance with the prayer call schedule. They also post traffic triangles throughout Camp Delta to remind task force members not to disrupt the 20-minute observation period, Mendez explained.*

See http://www.defense.gov/news/newsarticle.aspx?id=16267. Accessed July 19, 2012.

And another DOD news release, dated February 16, 2005, pointed out the numerous amenities provided the detainees, and then further noted:

> *During Ramadan, detainees were allowed to break their daily fast with water and dates at the appropriate time, and prayer calls are broadcast over loudspeakers five times a day.*

See http://www.defense.gov/news/newsarticle.aspx?id=25882. Accessed July 19, 2012.

[799] *Guantanamo Detainees*, accessed on July 18, 2012 at http://www.defense.gov/news/Apr2004/d20040406gua.pdf.

In January of 2003, DOD issued a memorandum laying out the Standard Operating Procedure (SOP) "for the handling and inspecting of detainee Korans." The copy of that memorandum included in this chapter was found at this DOD website:

http://www.defense.gov/news/Jun2005/d20050601KoranSOP.pdf.[800]

In the memorandum, MP means Military Police, and MSU means Maximum Security Unit.

As you read the memorandum you will see that our personnel were commanded to treat the Koran with "respect and reverence," and to "avoid handling or touching the detainee's Koran whenever possible." Generally, security inspections involving a Koran were to be done by the detainee holding the Koran and moving it around on the instructions of the inspector. If personnel had to touch the Koran, they were instructed to put on clean gloves "in full view of the detainees prior to handling" the Koran. And this was required to be done by non-Muslims in front of "rank-and-file *jihadists* who took up arms against the U.S."!

---

800 This website was accessed on July 18, 2012.

DEPARTMENT OF DEFENSE
JOINT TASK FORCE GUANTANAMO
HEADQUARTERS, JOINT DETENTION OPERATION GROUP (JDOG)
GUANTANAMO BAY, CUBA APO AE 09360

JTF-GTMO-JDOG-CO 19 JAN 03

MEMORANDUM FOR All personnel, JDOG

SUBJECT: Camp Delta Interim SOP Modification: Inspecting/Handling Detainee Korans Standard Operating Procedure (SOP)

1. **General.** The purpose of this SOP is to provide guidance and set specific procedures for the handling and inspecting of detainee Korans.

2. **Intent.** To ensure the safety of the detainees and MPs while respecting the cultural dignity of the Korans thereby reducing the friction over the searching the Korans. JTF-GTMO personnel directly working with detainees will avoid handling or touching the detainee's Koran whenever possible. When military necessity does require the Koran to be search, the subsequent procedures will be followed.

3. **Inspection.**

a. The MP informs the detainee that the Chaplain or a Muslim interpreter will inspect Koran. If the detainee refuses the inspection at any time, the noncompliance is reported to the Detention Operations Center (DOC) and logged appropriately by the block NCO.

b. The Koran will not be touched or handled by the MP.

c. The Chaplain or Muslim interpreter will give instructions to the detainee who will handle the Koran. He may or may not require a language specific interpreter.

d. The inspector is examining so as to notice an unauthorized items, markings, or any indicators that raises suspicion about the contents of the Koran.

e. The inspector will instruct the detainee to first open the one cover with one hand while holding the Koran in the other thus exposing the inside cover completely.

f. The inspector instructs the detainee to open pages in an upright manner (as if reading the Koran). This is a random page search and not every page is to be turned. Pages will be turned slowly enough to clearly see the pages.

g. The inspector has the detainee show the inside of the back cover of the Koran.

h. The detainee is instructed to show both ends of the Koran while the book is closed so that inspector can note the binding while closed paying attention to abnormal contours or protrusions associated with the binding. The intent is to deduce if anything may be in the binding without forcing the detainee to expose the binding, which may be construed as culturally insensitive or offensive given the significance of the Koran.

i. How the detainee reacted, observation by other detainees, and other potentially relevant observations will be annotated appropriately on the block significant activities sheet as well as staff journal.

4. **Handling.**

a. Clean gloves will be put on in full view of the detainees prior to handling.

b. Two hands will be used at all times when handling the Koran in manner signaling respect and reverence. Care should be used so that the right hand is the primary one used to manipulate any part of the Koran due to the cultural association with the left hand. Handle the Koran as if it were a fragile piece of delicate art.

c. Ensure that the Koran is not placed in offensive areas such as the floor, near the toilet or sink, near the feet, or dirty/wet areas.

5. **Removal.**

a. Korans should be left in the cell as a general rule (save in MSU), even when a detainee is moved to another cell or block. In principal, every cell (except MSU) will have a Koran "assigned" to it.

b. If a Koran must be removed at the direction the CJDOG, the detainee library personnel or Chaplain will be contacted to retrieve and properly store the Koran in the detainee library. The request for the librarian/Chaplain, as well as the retrieval itself, will be logged appropriately.

c. If the Chaplain, librarian, or Muslim interpreter, within the needs of the situation, cannot remove the Koran, then the MP may remove the Koran after approved by the DOC (who notes this in the MP Blotter) IAW the following procedures:

1) Clean gloves will be put on in full view of the detainees prior to handling

2) Two hands will be used at all times when handling the Koran in manner signaling respect and reverence.

3) Place a clean, dry, detainee towel on the detainee bed and then place the Koran on top of the clean towel in a manner, which allows it to be wrapped without turning the Koran over at any time in a reverent manner. Ensure that the Koran is not placed in offensive areas such as the floor, near the toilet or sink, near the feet, or dirty/wet area when doing this activity.

d. How the detainee reacted, observation by other detainees, and other potentially relevant observations will be annotated appropriately on the block significant activities sheet as well as staff journal.

e. The Koran shall be returned to the librarian, Chaplain, or DOC (in that order).

f. **Exception: Detainee in MSU may have a Koran if specifically authorized by a 508-1 or the Level 5 Block Entitlement Form.** Once detainee leaves MSU, the same handling/removing policies and procedures remain in effect.

6. Korans are the property of the U.S. Government and as such will remain in the cells only to be removed at the JDOG Commander's decision.

7. For further information or clarification, please contact the JDOG DOC @ 3239.

So how were these procedures working? Here is an excerpt from a preliminary report on May 26, 2005, by Brigadier General Jay Hood, then-Commander of Joint Task Force Guantanamo:

> *First off, I'd like you to know that we have found no credible evidence that a member of the Joint Task Force at Guantanamo Bay ever flushed a Koran down a toilet. We did identify 13 incidents of alleged mishandling of the Koran by Joint Task Force personnel.*
>
> *Ten of those were by a guard and three by interrogators.*
>
> *We found that in only five of those 13 incidents, four by guards and one by an interrogator, there was what could be broadly defined as mishandling of a Koran. None of these five incidents was a result of a failure to follow standard operating procedures in place at the time the incident occurred.*
>
> *We have determined that in six additional incidents involving guards that the guard either accidentally touched the Koran, touched it within the scope of his duties, or did not actually touch the Koran at all. We consider each of these incidents resolved.*
>
> *In two additional incidents, involving interrogators, we found that a Koran was either touched or stood over during an interrogation. The first incident does not to be -- appear to be mishandling, as it involved placing two Korans on a television. The Koran was not touched during the second incident, and the interrogator's action during the interrogation was accidental.*[801]

---

[801] See the DOD news transcript at: http://www.defense.gov/Transcripts/Transcript.aspx?TranscriptID=3853. Accessed on July 19, 2012.

So there were instances when a non-Muslim guard actually touched the Koran, accidently or not, and when a non-Muslim interrogator actually stood over the Koran. Unfortunately, the official policy of the United States government appeared to consider those as inappropriate behaviors! Does the word *Dhimmi* come to mind? The major difference is that this *Dhimmi* attitude was voluntarily ordered by the United States government in 2003.

In case you're wondering if these submissive attitudes toward Islam and the detainees still exist at Gitmo, the answer is yes. This is from the current *Overview* page at the official Gitmo website:

> ***Cultural sensitivity***
>
> *Detainees have the opportunity to pray five times each day. Prayer times are posted for the detainees and arrows are painted on the ground in each cell and in communal areas so the detainees know the direction to Mecca.*
>
> *Once prayer call sounds, detainees receive 20 minutes of uninterrupted time to practice their faith. The guard force strives to ensure detainees are not interrupted during the 20 minutes following the prayer call, even if detainees are not involved in religious activity. JTF Guantanamo schedules detainee medical appointments, interrogations and other activities mindful of the prayer call schedule.*
>
> *Every detainee at GTMO is issued a personal copy of the Quran. Strict measures are also in place throughout the facility to ensure that the Quran is handled appropriately by detention personnel.*
>
> *JTF Guantanamo recognizes Islamic holy periods, like Ramadan, by modifying meal schedules in observance of religious requirements.*

DoD personnel deployed to GTMO receive cultural training to ensure they understand Islamic practices.[802]

It is also interesting to notice how the description of the detainees has changed. Now, in 2012,

Detainees at GTMO include:

- *Terrorist trainers*
- *Terrorist financiers*
- *Bomb makers*
- *Osama Bin Laden bodyguards*
- *Recruiters and facilitators*[803]

What happened to the *jihadists* of 2004?

Fight against those who believe not in Allah, nor in the Last Day, nor forbid that which has been forbidden by Allah and His Messenger (Muhammad), and those who acknowledge not the religion of truth (i.e. Islam) among the people of the Scripture (Jews and Christians), until they pay the Jizyah with willing submission, and feel themselves subdued.

Koran, Chapter 9, Verse 29

---

802 See the Joint task Force Guantanamo website *Overview* section at: http://www.jtfgtmo.southcom.mil/xWEBSITE/fact_sheets/GTMO%20Overview.pdf, p. 4. Accessed on July 19, 2012.

803 Ibid., p. 2.

Chronology

Unless otherwise indicated, the information in this chronology is based mainly on *The Life of Muhammad, The Sealed Nectar*, and the relevant volumes of *The History of al-Tabari*. On occasion there are differences about when a particular event occurred, and this is discussed in the footnotes. When I have been unable to determine the general month of a particular event, I have included it at the end of the year in which it appeared to have taken place.

570	Muhammad (bin 'Abdullah) was born in Mecca. His father died before he was born.
576	Muhammad's mother, Aminah bint Wahb, died and his grandfather, 'Abdu'l-Muttalib, took over his care.
578	Muhammad's grandfather died, and Abu Talib, Muhammad's uncle, became his guardian.
595	Muhammad married 40 year old Khadija bint Khuwaylid, a widow and a merchant woman of great wealth in Mecca. They had seven children. Of these, only the four daughters lived to become Muslims and emigrate to Medina.
605	The Ka'bah in Mecca was torn down and rebuilt by the Quraysh tribe. Its new roof was made by a Christian Copt carpenter in Mecca using timber

	recovered from a wrecked Greek merchant ship. The sacred Black Stone was returned to its place by Muhammad.[804]
610	Muhammad received his first "revelation" during the month of *Ramadan*. His wife Khadija became the first convert to Islam. She was soon joined by Muhammad's cousin, Ali bin Abi Talib, who at the age of nine or ten became the first male convert to Islam.
613	Up until this time, Muhammad had kept his preaching about Islam relatively secret and hidden. The small number of additional Muslims who had joined him prayed away from the view of their fellow tribe members. Muhammad now received a "revelation" telling him to start openly preaching Islam in Mecca.
615	Due to anti-Muslim sentiment in Mecca, approximately 82 Muslim men, some with families, emigrated to Abyssinia. Muhammad stayed in Mecca under the protection of Abu Talib. Other Muslims also remained in Mecca.
619	Khadija and Abu Talib died. Even though

[804] Muhammad said that the Black Stone had descended from Paradise. When it had originally descended it was "more white than milk," but it became blackened as it absorbed the sins of the children of Adam who touched it. See *Jami' At-Tirmidhi*, Vol. 2, No. 877, pp. 290-291.

Muhammad had requested it, Abu Talib refused to convert to Islam on his death bad. Muhammad subsequently received protection in Mecca from Al-Mut'im b. 'Adi.

Muhammad married Sawdah bint Zam'ah b. Qays.

620 April: Muhammad married Aisha bint Abi Bakr al-Siddiq. Aisha was six years old.

Muhammad met with a group of six men on pilgrimage to Mecca from Medina. He converted them to Islam and they returned to Medina.[805] The growing Muslim community in Medina became known as the *Ansar* (Helpers).

---

[805] Al-Tabari points out a rather significant, non-religious reason for the conversion of these Medinans - self defense:

> *One of the things which God had done for them in order to prepare them for Islam was that the Jews lived with them in their land. The Jews were people of scripture and knowledge, while the Khazraj* [Medinan Arab tribe] *were polytheists and idolaters. They had gained the mastery over the Jews in their land, and whenever any dispute arose among them the Jews would say to them, "A prophet will be sent soon. His time is at hand. We shall follow him, and with him as our leader we shall kill you as 'Ad and Iram were killed." When the Messenger of God spoke to this group of people* [the Khazraj] *and called them to God, they said to one another, "Take note! This, by God, is the prophet with whom the Jews are menacing you. Do not let them be before you in accepting him."*

See *The History of al-Tabari: Muhammad at Mecca*, pp. 124-125. This reason was also noted in *The Life of Muhammad*, pp. 197-198.

621 First Pledge of al-'Aqabah. Twelve of the *Ansar* came to Mecca on pilgrimage and met with Muhammad. They took an oath of allegiance to Muhammad and pledged to accept and practice Islam. There was no consideration of fighting or providing protection to Muhammad, and therefore this first pledge was known as the "Pledge of Women."

622 June: Second Pledge of al-'Aqabah. 70-73 males and two females of the *Ansar* came to Mecca and met with Muhammad. They took an oath of allegiance to Muhammad and swore to protect him as they would their wives and children if he came to Medina. This oath included a pledge to wage war against all of mankind.[806] Prior to this,

---

806 Al-Tabari wrote:

> *When they gathered to take the oath of allegiance to the Messenger of God, al-'Abbas b. 'Ubadah b. Nadlah al-Ansari, the brother of the Banu Salim b. 'Awf, said, "People of the Khazraj, do you know what you are pledging yourselves to in swearing allegiance to this man?" "Yes," they said. He continued, "In swearing allegiance to him you are pledging yourselves to wage war against all mankind..."*

See *The History of al-Tabari: Muhammad at Mecca*, p. 134. This oath also meant that the *Ansar* would have to sever their ties with the Jews of Medina:

> *O Messenger of God, there are ties between us and other people which we shall have to sever (meaning the Jews). If we do this and God gives you victory, will you perhaps return to your own people and leave us?" The Messenger of God smiled and then said, "Rather, blood is blood, and blood shed without retaliation is blood shed without retaliation. You are of me and I am of you. I shall fight whomever you fight and make peace with whomever you make peace with."*

Muhammad had not been given permission by Allah to fight or to shed blood. After this second pledge, verses of the Koran were "revealed" to Muhammad that allowed the Muslims to start fighting.

July: The emigration of the Muslims from Mecca to Medina - the *Hijrah*. This became the first year of the Muslim calendar. Over a two month period about 70 Muslim males, with their wives and families, emigrated to Medina. The Muslims arriving from Mecca were known as the Emigrants (*Muhajirun*). The *Ansar* drew lots among themselves as to which of the Emigrants would stay with which of the *Ansar*.[807] Muhammad stayed in Mecca waiting for approval from Allah before he would emigrate.

September: Muhammad emigrated to Medina, accompanied by Abu Bakr.

Ibid., p. 133. The *Ansar* would later say

> *We are those who have given the Bai'a (pledge) to Muhammad for Jihad (i.e. holy fighting) as long as we live.*

See *Sahih Al-Bukhari*, Vol. 5, Book 63, No. 3796, p. 86. Another *hadith* mentioned the Emigrants as having also given that pledge - see *Sahih Al-Bukhari*, Vol. 4, Book 56, No. 2834, p. 71.

807 *Sahih Al-Bukhari*, Vol. 3, Book 52, No. 2687, p. 499.

623 March: First Muslim military expedition to intercept the caravans of the Quraysh - Expedition of Sif al-Bahr. No battle resulted. 30 Emigrant fighters.[808]

---

[808] With regard to these early military expeditions, W. Montgomery Watt made an interesting observation:

> *Some further points may be noted about these expeditions. All except that of Safawan, which was punitive, seem to have had the aim of intercepting a Meccan caravan and gaining booty...It is also to be noted that none but Emigrants took part in these early expeditions. Before he encouraged his Meccan followers to join him in making the Hijrah, Muhammad must have considered how they would make their living at Medina. They could hardly expect to be permanent guests of the Ansar, the Muslims of Medina, and they probably had no inclination to become farmers, though land seems to have been available. They had some expertise in trade with Gaza and Damascus, but attempts to trade would almost certainly lead to conflict with the Meccans. Therefore, the intercepting of Meccan caravans and disrupting of Meccan trade must have been seen at least as a possibility.*

See *The History of al-Tabari: The Foundation of the Community*, p. xx.

The Emigrants were described as "homeless, jobless and often penniless" whose number in Medina "was increasing day by day" - see *The Sealed Nectar*, p. 222. There was also initially some hunger among the Emigrants - see *Jami' At-Tirmidhi*, Vol. 4, Nos. 2365-2372, pp. 385-392, and Nos. 2473-2474, pp. 476-477. But Muhammad assured the "destitute" Emigrants that they would

> *precede the rich emigrants by forty years in getting into Paradise on the Day of Resurrection.*

Sahih Muslim, Vol. 8, No. 2979R1, p. 380.

And even Muhammad and his family did not have sufficient food on a regular basis:

Ibn 'Abbas said: "The Messenger of Allah would spend many consecutive nights and his family did not have supper, and most of the time their bread was barely bread."

Jami' At-Tirmidhi, Vol. 4, No. 2360 and Comments, pp. 382-383; for other *hadiths* in Vol. 4 about the shortage of food for Muhammad and his family, see Nos. 2356-2359, pp. 380-382; and No. 2471 and Comments, p. 475. Also see *Sahih Muslim*, Vol. 6, No. 2038, p. 364, and Nos. 2040R6-R7, pp. 367-368; and Vol. 8, Nos. 2970-2975, pp. 377-379.

This shortage of food for Muhammad and his family was also mentioned in:

Sunan Ibn Majah, Vol. 3, Nos. 2436-2439, pp. 396-397; Vol. 4, Nos. 3346-3347, pp. 364-365; and Vol. 5, Nos. 4144-4150, pp. 311-313;

Sahih Al-Bukhari, Vol. 3, Book 34, Nos. 2068-2069, p. 167; Vol. 3, Book 48, No. 2508, p. 398; Vol. 3, Book 51, No. 2567, p. 428; Vol. 5, Book 63, No. 3798, p. 87; Vol. 7, Book 70, No. 5416, p. 206; Vol. 7, Book 70, No. 5423, pp. 208-209; and Vol. 8, Book 81, No. 6458, p. 256;

Sunan An-Nasa'i, Vol. 5, No. 4437, p. 245.

And after Muhammad's death, his wife Aisha stated:

...there was nothing in my house that a living being could eat, except some barley lying on a shelf. So, I ate of it for a long period and measured it, and (after a short period) it was consumed.

See *Sahih Al-Bukhari*, Vol. 4, Book 57, No. 3097, p. 207. Aisha's statement was also reported in *Sunan Ibn Majah*, Vol. 4, No. 3345, p. 364. And this barley was provided by a Jew:

...Anas said that the Messenger of Allah died while his shield was mortgaged with a Jew in return for thirty Wasq (approximately 180 kg) of barley, which the Prophet bought on credit as provisions for his household.

See *Tafsir Ibn Kathir*, Vol. 2, p. 94. Another report stated that Muhammad had used his "coat of armor" as security for this barley - see *The Sealed Nectar*, p. 555.

April:	Military expedition of Rabigh. Exchange of arrows with Meccans, but no casualties. 60 Emigrant fighters.
May:	Muhammad consummated his marriage with Aisha bint Abi Bakr al-Siddiq.
May:	Military expedition to al-Kharrar to intercept a caravan. The caravan had already arrived and there was no contact. 20-21 Emigrant fighters.
August:	The first military expedition to be led by Muhammad. The expedition of al-Abwa (Buwat), searching for Quraysh and Bani Damrah. Treaty of Friendship signed with Bani Damrah. No fighting. 200 Emigrant fighters.
October:	Expedition to Buwat, led by Muhammad to intercept a Quraysh caravan of 100 men and 2,500 camels. No fighting. 200 Emigrant fighters.
November:	Expedition of al-'Ushayrah, led by Muhammad to intercept a Quraysh caravan. No fighting.

However, Muhammad would take advantage of food shortages to obtain the reward earned from engaging in a "voluntary fast":

> *It was narrated that 'Aishah said: "The Messenger of Allah would enter upon me and say: 'Do you have anything (any food)?' If we said: 'No,' he would say: 'Then I am fasting.' So he would continue fasting, then if we were given some food, he would break his fast." She said: "Sometimes he would fast and (then) break fast (i.e. combine fasting and breaking fast in one day."*

Sunan Ibn Majah, Vol. 2, No. 1701 and Comments, p. 504. This approach to voluntary fasting by Muhammad was also reported in *Sunan An-Nasa'i*, Vol. 3, Nos. 2324-2332, pp. 257-261.

December:	Expedition of Safwan (or Badr 1), led by Muhammad after the herds of Medina were raided. The raiders eluded Muhammad and there was no fighting.
December:	Expedition of Nakhlah. Muhammad sent 7-12 Emigrants out to look for Quraysh. They came upon a Quraysh caravan. However, it was the last day of a traditional pagan sacred month in which fighting was not allowed. But if the Muslims waited until the next day to attack, the caravan would be in the *Haram*, the sacred territory of Mecca and out of their reach. The Muslims decided to immediately attack, killing one and capturing two of the Quraysh. They seized the caravan and returned to Muhammad. This was the first plunder taken by the Muslims. However, fighting during a sacred month initially created a dilemma for Muhammad; he said he had not ordered it to be done and he impounded the plunder and the captives. Then he received a "revelation" from Allah saying that although it was bad to fight during a sacred month, it was worse to prevent people from following the way of Allah (Koran 2:217). Muhammad then divided the plunder, keeping 1/5 for Allah and himself and dividing the remainder between the Muslim warriors. This became the standard for dividing subsequent plunder, and it was later codified in the Koran (8:41) as a "revelation" to Muhammad after the Battle of Badr (see March 624). Muhammad would later say that he was the first prophet for whom war plunder had been made legal.[809]

---

[809] *Sahih Al-Bukhari*, Vol. 1, Book 8, No. 438, p. 280.

624	February:	The *Qiblah*, the direction Muslims face in prayer, was changed from Jerusalem (Syria) to Mecca, apparently initiated because of disparaging comments from some Jews.[810]
	March:	The Battle of Badr. Muhammad led an expedition to intercept a Quraysh caravan returning from Syria; the caravan was led by Abu Sufyan and accompanied by 70 horsemen.[811] Abu Sufyan

---

[810] Al-Tabari wrote:

> *The Prophet turned towards Jerusalem for sixteen months, and then it reached his ears that the Jews were saying, "By God, Muhammad and his companions did not know where their Qiblah was until we directed them." This displeased the Prophet and he raised his face toward Heaven, and God said, "We have seen the turning of your face to Heaven."*

The History of al-Tabari: The Foundation of the Community, p. 25. Also see the Koran (2:142-144, and 149-150) where the new *Qiblah* is mentioned. The changing of the *Qiblah* was also discussed in *The Life of Muhammad*, pp. 258-259, and 289.

[811] Al-Tabari explained:

> *When the Messenger of God heard about them he called together his companions and told them of the wealth they had with them and the fewness of their numbers. The Muslims set out with no other object than Abu Sufyan and the horsemen with him. They did not think that these were anything but (easy) booty and did not suppose that there would be a great battle when they met them.*

The History of al-Tabari: The Foundation of the Community, p. 29. Ibn Ishaq also noted that the Muslims' purpose for this expedition was to get the "booty" of the caravan - see *The Life of Muhammad*, pp. 289, 321 and 610. That same purpose was also noted in *Sahih Al-Bukhari*, Vol. 5, Book 64, No. 3951, p. 179, and Vol. 5, Book 64, No. 4418, p. 425. A modern biography of Muhammad noted that

heard about the Muslim expedition, sent to Mecca for help and changed his route. The Muslims missed the trading party but ended up fighting a relief force from Mecca consisting of 950 men. The Muslim force consisted of about 314 men, a combination of Emigrants (83) and *Ansar* (231); this was the first Muslim expedition that included *Ansar*. The Meccans were defeated, with 70 killed and 70 taken captive. The Muslims lost 14 men. The Muslims believed that angels had joined with them in the battle. Muhammad had promised the Muslim warriors they could "keep all the booty" they took, and those killed while

---

after he found out that the wealth of the lightly-guarded caravan amounted to 50 thousand gold dinars, he

> *immediately encouraged the Muslims to rush out and intercept the caravan to make up for their property and wealth they were forced to give up in Makkah. He did not give orders binding to everyone, but rather gave them full liberty to go out or stay back, thinking that it would be just a task on a small scale.*

The Sealed Nectar, p. 251.

So the Muslims intended this to simply be a raid on an easy target. The only reason there was a battle was because *Allah* had "willed it," as pointed out in Chapter 8, Verse 7 of the Koran:

> *And (remember) when Allah promised you (Muslims) one of the two parties (of the enemy, i.e. either the army or the caravan) that it should be yours; you wished that the one unarmed (the caravan) should be yours, but Allah willed to justify the truth by his Words and to cut off the roots of the disbelievers (i.e. in the battle of Badr).*

Also see *Sahih Muslim*, Vol. 8, No. 2769, p. 270.

	fighting would be admitted to Paradise.[812] Afterwards, Chapter 8 of the Koran, *Al-Anfal* (The Spoils of War), was "revealed" to Muhammad about events that happened during this battle.
March:	Expedition against the Bani Sulaym (or Expedition to Qarqarat al-Kudr), led by Muhammad. The Bani Sulaym fled and there was no fighting. The Muslims took 500 camels as plunder.
April:	Muhammad besieged the Bani Qaynuqa, one of the Jewish tribes in Medina, because they had refused to accept Islam and Muhammad felt threatened by them. After 15 days they surrendered. Muhammad originally wanted to kill the fettered captives, but he was talked out of it. The tribe was subsequently expelled from Medina and their property was divided among the Muslims.
April:	Expedition against the Bani Sulaym and Ghatafan. The Muslims killed some of the enemy and took their livestock. Three Muslims were killed.
June	The Expedition of al-Sawiq, led by Muhammad in pursuit of a Quraysh raiding party that had attacked Medina. The Quraysh escaped and there was no fighting. 200 Muslim fighters (Emigrants and *Ansar*).
July	The Raid of Dhu Amarr. Expedition to Najd

812 *The History of al-Tabari: The Foundation of the Community*, p. 55.

	against the Ghatafan, led by Muhammad. There was no fighting.
September	Expedition against the Quraysh and Bani Sulaym, led by Muhammad. There was no fighting.
September:	Muhammad ordered the murder of Ka'b b. al-Ashraf, a Jewish poet in Medina who had criticized Muhammad and had written poetry offensive to some Muslim women. Muhammad told the Muslim who was to kill al-Ashraf that it was acceptable to tell a lie to get close to al-Ashraf. Al-Ashraf was tricked into coming out of his fortified house and he was attacked and stabbed to death by a number of Muslims who had been waiting for him. This led to a great sense of fear among the Jews in Medina, the killing of another Jew on the general orders of Muhammad, and an interesting basis for a conversion to Islam.[813]

---

813 From al-Tabari:

The next morning, the Jews were in a state of fear on account of our attack upon the enemy of God [al-Ashraf], *and there was not a Jew there but feared for his life.*

The Messenger of God said, "Whoever of the Jews falls into your hands, kill him." So Muhayyisah b. Mas'ud fell upon Ibn Sunaynah, one of the Jewish merchants who was on close terms with them and used to trade with them, and killed him. Huwayyisah b. Mas'ud (his brother) at that time had not accepted Islam; he was older than Muhayyisah, and when (the latter) killed (the Jew), he began beating him and saying, "O enemy of God, have you killed him? By God, you have much fat in your belly from his wealth." Muhayyisah said, "I said to him, 'By God, if he who commanded me to kill him had commanded me to kill you, I would have cut off your head.'" And, by God, that was the beginning of Huwayyisah's acceptance of Islam.

October	Invasion of Buhran. Muhammad led a force of 300 Muslim warriors to Buhran, in the area of Al-Furu'. There was no fighting.
November	Expedition to al-Qaradah to attack a Quraysh caravan carrying silver and wares worth 100 thousand *dirhams*. The caravan was captured. There were 100 Muslim horsemen under the command of Zayd bin Harithah Al-Kalbi.
November:	Muhammad ordered the killing of Abu Rafi Sallam b. Abi al-Huqayq, a Jew who had supported al-Ashraf and who had also criticized Muhammad. A small group of Muslims gained access to Abu Rafi's fortified house in Khaybar and he was stabbed to death in front of his family. Muhammad's order to kill Abu Rafi appeared to have stemmed from tribal rivalry among the Ansar over who would be better Muslims in the eyes of Muhammad.[814]

> *He said, "If Muhammad had ordered you to kill me, you would have killed me?" and I replied, "Yes, by God, if he had ordered me to kill you I would have cut off your head." "By God," he said, "a faith which has brought you to this is indeed a marvel." Then Huwayyisah accepted Islam.*

The History of al-Tabari: The Foundation of the Community, pp. 97-98. This is also reported in *The Life of Muhammad*, p. 369; and a shorter version is in *Sunan Abu Dawud*, Vol. 3, No. 3002, p. 499.

[814] From al-Tabari:

> *One of the favours which God conferred upon his Prophet was that these two tribes of the Ansar, al-Aws and al-Khazraj, used to vie with one another like stallions as regards the Messenger of God; al-Aws did not do anything which benefited the Messenger of God without al-Khazraj saying, "By God, they will*

625 February: Muhammad married Hafsa bint 'Umar b. al-Khattab.

March: Expedition to (Battle of) Uhud, led by Muhammad, in response to an attack force of Quraysh who had stopped at Uhud on their way to Medina; this force was under the leadership of Abu Sufyan b. Harb. The Muslims had 700 fighters and the Quraysh had 3,000. The "motto" of the Muslims on this day was, "I seek death, I seek death."[815] The Muslims were initially victorious and started to plunder the abandoned Quraysh camp. A rear guard of 50 Muslim

---

> *not gain superiority over us in Islam in the eyes of the Messenger of God by doing this," and they would not cease until they had done something similar. When al-Khazraj did something, al-Aws said* [sic] *the same. Thus, when al-Aws killed Ka'b b. al-Ashraf on account of his hostility to the Messenger of God, al-Khazraj said, "They will never take superiority from us by doing that." They conferred together to find a man comparable to Ibn al-Ashraf in hostility to the Messenger of God and called to mind Ibn Abi al-Huqayq, who was in Khaybar. They then asked the Messenger of God for permission to kill him, and this he gave.*

The History of al-Tabari: The Foundation of the Community, p. 101; this deadly competition between *al-Aws* and *al-Khazraj* was also noted in *The Life of Muhammad*, p. 482, and in *The Sealed Nectar*, p. 380.

There is some debate about when the killing of Abu Rafi actually happened; al-Waqidi maintained it happen in May of 626 - see *The History of al-Tabari: The Foundation of the Community*, p. 101. On the other hand, Ibn Ishaq wrote that it apparently happened shortly after the defeat of the Bani Qurayzah, which would be around April of 627 - see *The Life of Muhammad*, p. 482. April of 627 was also the time period given for this incident in *The Sealed Nectar*, p. 381.

[815] *The Sealed Nectar*, p. 308.

archers had been ordered to maintain their position, but when they saw the Quraysh camp being plundered they left to join in the plunder. This allowed the Quraysh to counterattack and defeat the Muslims. The Muslims returned to Medina and the Quraysh started back to Mecca. During the fighting at Uhud, an *Ansar* named al-Harith b. Suwayd b. Samit killed another *Ansar* to settle an old blood feud. Al-Harith then joined the Quraysh and went to Mecca. He later sought forgiveness from Muhammad so he could return to his tribe. When al-Harith appeared before Muhammad, he was beheaded on Muhammad's order. When Abu 'Afak, another *Ansar*, expressed his displeasure about al-Harith's death, Abu 'Afak was killed on Muhammad's order.

March: Expedition of Hamra al-Asad, led by Muhammad. The purported purpose was to go in pursuit of the Quraysh. However, the Muslims travelled only to Hamra al-Asad, which was eight miles from Medina. They camped there for three days and then returned to Medina. There was no fighting.

March: Muhammad married Zaynab bint Khuzaymah; she died eight months later.

April: Muhammad ordered the killing of 'Asma bint Marwan, a poetess in Medina who was married to a man of the B. Khatma tribe. Because of her displeasure about the killing of Abu 'Afak, she had written a poem criticizing Muhammad and Islam. At Muhammad's request, 'Umayr b. 'Adiy went to her house at night and killed her. When 'Umayr reported back, Muhammad said, "You have helped God and His apostle, O 'Umayr!" The fear created by this killing caused the men of

B. Khatma to quickly convert to Islam "because they saw the power of Islam."[816]

July: The Expedition of al-Raji. At the request of a group of men from 'Adal and al-Qarah, Muhammad sent six Muslims back with them to teach their people about Islam. The six Muslims were betrayed at the watering placed of al-Raji. Three were killed and three were taken prisoner. The three prisoners were later killed at separate times. One of those three, Khubayb b. 'Adi, was beheaded outside Mecca and then tied to a "cross."[817]

---

816 Ibn Ishaq wrote:

Now there was a great commotion among the B. Khatma that day about the affair of Bint Marwan. She had five sons, and when 'Umayr went to them from the apostle he said, 'I have killed Bint Marwan, O sons of Khatma. Withstand me if you can; don't keep me waiting.' That was the first day that Islam became powerful among B. Khatma; before that those who were Muslims concealed the fact. The first of them to accept Islam was 'Umayr b. 'Adiy who was called 'the Reader', and 'Abdullah b. Aus and Khuzayma b. Thabit. The day after Bint Marwan was killed the men of B. Khatma became Muslims because they saw the power of Islam.

The Life of Muhammad, p. 676.

817 Al-Tabari noted the report of a Muslim sent by Muhammad as a spy:

The Messenger of God sent him alone to Quraysh as a spy. He said, "I came to the cross to which Khubayb was bound, frightened that someone might see me, climbed up it, and untied Khubayb. He fell to the ground, and I withdrew a short distance. Then I turned round, and I could not see a trace of Khubayb - it was as though the earth had swallowed him up. Nothing has been heard of Khubayb to this day.

July: The Mission of 'Amr b. Umayyah against Abu Sufyan. Muhammad sent two Muslims to Mecca to kill Abu Sufyan. While in Mecca, one of the Muslims, 'Amr b. Umayyah, was recognized. They were chased and hid in a cave to elude their pursuers. A Meccan rode too close to the cave and was killed by 'Amr. After hiding in the cave for two days, the Muslims went out and came upon Khubayb's body hanging on a cross at al-Tan'im. They were discovered while taking down Khubayb's body. One Muslim got on his camel and rode back to Medina. 'Amr hid in a cave overlooking Ghalil Dajnan. While he was in the cave, a one-eyed sheepherder came in driving some sheep. They identified themselves by tribal affiliation, and, although there had been no mention of Islam, the sheepherder volunteered that he would never become a Muslim. After the sheepherder went to sleep, 'Amr killed him "in the most dreadful way."[818] While en route back to

---

The History of al-Tabari: The Foundation of the Community, pp. 146-147; also see p. 149 for another version of how Khubayb was taken down from the cross.

Ibn Ishaq provided another version of the story. He wrote that Khubayb was "crucified" by being bound to and "raised on the wood." Khubayb was then killed by repeated lance thrusts. See *The Life of Muhammad*, pp. 428 and 674. It was also mentioned that Khubayb was "crucified" by being bound to "a lofty trunk" in *The Sealed Nectar*, pp. 350-351.

[818] From al-Tabari:

> *There I went into a cave with my bow and arrows. While I was in it a tall one-eyed man from the Banu al-Dil b. Bakr came in driving some sheep. He said, "Who is there?" and I said, "One of the Banu Bakr." He said, "I am from the Banu Bakr, one of the Banu al-Dil." Then he lay down next to me, and raised his voice in song:*

Medina, 'Amr killed one Quraysh and captured another. When he told Muhammad what all he had done, Muhammad said, "Well done," and prayed for 'Amr to be blessed.[819]

July: The Expedition to Bi'r Ma'unah. Muhammad sent 40-70 Muslims to call the people of Najd to Islam. The Muslims stopped at Bi'r Ma'unah, where they were attacked by non-Muslims. There were varying accounts about whether all of the Muslims were killed, or whether it was all but one or two.

August: Muhammad besieged the Bani al-Nadir, one of the Jewish tribes of Medina, because they were supposedly plotting to kill him.[820] After 15 days the Bani al-Nadir surrendered. They were forced to leave Medina taking with them only what their camels could carry. Some settled in the Jewish community of Khaybar (see the May 628 entry for

---

I will not be a Muslim as long as I live, and will
not believe in the faith of the Muslims.

I said, "You will soon see!" Before long the beduin [sic] *went to sleep and started snoring, and I went to him and killed him in the most dreadful way that anybody has ever killed anybody. I leant over him, stuck the end of my bow into his good eye, and thrust it down until it came out of the back of his neck.*

The History of al-Tabari: The Foundation of the Community, pp. 149-150. The same story is related in *The Life of Muhammad*, pp. 674-675.

819 *The History of al-Tabari: The Foundation of the Community*, p. 150.

820 There was some disagreement about when this siege against the Bani al-Nadir actually took place. There was one report that it took place around September of 624. See *Sahih Al-Bukhari*, Vol. 5, Book 64, Chapter 14, p. 215.

Khaybar). All of the personal and physical property they left behind was given to Muhammad as his personal property. Muhammad then divided that property almost exclusively among the Emigrants. Only two poor Ansar received any share of it. However, there was another report that from this property Muhammad "kept for himself food for one year, and what was left he spent on cavalry and weapons, equipment for the cause of Allah."[821] Afterwards, Chapter 59 of the Koran, *Al-Hashr* (The Gathering), was "revealed" to Muhammad about the defeat of the Bani al-Nadir.

October: The Expedition of Dhat al-Riqa, led by Muhammad against the Bani Muharib and the Bani Tha'labah. They met an opposing force at Nakhlah, but no fighting took place. The Prayer of Fear was first introduced by Muhammad. It was a shortened form of prayer for Muslim warriors confronting an enemy.[822]

---

[821] *Sunan An-Nasa'i*, Vol. 5, No. 4145, pp. 98-99. Also reported in *The Sealed Nectar*, p. 357.

[822] Al-Waqidi stated that this expedition took place around July of 626 - see *The History of al-Tabari: The Foundation of the Community*, p. 161. But some claimed that this expedition actually occurred sometime after the Muslim conquest of Khaybar, which occurred around May of 628. See *Sahih Al-Bukhari*, Vol. 5, Book 64, Chapter 32, pp. 272-273; and *The Sealed Nectar*, p. 446.

Although there was no fighting, the presence of 400-700 Muslim warriors in the area of Nakhlah had a decisive impact on the non-Muslim bedouins:

> *The victory at the Invasion of Dhat-ur-Riqa' had a tremendous impact on all the bedouins. It cast fear into their hearts and made them too powerless to annoy the Muslim society in Madinah. They began to adjust in the prevailing situation and prepared themselves to accept the new geo-political conditions*

626	January:	The Expedition of al-Sawiq (or Badr al-Maw'id), led by Muhammad. The Muslims had 1,500 fighters on foot and ten horsemen. The purpose was to again meet and fight the Quraysh at Badr . However, the Quraysh, under Abu Sufyan, stopped short of Badr and returned to Mecca. There was no fighting.
	March:	Muhammad married Hind bint Abi Umayyah (Umm Salamah).
	August:	Expedition to Dumat al-Jandal, led by Muhammad against an enemy force that had reportedly gathered there. There was no contact and no fighting. Muhammad had 1,000 Muslim warriors.
627	February:	The Battle of the Trench (The Attack of the Allied Parties).[823] A group of Jews, from the expelled Bani al-Nadir, met with the Quraysh and the tribe of Ghatafan and invited them to make a combined attack on Muhammad. They all agreed. The Bani Qurayzah, the last remaining major Jewish tribe in Medina, subsequently joined the alliance. The

---

working in favor of the new religion. Some of them even embraced Islam and took an active part in the conquest of Makkah and the battle of Hunain, and received their due shares of the war booty.

The Sealed Nectar, p. 446.

[823] This battle was also known as the *Ghazwa of Al-Khandaq* and the Battle of *Al-Ahzab* (the Confederates). There was a report that this battle actually took place around March of 626 - see *Sahih Al-Bukhari*, Vol. 5, Book 64, Chapter 30, p. 259.

	Quraysh were led by Abu Sufyan. The combined forces of the allies numbered 10,000, and outnumbered all of the Muslims in Medina.[824] When Muhammad heard about this, he had a protective trench dug along the northern approaches to Medina. He had 3,000 Muslim warriors. There was some minor fighting. Nu'aym b. Mas'ud, a Ghatafan who had secretly converted to Islam, came to Muhammad and asked what he could do. Muhammad said that war was deception and sent Nu'aym to spread rumors and distrust among the allies, who did not know of Nu'aym's conversion. The alliance soon crumbled, with the Quraysh and Ghatafan returning to their lands.
March:	The Expedition against the Bani Qurayzah. Muhammad besieged the Bani Qurayzah for 25 days. They surrendered. 600-900 males (all males who had reached puberty) were beheaded.[825] Their property, women and children were divided among the Muslims, with some of the female captives being sold in Najd for horses and weapons. Muhammad took one of the captives, Rayhanah bint 'Amr b. Khunafah, as his concubine, and she remained in his possession

---

[824] *The Sealed Nectar*, p. 363.

[825] There was one female captive that was also beheaded. One report was that she was beheaded because she had "verbally abused and insulted" Muhammad - see *Sunan Abu Dawud*, Vol. 3, No. 2671 and Comment, pp. 296-297. Another report said that it was because she had thrown a millstone during the siege and killed a Muslim warrior - see *The Life of Muhammad*, pp. 464-465, and p. 765, n.711. This latter reason was also mentioned in *The Sealed Nectar*, p. 378.

until his death. Muhammad subsequently drove all of the Jews out of Medina.[826]

April: Muhammad married Zaynab bint Jahsh.

May: Muhammad sent 30 Muslims under the command of Muhammad bin Maslamah on a military mission into the area of the Bani Bakr bin Kilab. The Muslims attacked, scattered their opponents, and obtained a large amount of spoils.

July: Expedition to Dhu al-Qassah. A party of 11 Muslims, under the command of Muhammad bin Maslamah, was sent against the Bani Tha'labah tribe in Dhu al-Qassah. The Muslims were surprised as they were sleeping by 100 enemy soldiers. Ten of the Muslims were killed, and bin Maslamah was wounded, but escaped.

August: Expedition to al-Ghamr. About 41 Muslims under the command of 'Ukashah bin Al-Mihsan were sent against the Bani Asad tribe in al-Ghamr. However, the enemy fled. The Muslims were able to capture 200 camels, which they took back to Medina.

August: Expedition to Dhu al-Qassah. In retaliation for the July attack against bin Maslamah's small force, Muhammad sent a "raiding party" of 40-41 Muslims, under the command of Abu 'Ubaidah bin Al-Jarrah, against the Bani Tha'labah. The Muslims conducted a surprise attack in the morning, and the Bani Tha'labah all fled. The Muslims captured "cattle, old clothes, and a single

---

826 *Sunan Abu Dawud*, Vol. 3, No. 3005, p. 503.

man." The man became a Muslim and was released.

September: The Expedition against the Bani Lihyan, led by Muhammad, in retaliation for the six Muslims killed during the Expedition of al-Raji (July 625). However, when the 200 Muslim warriors arrived at the settlements they found the Bani Lihyan had already taken secure positions on the mountain tops. There was no fighting.

September: The Expedition to Dhu Qarad, led by Muhammad. This was in response to a raid by Ghatafan on Muhammad's milk camels while the Muslims were in the territory of the Bani Lihyan. Some of the raiders were killed and camels were recovered.

September: The Expedition to al-'Eis. 170 Muslim horseman under the command of Zayd bin Harithah set out for al-'Eis and intercepted a Quraysh caravan led by Abu Al-'As, who was married to Muhammad's daughter Zaynab (he lived in Mecca and was not yet a Muslim). The Muslims looted the caravan. Abu Al-'As escaped and took refuge in Zaynab's house in Medina. At Zaynab's request, Muhammad recommended that the Muslims return the property to Abu Al-'As. They did so. Abu Al-'As returned to Mecca, gave the property to those entitled to it, converted to Islam and joined Zaynab in Medina.

October: Expedition to al-Taraf. 15 Muslim warriors under the command of Zayd bin Harithah raided the Bani Tha'labah at al-Taraf. The Bani Tha'labah fled and the Muslims captured 20 of their camels.

October:	Expedition to Hisma. Dihyah al-Kalbi was returning with merchandise and clothing and stopped at Hisma. There he was robbed. Dihyah returned to Medina and informed Muhammad. Muhammad sent a "raiding party" to Hisma.
November:	A "raiding party" of 15 Muslim warriors under the command of Zayd bin Harithah went to Wadi al-Qura. The people there attacked the Muslims, killing nine of them. Zayd bin Harithah and the others escaped.
December:	The Expedition against the Bani al-Mustaliq, led by Muhammad in response to a report that the Bani al-Mustaliq were gathering against him to attack Medina. The Muslims attacked "without warning" while the Bani al-Mustaliq were watering their cattle.[827] The Bani Al-Mustaliq

[827] *Sahih Al-Bukhari*, Vol. 3, Book 49, No. 2541, p. 413. This *hadith* about the surprise attack on the Bani al-Mustaliq was also reported in *Sahih Muslim*, Vol. 5, No. 1730, p. 162. The fact that the Bani al-Mustaliq were attacked "while they were unprepared" and watering their cattle was also pointed out in *The Mainstay Concerning Jurisprudence*, p. 314.

It is interesting to contrast this with how a modern biography of Muhammad depicts the same event:

> *The two armies were stationed at a well called Muraisi'. Exchange of arrow fire continued for an hour, and then the Muslims rushed and engaged the enemy in a battle that ended in a complete victory for the Muslims.*

The Sealed Nectar, p. 386. That there had been mutual combat was also stated by al-Tabari in his brief description of the matter:

> *The people advanced toward each other and fought fiercely. God put the Banu al-Mustaliq to flight and killed some of them.*

were defeated, and their property, women and children were divided among the Muslims.[828] Muhammad married one of the captured women, Juwayriyyah bint al-Harith. The war-cry of the Muslims that day was, "O victorious one, slay, slay!"[829]

December: A Muslim "raiding party," under the command of 'Abdur-Rahman bin 'Auf, went to Dumat al-Jandal to "invite" the people to become Muslim. They accepted the invitation.

December: A 100-man Muslim "raiding party" under the command of 'Ali bin Abi Talib was sent to Fadak to confront a clan of the Bani Sa'd b. Bakr. Muhammad had heard that a force from this tribe intended to aid the Jews of Khaybar. The Muslims attacked. but the clan escaped. The Muslims captured 500 camels and 2,000 goats.

> *He gave their children, women, and property to the Messenger of God as booty - God gave them to him as spoil.*

The History of al-Tabari: The Victory of Islam, p. 51.

Ibn Ishaq simply wrote that the Muslims

> *met them at a watering place of theirs called al-Muraysi' in the direction of Qudayd towards the shore. There was a fight and God put the B. al-Mustaliq to flight and killed some of them and gave the apostle their wives, children, and property as booty.*

The Life of Muhammad, p. 490.

828 The fate of the captured women is discussed in Chapter 11, *Whom Your Right Hands Possess*.

829 *The Life of Muhammad*, p. 768, n. 738.

--------- Expedition to al-Jamum. A Muslim "raiding party," under the command of Zayd bin Harithah, was sent to al-Jamum. They captured cattle, sheep, and took prisoners.

628 January: A Muslim "raiding party" under the command of Zayd bin Harithah, went out against the Bani Fazarah and fought them at Wadi al-Qura. Among the captives was Umm Qirfah, a very old woman who was cruelly killed by the Muslims, and her daughter, "among the fairest of the Arabs," who was given to Muhammad by the Muslim who had captured her. Muhammad then gave the daughter to his uncle.[830]

---

[830] Al-Tabari wrote:

> *Zayd b. Harithah ordered Qays to kill Umm Qirfah, and he killed her cruelly. He tied each of her legs with a rope and tied the ropes to two camels, and they split her in two. Then they brought Umm Qirfah's daughter and 'Abdallah b. Mas'adah to the Messenger of God...The Messenger of God asked Salamah* [who had captured the daughter originally] *for her, and Salamah gave her to him. He then gave her to his maternal uncle, Hazn b. Abi Wahb, and she bore him 'Abd al Rahman b. Hazn.*

See *The History of al-Tabari: The Victory of Islam*, pp. 96-97. The same story is related in *The Life of Muhammad*, p. 665; but in this source it appeared that Salamah asked Muhammad for her, and Hazn appeared to be the uncle of Salamah, not Muhammad.

It is interesting to note that the killing of Umm Qirfah was entirely left out when this battle was mentioned in a modern biography of Muhammad. Additionally, in this biography the daughter of Umm Qirfah met a different fate: Salamah stated that Abu Bakr had given him Umm Qirfah's daughter. Salamah continued,

February:	A "raiding party" of 20 Muslims set out against members of the Bani 'Uraynah who had killed Muhammad's herdsman and driven off some camels. The Muslims captured them. Muhammad ordered that they be blinded and their hands and feet be cut off. They were left to die.
March:	Treaty of Al-Hudaybiyah. Muhammad, accompanied by about 1,400 Muslims, travelled to Mecca to perform the "lesser pilgrimage" and visit the Ka'bah. The Quraysh did not want him to enter Mecca and sent out a force. Muhammad evaded the force and camped at al-Hudaybiyah, making no effort to enter Mecca. This resulted in a treaty between Muhammad and the Quraysh that, among other things, guaranteed a ten year peace between them and would allow Muhammad to make the pilgrimage to Mecca the following year. Muhammad returned to Medina. Afterwards, Chapter 48 of the Koran, *Al-Fath* (Victory) was revealed to Muhammad about this treaty.
May:	Muhammad married Ramlah bint Abi Sufyan (Umm Habibah), the daughter of Abu Sufyan.
May:	The Expedition to Khaybar. Muhammad led a

So, I had not yet disrobed her when Allah's Messenger asked about the daughter of Umm Qirfah. So she was sent to Makkah and exchanged for some Muslim captives there.

The Sealed Nectar, pp. 395-396. This is the same version as mentioned in *Sahih Muslim*, Vol. 5, No. 1755, p. 175.

Muslim army of 1,400 (including 200 horsemen) against the Jewish community of Khaybar. The Muslims camped between Khaybar and the location of the Ghatafan tribe, to prevent the Ghatafan from joining the Jews of Khaybar. The Muslims attacked at daybreak, as the townspeople were coming out of their houses to go to their jobs. Khaybar was conquered, and the "women of Khaybar were distributed among the Muslims."[831] The war-cry of the Muslims had been, "O victorious one, slay, slay!"[832] The Jews' property and many of their people were divided among the Muslims; others of the Jews were banished or allowed to remain on their land and work it, giving half a share of the results of their labor to the Muslims. Muhammad married one of the captives, Safiyyah bint Huyayy, after ordering the torture and beheading of her husband, Kinanah b. al-Rabi' b. Abi al-Huqayq. Kinanah b. al-Rabi' had refused to reveal the location of the rest of the treasure of the Bani al-Nadir, the Jewish tribe that had been expelled from Medina in August 625, and some of whom had subsequently settled in Khaybar. Safiyyah's father had also been killed during the battle.

June: The Expedition to Wadi al-Qura. On the way back to Medina from Khaybar, Muhammad stopped in Wadi al-Qura and besieged its people for a number of nights. The Muslims obtained a large amount of plunder.

---

831 *The Life of Muhammad*, p. 511. That day Muhammad prohibited "carnal intercourse with pregnant women who were captured." See Ibid., p. 512.

832 Ibid., p. 770, n. 760.

	December:	Muhammad sent a Muslim "raiding party" to Najd. A nonparticipant later stated, "We have not seen an expedition quicker in return or greater in spoils than this expedition."[833]
	December:	Expedition to the Bani Murrah. A Muslim "raiding party" of 30 men under the command of Bashir bin Sa'd Al-Ansari was sent to fight the Bani Murrah at Fadak. The Muslims initially killed many of the Bani Murrah and seized many of their camels and cattle. However, as the Muslims were returning to Medina, the Bani Murrah attacked and killed all of the Muslims except Bashir, who took refuge with Jews in Fadak until his wounds healed and he could return to Medina.
	December	Expedition to the Hawazin tribe at Turabah. A party of 31 Muslims under the command of 'Umar bin Al-Khattab was sent against the Hawazin. However, the Hawazin heard of their approach and fled. There was no fighting.
629	January:	A Muslim "raiding party" went to al-Mayfa'ah.
	January:	A Muslim force of 130 men under the command of Ghalib bin 'Abdullah Al-Laithi was sent against the Bani 'Uwal and the Bani 'Abd bin Tha'labah. The Muslims killed a number of the enemy and captured cattle and camels.
	February:	Expedition to Yumn and Jinab. Muhammad sent

---

[833] *Jami' At-Tirmidhi*, Vol. 6, No. 3561, p. 267.

a Muslim "raiding party" against the Ghatafan in response to a report that they were gathering to attack the Muslims. They encountered the Ghatafan army and put them to flight. The Muslims returned to Medina with captured camels and sheep.

March: Muhammad and a group of Muslims performed the "Fulfilled Pilgrimage" to Mecca;[834] they stayed there for three days. They left after that allotted time and returned to Medina.

March: Muhammad married Maymunah bint al-Harith.

April: The "raid" against the Bani Sulaym. After he returned from Mecca, Muhammad sent a force of 51 Muslim fighters against the Bani Sulaym. The Muslims were defeated and all, or all but one, were killed.

June: The Expedition against the Bani al-Mulawwih.

---

[834] This pilgrimage is also known as the *Umratul-Qada'* (the restitutive or compensatory visitation). As Muhammad entered Mecca, one of the Muslims, 'Abdullah bin Rawahah, walked before him reciting

> *Get out of his way, you unbelievers, make way.*
> *Today we will fight about its revelation*
> *With blows that will remove heads from shoulders*
> *And make friend unmindful of friend.*

'Umar criticized 'Abdullah for reciting poetry in front of Muhammad, but Muhammad said to 'Umar, "Let him do so, for what he is saying is more effective than shooting arrows at them." See *Sunan An-Nasa'i*, Vol. 3, No. 2876, p. 538. The above recitation, with almost the same wording, was reported in *The Sealed Nectar*, pp. 449-450. A longer version of this recitation is in *The Life of Muhammad*, p. 531, where it was also pointed out that 'Abdullah was holding the halter of Muhammad's camel as he was reciting the verses.

Muhammad sent out a "raiding party" of 13-19 Muslims. They attacked after the people had gone to sleep.[835] The battle cry of the raiding party that night was "Kill! Kill!"[836]

June: The Expedition to the Bani 'Amir. A Muslim "raiding party" of 24 men raided the Bani 'Amir and took camels and sheep.

June: A force of 25 Muslims under the command of Shuja' bin Wahb Al-Asadi was sent to attack the Bani Hawazin. There was no fighting, but the Muslims obtained some plunder.

September: The Expedition to Mu'tah. Muhammad sent a force of 3,000 Muslims under the command of Zayd bin Harithah to Syria. At Mu'tah they encountered a force of Byzantines and Arab auxiliaries numbering 200,000. The Muslims were surprised at the size of this force. They were defeated and returned to Medina. A modern biography of Muhammad described this battle as

---

835 From al-Tabari:

> *We gave them until their herds had come back from pasture in the evening. After they had milked the camels, set them to rest by the watering trough, and had stopped moving around, after the first part of the night had passed, we launched the raid on them. We killed some of them, drove away the camels, and set out to return.*

The History of al-Tabari: The Victory of Islam, p. 141. Also see *The Life of Muhammad*, pp. 660-661. There was another report that this raid actually happened around June or July of 628 - see *The Sealed Nectar*, p. 446.

836 *The History of al-Tabari: The Victory of Islam*, p. 142.

the most significant and the fiercest battle during the lifetime of Allah's Messenger, a beginning and a start to the great conquests of the land of the Christians.[837]

September: Expedition of Dhat al-Salasil. Muhammad sent a force of 500 Muslims to the territory of the Bani Quda'ah. The Muslims attacked and defeated the Bani Quda'ah.

October: The Expedition known as Al-Khabat (the *Ghazwa* of the Seacoast). Muhammad sent a force of 300 Muslims to the area of the tribe of Juhaynah to watch for a Quraysh caravan. They waited for about two weeks and then started to run out of food. However, they were along the seacoast and survived by eating a whale. They then returned to Medina. There was no fighting.

November: Expedition of Ibn Abi Hadrad to al-Ghabah. A large group of the Jusham, under the command of Rifa'ah b. Qays, had camped at al-Ghabah. Muhammad sent three Muslims to gather information or to bring back Rifa'ah. The three Muslims watched over the encampment as night fell. Rifa'ah went out alone to check on a missing herdsman. Ibn Abi Hadrad killed him with an arrow and then beheaded him. The three Muslims then attacked the encampment; the surprised inhabitants ran away. The Muslims went back to Medina with camels, goats, and sheep, and presented Rifa'ah's head to Muhammad.

November: The Khadrah Mission. In response to news about

---

837 *The Sealed Nectar*, p. 452.

the gathering of Bani Ghatafan troops, Muhammad sent 15 Muslim fighters under the command of Abu Qatadah against them. The Muslims were victorious and returned with prisoners and plunder.

December: The Expedition to Idam. Muhammad sent eight Muslims to raid the lowland of Idam.

--------- A Muslim "raiding party" of 16 men went to Dhat Atlah. They met a large force, whom they summoned to Islam. The large force responded by attacking and killing all of the Muslims but one.

630 January: The Conquest of Mecca.[838] Muhammad led a

---

838 Year 9 of the Muslim calendar covered the time period April 20, 630 - April 8, 631. During this year (The Year of the Deputations) and Year 10 (April 9, 631 - March 28, 632) representatives of the Arab tribes starting coming to Medina in succession to accept Islam. Their frequency increased in Year 10. Ibn Ishaq explained this growing acceptance of Islam:

> *In deciding their attitude to Islam the Arabs were only waiting to see what happened to this clan of Quraysh and the apostle. For Quraysh were the leaders and guides of men, the people of the sacred temple* [the Ka'bah], *and the pure stock of Ishmael son of Abraham; and the leading Arabs did not contest this. It was Quraysh who had declared war on the apostle and opposed him; and when Mecca was occupied and Quraysh became subject to him and he subdued it to Islam, and the Arabs knew that they could not fight the apostle or display enmity towards him they entered into God's religion 'in batches' as God said, coming to him from all directions.*

The Life of Muhammad, p. 628. This practical attitude of the Arabs was also pointed out in *Winning the Hearts and Souls*, p. 165. This rush by Arab tribes to convert to Islam even led to a young boy becoming the *imam* of his tribe:

force of 10,000 Muslim warriors against Mecca.[839] Abu Sufyan met him outside of Mecca and

---

Narrated 'Amr bin Salama:...So, when Makkah was conquered, then every tribe rushed to embrace Islam, and my father hurried to embrace Islam before (the other members of) my tribe. When my father returned (from the Prophet) to his tribe, he said, "By Allah, I have come to you from the Prophet for sure!" The Prophet afterwards said to them, "...and let the one amongst you who knows the Qur'an most should [sic] *lead the Salat (prayer)." So they looked for such a person and found none who knew more of the Qur'an than I because of the Quranic verses which I used to learn from the caravans. They therefore made me their Imam [to lead the Salat (prayer)] and at that time I was a boy of six or seven years..."*

Sahih Al-Bukhari, Vol. 5, Book 64, No. 4302, pp. 359-360. This was also reported in *Sunan Abu Dawud*, Vol. 1, No. 585, p. 359; and *Sunan An-Nasa'i*, Vol. 1, No. 790, p. 466.

839 It should be noted that less than eight years earlier, at the time of the emigration to Medina in the latter part of 622, Muhammad had managed to convert only around 200 Meccans to Islam. A factor in this subsequent exponential growth in Islam was commented on in *Jami' At-Tirmidhi*:

In the days following the military conquests, Allah had opened for Muslims the doors of abundance and plenty...

Jami' At-Tirmidhi, Vol. 4, Comments on p. 385. In another comment, this life of abundance was contrasted with the early years of the Emigrants in Medina; this was pointed out after *Hadith* No. 2473 described how Ali bin Abi Talib, who later became the fourth caliph, was so hungry that he drew water from a well for a Jew, who gave him one date to eat for each bucket:

The Hadith gives us an idea as to how very hard pressed financially were the Companions in the early years of emigration in Al-Madinah. Prosperity and affluence only came to them after Allah granted them victories in military campaigns over their enemies.

Jami' At-Tirmidhi, Vol. 4, Comments on p. 477. A similar comment pointed out:

> *After Emigration some of the Companions died before the conquests started and the wealth started pouring in...*

Jami' At-Tirmidhi, Vol. 6, Comments to *Hadith* No. 3853, p. 477.

After the Battle of Hunayn, Abu Qatada, a Muslim warrior, noted what he had done with his share of the spoils:

> *...I bought a garden with its price, and that was my first property which I owned through the war booty.*

See *Sahih Al-Bukhari*, Vol. 9, Book 93, No. 7170, p. 179. Muhammad used his share of the spoils from Hunayn to pay back a loan - see *Sunan Ibn Majah*, Vol. 3, No. 2424, p. 387.

For comments noting how the conditions of Muhammad's household improved after the conquest of the two Jewish tribes in Medina and of the Jews in Khaybar, see *Sahih Al-Bukhari*, Vol. 4, Book 57, No. 3128, p. 220; Vol. 5, Book 64, No. 4242, pp. 334-335; *Sahih Muslim*, Vol. 5, No. 1771R1, p. 192; and *Jami' At-Tirmidhi*, Vol. 4, Comments for *Hadith* No. 2362, p. 383.

And after defeating the Jews in Khaybar, Muhammad and the Emigrants used the spoils from that battle to pay back the *Ansar* for the earlier assistance they had received upon first arriving in Medina - see *Sahih Muslim*, Vol. 5, No. 1771, pp. 191-192; *Sahih Al-Bukhari*, Vol. 3, Book No. 51, No. 2630, p. 459; and *The Sealed Nectar*, p. 440.

Muslim warriors were also able to use "war booty" to pay in advance for food and oil - see *Sahih Al-Bukhari*, Vol. 3, Book 35, Nos. 2254-2255, p. 249. And with his share of the spoils, Muhammad offered to pay the debt left behind after a Muslim died - see *Sunan An-Nasa'i*, Vol. 3, Nos. 1964-1965, pp. 90-91. This new found wealth among the Muslims was likely a factor in the rising of prices that Muslims complained about during the time of Muhammad - see *Sunan Ibn Majah*, Vol. 3, Nos. 2200-2201, pp. 258-259.

The wealth continued after Muhammad's death:

> *During the period of the Rightly-Guided Caliphs, military conquests brought abundant wealth, and people were able to live in nice houses and wear fine clothes. They even blew their*

became a Muslim.[840] There was some fighting when the Muslims entered Mecca. Muhammad ordered the killing of certain individuals, even if they had sought refuge in the Ka'bah.[841] The

---

noses in fine pieces of cloth. This change of fortunes astonished Abu Hurairah.

Jami' At-Tirmidhi, Vol. 4, Comments to *Hadith* No. 2367, p. 387.

840 Abu Sufyan was initially uncertain about whether or not Muhammad was really the Messenger of Allah. However, when threatened with being beheaded, he decided that Muhammad was the Messenger of Allah and he became a Muslim. See *The History of al-Tabari: The Victory of Islam*, p. 173, and *The Life of Muhammad*, p. 547.

841 The individuals were:

'Abdallah b. Sa'd b. Abi Sarh: An apostate from Islam who used to be a scribe for Muhammad and write down his "revelations." He was saved only because of the inaction of the *Ansar*:

> *He* ['Abdallah] *fled to 'Uthman, who was his foster-brother, and 'Uthman hid him. 'Uthman later brought him to the Messenger of God after the people of Mecca had become calm. He asked the Messenger of God to grant him a promise of safety. The Messenger of God is said to have remained silent for a long time and then to have said yes. After 'Uthman had taken him away, the Messenger of God said to his companions who were around him, "By God, I kept silent so that one of you might go up to him and cut off his head!" One of the Ansar said, "Why didn't you give me a signal, Messenger of God?" He replied, "A prophet does not kill by making signs."*

See *The History of al-Tabari: The Victory of Islam*, pp. 178-179. This story is also mentioned in *The Life of Muhammad*, p. 550; *Sunan Abu Dawud*, Vol. 5, No. 4359, pp. 19-20; and *Sunan An-Nasa'i*, Vol. 5, No. 4072, p. 64.

It was alleged that 'Abdallah arbitrarily altered "revelations" received by Muhammad, or had boasted about doing so after he became an apostate. This was an additional reason why Muhammad wanted him killed. 'Abdallah returned to Islam the day of the conquest of Mecca. See *The History of al-Tabari: The Last Years of the Prophet*, p. 148, and n. 979.

Similarly, there was a Christian convert to Islam that used to write down the "revelations" for Muhammad. Later on he returned to Christianity and used to say, "Muhammad knows nothing but what I have written for him." He later died, but it was reported that the earth refused to accept his body. See *Sahih Al-Bukhari*, Vol. 4, Book 61, No. 3617, p. 492.

'Abdallah b. Khatal: An apostate from Islam. Muhammad was advised that Khatal was "clinging to the curtain of the Ka'bah." Muhammad said, "Kill him," and Khatal was killed. See *Sahih Al-Bukhari*, Vol. 3, Book 28, No. 1846, pp. 59-60; Vol. 4, Book 56, No. 3044, pp. 173-174; and Vol. 5, Book 64, No. 4286, p. 353. Also see: *Sahih Muslim*, Vol. 4, No. 1357, p. 320; *Sunan Abu Dawud*, Vol. 3, No. 2685, p. 307; *Jami' At-Tirmidhi*, Vol. 3, No. 1693, p. 431; *Sunan An-Nasa'i*, Vol. 3, No. 2870, p. 536; and Vol. 5, No. 4072, p. 63; and *Winning the Hearts and Souls*, pp. 43 and 46.

Fartana and Quraybah: Two singing girls who belonged to 'Abdallah b. Khatal and used to sing satire about Muhammad. There were reports that Quraybah was killed, while Fartana accepted Islam and was granted safety, only to die later after being run over by a horse, possibly intentionally.

Sarah: Used to insult Muhammad when he was in Mecca. There were reports that she was either killed, or she was granted safety and later trampled by a horse.

Al-Huwayrith b. Nuqaydh: Used to insult Muhammad when he was in Mecca. He also had poked the camel upon which two of Muhammad's daughters had been riding, causing them to fall off. He was killed by Ali bin Abi Talib (*Winning the Hearts and Souls*, p. 46.)

Miqyas b. Subabah: Pretended to have converted to Islam. Went to Medina and collected "blood money" from Muhammad for his brother, who had been mistakenly killed by an *Ansar*. Miqyas then killed the *Ansar* and returned to Mecca. He was killed.

Ikrimah b. Abi Jahl: Fought against the Muslims in earlier battles. Converted to Islam and lived.

people of Mecca swore allegiance to Muhammad and converted to Islam.

January: Expedition against the Bani Jadhimah. Muhammad sent out Muslim detachments to areas around Mecca to summon the people to Islam; he did not order the detachments to fight. A detachment under Khalid bin al-Walid came upon the Bani Jadhimah. Khalid told them they could put down their weapons because people had become Muslims. Believing that, as a result, war had ended and people were at peace, the Bani Jadhimah laid down their weapons. The Muslims bound them and beheaded many of them. When Muhammad heard this, he sent an envoy with money to pay "blood money" and compensation for property that had been taken.

January: Expedition to Nakhlah. Muhammad sent a Muslim expedition under Khalid bin al-Walid to destroy the temple of the pagan goddess al-'Uzza. Khalid destroyed the temple and broke the idol. A "naked, wailing Ethiopian woman came out before him." Khalid killed her and took the jewels she was wearing. Muhammad claimed that the woman had been al-'Uzza.[842]

January: Battle of Hunayn. Muhammad led a force of

Hind bt. 'Utbah b. Rabi'ah: Wife of Abu Sufyan. She had mutilated Muslim corpses, including that of Muhammad's uncle Hamzah, at the Battle of Uhud. Converted to Islam and lived.

[842] *The History of al-Tabari: The Victory of Islam*, p. 187.

	12,000 Muslims (including 2,000 Meccans[843]) from Mecca against the Hawazin and Thaqif tribes, who had banded together to march on Mecca. They met at the valley of Hunayn.[844] The Muslims were initially put to flight. However, they were able to rally and defeat the Hawazin and Thaqif; their women, children and flocks were divided among the Muslims. It was alleged that the captives from the Hawazin alone numbered 6,000. Some of the Hawazin tribe soon converted to Islam and the captives were set free. However, Muhammad did give Ali, Uthman and Umar (the other Rightly Guided Caliphs after Abu Bakr- see June 7, 632) each a female captive. Umar subsequently gave his female captive to his son. Groups of Hawazin fled from the battlefield and escaped to either Awtas or Al-Ta'if.
February:	Muhammad sent a Muslim force under the command of Abu 'Amir Al-Ash'ari to Awtas. The Hawazin there were defeated and some of their married women were captured by the Muslims. The question about whether or not the Muslims

---

[843] It was reported that a large number of these Meccans went along "not for the religious intention, but as spectators and in quest for war booty." See *Winning the Hearts and Souls*, p. 81.

[844] A horseman who had ridden ahead returned to the Muslim encampment the evening before the battle with a report for Muhammad:

> *'O Messenger of Allah! I traveled ahead of you until I ascended such and such mountain, and I saw Hawazin, all together with their women, cattle, and sheep gathered at Hunain.' The Messenger of Allah smiled and said: 'That will be spoils for the Muslims tomorrow, if Allah wills.'*

Sunan Abu Dawud, Vol. 3, No. 2501, p. 204.

could have sexual relations with married female captives led to the "revelation" of Koran Chapter 4, Verse 24, which made sex with these captives permissible. For details about this see Chapter 11, *Whom Your Right Hands Possess*.

February: The Siege of Al-Ta'if. Muhammad led the Muslims from Hunayn to lay siege to the Thaqif fortress at Al-Ta'if; the Thaqif had retreated from Hunayn to this location. The siege lasted for about 14-19 days, and for the first time a catapult was used by the Muslims. But the fortress held. However, the surrounding people outside the fortress surrendered to Muhammad. The Muslims returned to Medina.

April: Muhammad sent 50 Muslim horsemen under the command of 'Uyainah bin Hisn Al-Fazari against the Bani Tamim, who had urged other tribes not to pay the tribute (*Jizyah*) to the Muslims. The Muslims attacked, captured many prisoners, and returned to Medina. The Bani Tamim soon embraced Islam and the prisoners were returned.

May: Muhammad sent 20 Muslim fighters under the command of Qutbah bin 'Amir against the Khath'am tribe in Tabalah. The Muslims were victorious and returned to Medina with women, camels and sheep.

June: Muslim fighters were sent to the Bani Kilab to call that tribe to embrace Islam. They refused, fought the Muslims and were defeated.

July: *Sariyyat* 'Ali to Fulus. Muhammad sent a Muslim army (*sariyyah*) under the command of Ali bin Abi Talib to the land of Tayyi'. They raided the land, took captives and seized two swords that were in the temple of Fulus.

October: The Military Expedition to Tabuk. Muhammad led an army of 30,000 Muslims against the Byzantines. The Muslims went to Tabuk, waited several days, and then returned to Medina. There was no contact with the Byzantines.

December: A deputation of Thaqif came to Medina from al-Ta'if to meet with Muhammad. The Thaqif realized that the Arabs around them had embraced Islam and the Thaqif did not have the military strength to fight them. The delegation tried to negotiate with Muhammad about accepting only certain aspects of Islam, but Muhammad refused. They subsequently embraced Islam and signed a treaty with Muhammad. On Muhammad's orders, two Muslims from Medina accompanied the delegation back to al-Ta'if. One of these Muslims used a pickaxe to destroy the Thaqif's pagan idol *al-Lat*, whose sanctuary was near al-Ta'if.

631 August: The Expedition to the Bani al-Harith b. Ka'b. Muhammad sent Khalid bin al-Walid with a force of 400 Muslims. Khalid was ordered to spend three days inviting the Bani al-Harith to Islam. If they accepted, he was to stay with them and teach them about Islam. If they declined, he was to fight them. The Bani al-Harith accepted Islam.

December: Muhammad sent a Muslim army under the command of Ali bin Abi Talib to the Arab tribes in the Yemen. A Muslim expedition under the command of Khalid bin al-Walid had spent the previous six months inviting those tribes to Islam, without much success. The people of Yemen heard of Ali's approach, and the Hamdan tribe embraced Islam in one day. Upon hearing this, the rest of the people of Yemen accepted Islam.

--------- Surad b. 'Abdallah al-Azdi led a delegation from the al-Azd tribe to Medina and converted to Islam. Muhammad ordered Surad to lead a Muslim army against the fortified Yemeni town of Jurash. The Muslims besieged the town for about one month, with no success. Surad then led his army away. The Jurash believed the Muslims were fleeing from them, and they went in pursuit. When they overtook the Muslims, Surad's army turned on them and inflicted heavy losses on the Jurash. The Jurash soon embraced Islam.

632 January: Muhammad sent 150 cavalry men under the command of Jarir bin 'Abdullah Al-Bajali to destroy Dhul-Khalas, a pagan shrine in Yemen. They destroyed the shrine and killed whoever they found there. They returned and informed Muhammad; he "invoked good" upon them for what they had done.[845]

February: Muhammad made his Farewell Pilgrimage to Mecca. He then returned to Medina.

April: Muhammad ordered an expedition to Syria under the command of Usama bin Zayd. However, Muhammad became very ill and the expedition was delayed. News of Muhammad's illness

---

845 *Sahih Al-Bukhari*, Vol. 5, Book 63, No. 3823, p. 99.

spread and there were uprisings and counter-claims of prophethood by al-Aswad in the Yemen, Musaylimah in al-Yamamah, and Tulayhah in Asad. The uprisings were put down, with al-Aswad killed, and Musaylimah and Tulayhah driven away. Tulayhah later embraced Islam, and Musaylimah was killed fighting the Muslims during the Wars of Apostasy.

June 7: Muhammad died in Medina. His last injunction was reportedly, "Let not two religions be left in the Arabian peninsula." There was initially some dissension, with some of the *Ansar* giving consideration to selecting one of their own to lead the Medinan Muslims. However, most of the Muslims, including the *Ansar*, were quickly convinced to give their oath of allegiance to Abu Bakr, an Emigrant, and Muhammad's father-in-law and close companion.[846] Abu Bakr was the

---

[846] Fred M. Donner noted the significance of the selection of Abu Bakr:

> *In agreeing to recognize Abu Bakr as their leader following the Prophet's death, the Muslims also decided that they were to continue not only as a religious community but also as a unified polity. This decision was of the utmost importance. Had they decided otherwise, it is fair to assume that Islam would never have spread as it did, for the initial Islamic conquest movement was not primarily the expansion of a new faith, but rather the expansion of a new state - albeit a state whose coalescence was intimately linked with the new faith, which would come to be called Islam. It was under the shelter of this state ruled by Muslims that Islam first struck deep roots outside Arabian soil; without this shelter, Islam might well have remained a purely local Arabian cult, very different from what it eventually became as a result of its later evolution in the highly cultured regions of Mesopotamia, Syria, Egypt, and Iran.*

See *The History of al-Tabari: The Conquest of Arabia*, p. xii.

first of the "Four Rightly Guided Caliphs". But it was not until six months later that Ali bin Abi Talib and his followers swore allegiance to Abu Bakr.

June: In spite of concerns about potential uprisings, Abu Bakr ordered Usama bin Zayd to take his army into Syria because that is what Muhammad had wanted. Usama went on a 40 day campaign during which his army took plunder and captives. While the army was away, uprisings and apostasy against Islam started occurring among the Arab tribes. There were even two thwarted attacks on Medina. This began a period known as the Wars of Apostasy (*Riddah* Wars).

July: Usama's army returned to Medina. Additional Muslim warriors were gathered, and Abu Bakr sent 11 Muslim armies out to deal with the various uprisings. The Muslim armies marched not only against apostate tribes, but also against Arab tribes that had not been previously conquered during the time of Muhammad.

634 Islam was victorious on the Arabian Peninsula. Abu Bakr died from an illness. 'Umar bin al-Khattab became the second Caliph.

638 Jerusalem was conquered by the Muslims.

641 Egypt was conquered by the Muslims.

644	'Umar was killed by a Persian slave. 'Uthman bin Affan became the third Caliph.
656	'Uthman was assassinated. Ali bin Abi Talib became the fourth Caliph.
661	Ali, the last of the Four Rightly Guided Caliphs, was assassinated.
711	Muslim armies, having conquered much of the Middle East and a swath of land across Northern Africa, invaded Spain.
718	The Muslim conquest of Spain was virtually complete.

Bibliography
(arranged by title)

Malik ibn Anas ibn Malik ibn Abi 'Amir al-Asbahi, *Al-Muwatta of Imam Malik ibn Anas: The First Formulation of Islamic Law*, trans. Aisha Abdurrahman Bewley (Inverness, Scotland: Madinah Press, 2004)

Abu'l-Hasan 'Ali ibn Ahmad ibn Muhammad ibn 'Ali al-Wahidi, *Al-Wahidi's Asbab al-Nuzul*, trans. Mokrane Guezzou (Louisville, KY: Fons Vitae, 2008)

Steven Emerson, *American Jihad: The Terrorists Living Among Us* (New York: The Free Press, 2002)

"An American take on the Quran," *Des Moines Register*, February 11, 2012, p. 1E.

Abdul-Halim ibn Muhammad Nassar As-Salafi, *Description of Paradise in the Glorious Qur'an* (Riyadh, Kingdom of Saudi Arabia: Darussalam, 2010)

Mahmoud Ismail Saleh, *Dictionary of Islamic Words & Expressions*, 3rd ed. (Riyadh, Kingdom of Saudi Arabia: Darussalam, 2011)

Encyclopedia of Islamic Law: A Compendium of the Views of the Major Schools, adapted by Laleh Bakhtiar (Chicago: Kazi Publications, Inc., 1996)

Abu 'Eisa Mohammad Ibn 'Eisa at-Tirmidhi, *Jami' At-Tirmidhi*, trans. Abu Khaliyl, 6 Volumes (Riyadh, Kingdom of Saudi Arabia: Darussalam, 2007)

Sa'd Yusuf Abu 'Aziz, *Men and Women Around the Messenger*, trans. Suleman Fulani (Riyadh, Kingdom of Saudi Arabia: Darussalam, 2009)

Muslim Americans: A National Portrait, The Muslim West Facts Project, November 2010

Muslim Americans, Middle Class and Mostly Mainstream, Pew Research Center, May 22, 2007

Muslim Americans: No Signs of Growth in Alienation or Support for Extremism, Pew Research Center, August 30, 2011

Ahmad ibn Naqib al-Misri, *Reliance of the Traveller (Umdat al-Salik), A Classic Manual of Islamic Sacred Law*, edited and translated by Nuh Ha Mim Keller (Revised Edition 1994; rpt. Beltsville, Maryland: Amana Publications, 2008)

Muhammad bin Ismail bin Al-Mughirah Al-Bukhari, *Sahih Al-Bukhari*, trans. Muhammad Muhsin Khan, 9 Volumes (Riyadh, Kingdom of Saudi Arabia: Darussalam, 1997)

Abu'l Hussain 'Asakir-ud-Din Muslim bin Hajjaj al-Qushayri al-Naisaburi, *Sahih Muslim*, trans. Abdul Hamid Siddiqi, 8 Volumes (New Delhi: Adam Publishers and Distributors, 2008)

Dr. Mamdouh N. Mohamed, *Salaat: The Islamic Prayer from A to Z* (Fairfax, VA: B 200 Inc., 2005)

Abu Dawud Sulaiman bin Al-Ash'ath bin Ishaq, *Sunan Abu Dawud*, trans. Yaser Qadhi, 5 Volumes (Riyadh, Kingdom of Saudi Arabia: Darussalam, 2008)

Abu Abdur Rahman Ahmad bin Shu'aib bin 'Ali An-Nasa'i, *Sunan An-Nasa'i*, trans. Nasiruddin al-Khattab, 6 Volumes (Riyadh, Kingdom of Saudi Arabia: Darussalam, 2007)

Muhammad Bin Yazeed Ibn Majah Al-Qazwini, *Sunan Ibn Majah*, trans. Nasiruddin al-Khattab, 5 Volumes (Riyadh, Kingdom of Saudi Arabia: Darussalam, 2007)

Salahuddin Yusuf, *Tafsir Ahsanul-Bayan*, trans. Mohammad Kamal Myshkat, 4 Volumes (Riyadh, Kingdom of Saudi Arabia: Darussalam, 2010)

Salahuddin Yusuf, *Tafsir Ahsanul-Bayan(Part 30)* (Riyadh, Kingdom of Saudi Arabia: Darussalam, 2010)

Jalalu'd-Din Al-Mahalli and Jalalu'd-Din As-Suyuti, *Tafsir Al-Jalalayn*, trans. Aisha Bewley (London: Dar Al Taqwa Ltd., 2007)

Abu 'Abdullah Muhammad ibn Ahmad al-Ansari al-Qurtubi, *Tafsir Al-Qurtubi: Classical Commentary of the Holy Qur'an*, Vol. 1, trans. Aisha Bewley (London: Dar Al Taqwa Ltd., 2003)

Tafsir Ibn 'Abbas, trans. Mokrane Guezzou (Louisville, KY: Fons Vitae, 2008)

Abu Al-Fida' 'Imad Ad-Din Isma'il bin 'Umar bin Kathir Al-Qurashi Al-Busrawi, *Tafsir Ibn Kathir* (Abridged), trans. Jalal Abualrub, et al., 10 Volumes (Riyadh, Kingdom of Saudi Arabia: Darussalam, 2000)

The American Mosque 2011: Activities, Administration and Vitality of the American Mosque, US Mosque Survey 2011, May 2012

The American Mosque 2011: Basic Characteristics of the American Mosque, Attitudes of Mosque Leaders, US Mosque Survey 2011, January 2012

Muhammad ibn Sulayman at-Tamimi, *The Book of Major Sins*, trans. Dr. Ibraheem as-Selek (Riyadh, Kingdom of Saudi Arabia: International Islamic Publishing House, 2007)

The Global Gender Gap Report 2011, World Economic Forum, November 2011

Abu Ja'far Muhammad b. Jarir al-Tabari, *The History of al-Tabari: The Conquest of Arabia*, Vol. X, trans. and annotated Fred M. Donner (Albany, New York: State University of New York Press, 1993)

Abu Ja'far Muhammad b. Jarir al-Tabari, *The History of al-Tabari: The Foundation of the Community*, Vol. VII, trans. M. V. McDonald and annotated W. Montgomery Watt (Albany, New York: State University of New York Press, 1987)

Abu Ja'far Muhammad b. Jarir al-Tabari, *The History of al-Tabari: The Last Years of the Prophet*, Vol. IX, trans. and annotated Ismail K. Poonawala (Albany, New York: State University of New York Press, 1990)

Abu Ja'far Muhammad b. Jarir al-Tabari, *The History of al-Tabari: Muhammad at Mecca*, Vol. VI, trans. and annotated W. Montgomery Watt and M. V. McDonald (Albany, New York: State University of New York Press, 1988)

Abu Ja'far Muhammad b. Jarir al-Tabari, *The History of al-Tabari: The Victory of Islam*, Vol. VIII, trans. and annotated Michael Fishbein (Albany, New York: State University of New York Press, 1997)

The Honorable Wives of the Prophet, ed. Abdul Ahad (Riyadh, Kingdom of Saudi Arabia: Darussalam, 2004)

Abu Hanifah Nu'man ibn Thabit ibn Nu'man ibn al-Marzuban ibn Zuta ibn Mah, *The Kitab al-Athar of Imam Abu Hanifah: The Narration of Imam Muhammad Ibn Al-Hasan Ash-Shaybani*, trans. 'Abdassamad Clarke (London: Turath Publishing, 2007)

Samuel M. Zwemer, *The Law of Apostasy in Islam* (1924; rpt. Cornwall, United Kingdom: Diggory Press Ltd., 2006)

Muhammad Ibn Ishaq, *The Life of Muhammad (Sirat Rasul Allah)*, trans. Alfred Guillaume, (Karachi: Oxford University Press, 2007)

Imam Muwaffaq ad-Din Abdu'llah ibn Ahmad ibn Qudama al-Maqdisi, *The Mainstay Concerning Jurisprudence (Al-Umda fi 'l-Fiqh)*, trans. Muhtar Holland (Ft. Lauderdale, FL: Al-Baz Publishing, Inc., 2009)

The Meaning of the Glorious Koran, trans. Marmaduke Pickthall (1930; rpt. New York: Alfred A. Knopf, 1992)

The Message of the Qur'an, trans. Muhammad Asad, (Bristol, England: The Book Foundation, 2003)

The Mosque in America: A National Portrait, A Report from the Mosque Study Project, April 26, 2001

The Noble Qur'an, trans. Muhammad Muhsin Khan and Muhammad Taqi-ud-Din Al-Hilali (Riyadh, Kingdom of Saudi Arabia: Darussalam, 2007)

Jalal-al-Din 'Abd al-Rahman al-Suyuti, *The Perfect Guide to the Sciences of the Qur'an*, trans. Hamid Algar, et al. (Reading, UK: Garnet Publishing, 2011)

Safiur-Rahman Al-Mubarakpuri, *The Sealed Nectar* (Riyadh, Kingdom of Saudi Arabia: Darussalam, 2008)

The World Fact Book [on-line], Central Intelligence Agency

Majid Khadduri, *War and Peace in the Law of Islam* (Clark, NJ: The Lawbook Exchange Ltd., 2006)

'Imaduddeen Isma'eel Ibn Katheer Al-Qurashi, *Winning the Hearts and Souls: Expeditions and Delegations in the Lifetime of Prophet Muhammad*, trans. Research Department of Darussalam (Riyadh, Kingdom of Saudi Arabia: Darussalam, 2010)

110 Ahadith Qudsi: Sayings of the Prophet Having Allahs Statement, 3rd ed., trans. Syed Masood-ul-Hasan (Riyadh, Kingdom of Saudi Arabia: Darussalam, 2006)

Made in the USA
Lexington, KY
07 February 2015